KALEIDOSCOPE

A Plain Person's Panorama of the Bible

By Michael Huxtable

Private publication printed by
Phillips (Print & Stationery) Limited
115 High Street Crediton Devon

To my lovely Family, and my Friends

"Let this be written for a future generation, that a people not yet created may praise the **LORD**." (NIV) Psalm 102:18

Michael Huxtable

Copyright © Michael Huxtable 2011 All rights reserved. ISBN 978-1-4467-6708-5

Introduction:

The Aim of Kaleidoscope:

Kaleidoscope seeks to present a synthesis, so that the whole story of our Rescue is seen in unity. The Aim is to show in the Bible the love of God in Jesus Christ for all humanity, so that we read with understanding and enthusiasm, are enlightened by the Holy Spirit, and move in response.

<u>Please do have a Bible at hand when reading this book.</u>

This panorama of the Bible comes from my own amateur observations of the Bible text and from source books. It is a synthesis; I have not followed other similar writings, often analytical, but put it all together as I have felt the Lord extending my knowledge. Inevitably, my background has been part of it, and this is Physics, Chemistry and Botany, with which I have sought to continue acquaintance while working as a school teacher. I came to the Lord at age 16 through a lively conservative and biblical work, and I have read the Bible consistently and increasingly since 1945.

We are to learn the ways of God in his rescue of humanity from the blend of individual ingredients. We are to look beyond the events to the care and love and pain and purpose of our God behind it all, and to his total involvement in our scene.

When the risen Jesus walked home with the two disciples to Emmaus on Easter Day, perhaps for 2 hours, "he explained to them what was said in all the scriptures concerning himself." [Luke 24:27 NIV] This made their hearts burn within them! [v.32] May this be so for us. We need to listen to the Holy Spirit in our hearts as we peruse the passages; we need to weave the sacred scriptures together as we learn a little background geography and history, and as we consider modern ideas of our planet, our universe, our creation. As well, we find much human failure in the Bible, which is mirrored in our world today, so we need to become informed doers of the word of God to us and be moved to choose to behave and live and operate as God calls us in Christ. [See James 1:22-25]. May we determine to "grow in the grace and knowledge of the Lord Jesus Christ," as Peter prayed in the last verse of 2 Peter.

This may be helpful. It is extracted from an expert, writing in a pastoral journal for theological students: (from Moberly – "Story in the OT" in Themelios April 1986)

"Enter the story with imagination, as it can communicate through assumption, suggestion, and absorption. See the patterns of how God works, and receive what is left unsaid, where a meaningful silence communicates a sense of background, of mystery, or of God's presence, his guiding, his purposing. Let us allow the stories to appeal to our imagination and intuition; there are large areas of our personalities which are left untouched by reason, will and proclamation."

Faith and Science

Science has penetrated superstition: Galileo fell foul of the church which insisted that the sun went round the earth, alleged to be the centre of the universe. The church relied on their understanding of Bible texts, such as "He hath made the round world so sure: that it cannot be moved." (BCP Psalter for Ps 93:2) This was taken to mean that God made the Earth motionless in absolute terms.

Today, Science has been hijacked by some media-savvy atheists. Darwin's theory of the Evolution of the biological species challenged the church teaching of the inviolability of species, and some church leaders agreed with Darwin. But Evolution was seized by some atheists as a battering ram to demolish religion. However, Darwin himself was not an atheist, but a respectful scientist, perhaps an agnostic. Paley's argument from Design (1802) was disputed, and Darwin offered Natural Selection (1859) as an alternative to the "designer God". In fact you cannot prove logically that God is, and Darwin knew this. God has to be encountered through Jesus who is the image of God, the word of God. [Colossians 1:13-20 refers] We need insight both into Jesus and into Science.

I have followed the controversy of Science v. Religion in books and journals since university days, and I have been upset at the level of misunderstanding and misrepresentation. Many Christians hold that Science is a consistent, truthful, and intelligent description of God's amazing activity, in both physical and biological sciences; that scientific truth is in complete agreement with God's revealed truth in the Bible about his creation, and about human beings in relation to himself. Yet I am aware that both some scientists and also some Christians hold contrary views to this.

For about 150 years, as an absolute article of faith, the Young Earth Creationists of the USA identify the 'day' of Genesis 1 with 24 hours, and state that a 'miraculous' Creation in 6 consecutive days of 24 hours each occurred about 6,000 years ago. In order to maintain this position, they have to rely on God playing deceitful tricks, such as his planting fossils to mislead, and beaming light from stars with a false time indication. They reject the present conclusions of Physics, Astronomy, and Biology. But the word "day" has more than the restricted meaning of 24 hours. Thus, Shakespeare in his day wrote 39 plays and over a 100 sonnets – not all in one day. Hitler in his day murdered 6 million Jews – not all in 24 hours. In Genesis 1 the word "day" does not need to mean 24 hours; it can mean a period of time, an age when something was happening. Genesis is theological, not a science journal; it is unfair to load it with this kind of numerical meaning. This does not deny the miraculous in God's creation. The whole enterprise is miraculous whether it was accomplished in 144 hours or within a million million years!

The grandest of all God's miracles is the physical and bodily Resurrection of Jesus Christ from death, in history, in person, the fact of which has entirely transformed human life, and challenged mortal mind-sets.

[I mention Sir Fred Hoyle in chapter 2: As an undergraduate, I met him in 1949 for a few Tutorials. At that time, he was regarded as a formidable atheist by the active Christians! But by 1959 he had changed his stance. He admitted "A superior intelligence has been monkeying with the universe," and "the universe is a put-up job!" He coined the words "Big Bang" to be in contrast to his theory of "Continuous Creation." He died in 2003.]

I pay warm tribute and profound gratitude to my friend John Bryant, emeritus professor, Exeter University, himself a published author, for his patient guidance and advice over making this book presentable for publication.

Acknowledgements

Moberly	An article	Themelios
JD Barrow	The Constants of Nature	Vintage 2003
FS Collins	The Language of God	Simon & Schuster
CJ Humphries	The Miracles of Exodus	Continuum 2008
JW Harmer (ed)	The Scripture Lesson	Tyndale 1960
A Edersheim	The Life and Times of Jesus the Messiah	Longmans 1894
J John	Ten	Kingsway
R Baukham	Is the Bible Male?	Grove 1996
D Ronsa	An article	Fire, 1997
A Marshall	1 Timothy 2:11-12 RSV Interlinear NT	Marshall Pickering
JGSS Thomson	The Book of Psalms	New Bible Dictionary
BW Anderson	The Living World of the Old Testament	Longman 1978
D Lennon	Encounter God in Job	Scripture Union
H Marshall	An article The Bible in Transmission	Bible Society
JN Anderson	Resurrection	IVP 1950
R Watts	Resurrection or Nothing	Scripture Union
H Chadwick	The Early Church	Pelican 1981
G Bray	Creeds, Councils, and Christ	IVP 1984
EMB Green	The Books the Church Suppressed	Monarch 2005
RH Bainton	Here I Stand	Mentor 1953
RT France	Translating the Bible	Grove 1997
GD Fee & D Stuart	How to Read the Bible for All its Worth	Zondervan

Except where indicated, Scripture is taken from the HOLY BIBLE, NEW INTERNATIONAL VERSION NIV. Copyright 1973,1978, 1984 by International Bible Society. Used by permission of International Bible Society. All rights reserved worldwide.

"NIV" and "NEW INTERNATIONAL VERSION" are trademarks registered in the United States Patent and Trademark Office by International Bible Society.

CONTENTS
Chapter   page

Chapter	Title	Page
1:	Off to a Very Good Start	2
2:	Cosmological matters and Planet Earth	8
3:	Tectonic Plates	20
4:	Love forsaken, Paradise Lost	29
5:	God's unilateral Grace – the Covenant	35
6:	That "Multicolour dreamcoat" and an Egyptian story	44
7:	Exodus at Moses' hand	51
8:	How to Worship God!	63
9:	The Power of Doubt	75
10:	The Promised Land	82
11:	Samuel, Saul, David, and Solomon	99
12:	Wisdom	111
13:	Military powers in motion	122
14:	Men of Conviction	132
15:	A Kind of Restoration!	144
16:	**God's Son**	156
17:	Truth, the Resurrection and the Apostles' Testimony	172
18:	The New Covenant	181
19:	The New Testament Writings	194
20:	Witnesses to the ends of the earth	211
21:	Preserving Scripture	221
22:	"Be faithful, even to death…"	235
23:	The Second Coming	242
	Appendix	256

Suggestion: Read chapter 16 first; then begin chapter 1. 'Creation' has brought controversy and this can divert attention from the big panorama story line.

Chapter 1   Off to a Very Good Start

> Truth, Grace, and Peace pervade this creation work of God Most High. He is deeply involved at every stage, and the created Man-Woman pair receive intelligence and speech, with free-will. They, and we, can have knowledge of God, because God reveals this; also we may have understanding of the natural world through intelligent scientific observation.

(As a refreshing exercise for encountering the story of Creation in **Genesis 1:1-2:3**, listen to two voices reading alternately the odd and even numbered Days of creation in succession.)

This awesome description is narrated as if by an observer located on Earth, starting with gloom, then with light and clearing skies as creation unfolds. It reveals God as majestic in human terms, monotheistic in plurality ("God said [singular]... let us [plural] make man in our image"v.26). He appointed the human pair together as his agency (v.28), to lead all creatures with industry, intelligence, integrity, to be his assistants, knowing God and sharing with him the excitement and joy of this new venture.

Day 1 (vv.1-5)   Earth's surface was indistinct, dark, with stormy waters. At God's command, Light broke through; then the regular rhythm of day-light and night-time became apparent.

Day 2 (6-8)   At God's command, the obscuring mists broke to reveal the sky, so that the water-bearing clouds were visibly separated from the ocean waters.

Day 3 (9-13)   At God's command, dry land emerged from the seas. Then he created vegetative Life, with plants and trees, seeds and fruits.

Day 4 (14-19)   At God's command, the sky cleared to reveal stars and moon at night, and sun for the day time. Their motions were to be signs of seasons and days and years. So intelligent observers need to be stargazers! Note that God is the extravagant creator. Our galaxy, the Milky Way contains ten thousand million stars, of which our Sun is but one. The universe contains ten thousand million galaxies.

<u>Day 5 (20-23)</u> At God's command, the seas became full of sea creatures, big and small, and the air was populated with flying birds.

<u>Day 6 (24,25)</u> At God's command, the land produced mobile animals of all kinds, farm livestock, wild animals, and all other kinds.

After each creative action, God had pronounced it "Good!" Now, still in Day 6 (26-39), God created human beings, to be in his image, to rule all the living creatures of sea, air, and land. God blessed them, and charged them to increase in number, and to rule over everything living. He resourced them with food from green plants and fruits of trees.

Finally God pronounced his whole creation, together with the human beings, to be "Very Good!"

<u>Day 7 (Genesis 2:1-4)</u> God blessed the Seventh Day, made it holy, and rested from his work of creation.

Amongst the earliest known peoples, there were several accounts of Creation, and most have an elaborate mythology of fighting gods who were to be placated on earth by sacrifices. The compiler of Genesis, traditionally Moses, under the Holy Spirit of God Most High, recorded what God revealed as the simple truth by the Spirit. The Genesis narrative is quite different from and far superior to all other ancient narratives.

(In our day, we have an edited and translated version of what the compiler wrote. In the Appendix, there is comment on "editing" original scripture and its transmission to readers as the inspired word of God.)

The Jewish Calendar:
the day is solar, determined by the Sun setting and rising
the week is 7 days, ending on Shabbat, the seventh day.
In the creation story, this day was made holy (2:13) in contrast to Babylonian myths where the seventh day was dangerous!
the month is lunar, determined by the moon waxing and waning.

The year is seasonal, starting in spring. For this, Babylonians and Egyptians observed when the constellation Aries was in position.

Jewish Lunar months were determined by priestly observation, and promulgated by blowing rams horns [Psalm 81:3 Book of Common Prayer: "Blow up the trumpet in the New Moon"!]. The first day of the month began when the crescent new Moon was first seen in the evening – Jewish days start in the evening. The lunar month is 29.5 days, so some months are 29 days long and others 30. 12 lunar months are 354 days; 11 days were added to the 12th month (or sometimes the 6th) to ensure that the 1st day of the 1st month fell in spring. So the priests were making careful astronomical observations!

Genesis 2:4-25. This is a second Creation story with its focus on the human beings. It was perhaps written down earlier than the Genesis 1 account. The Hebrew word for Man is ADAM. When used with the definite article it is not a name, but is 'the man,' that is 'mankind', the human race. The OT has 500 occurrences of this use. (eg: What is *man* that you are mindful of him? Psalm 8:4) The Hebrew word for 'ground', the fruitful arable soil, is 'ADAMAH', from which the Lord God formed the 'ADAM'. [Genesis 2:7] Then notice 3:17-19, where the curse pronounced on the fallen ADAM was explicit in returning the living creature ADAM to the lifeless ADAMAH. [Also Psalm 90:3]

The rich soil was irrigated by the rivers [Genesis 2:10-14] and supported plant and animal life. From this soil the man was created and set to work to bring order in the Garden for the Lord God. Adam was an intelligent person; in the naming of the creatures he observed and accepted the charge to rule or minister. He had the power of speech and was able to communicate with his Lord, and with his wife. When Adam spoke, [Genesis 2:23] he described himself as 'ISH', ie Being, indicating self-awareness and a perception of life. He described his new companion as 'ISHAH', ie Female being, indicating that the woman matched the man, unlike any of the animals he had encountered previously. The humans responded to God, taking authority for plants and animals; God cared for their deep personal needs through marriage. Marriage is a creation ordinance of God.

Marriage, as a public commitment, is common to virtually all races, nations, and faiths. Ceremonies may vary, but universally, as well as the bride and groom taking each other, the whole community is involved and invited to support the pair. Marriage has become enshrined in national laws, so that children born into the new family have recognition and security. For Christians, Jesus most emphatically endorsed marriage as a lifelong estate. (It is speculation to consider the future of the children now born into unwedded situations, according to the strong individualism which rejects the received traditions of former generations. Such choice has come to depend on the rather depersonalised institutions of nursery and school.)

God has a longing loving heart for people, to bless and guide, that they may love and follow him freely and willingly. So he created the human pair with **free-will.** This is an essential ingredient if these purposes of God are to be realised. He loved them totally, and wanted them to love him equally totally. And not only that, but he even also had prepared an action-plan for the event that human beings chose not to follow their Creator. [1 Peter 1:18-21, Revelation 13:8]

Above is set down the Jewish Calendar, and we noted that the priests were responsible for maintaining it by making careful astronomical observations!

Today, Science, by careful intelligent observation, is finding how God operated. From Astronomy, Physics, and Biological sciences, it seems that it all started with the Big Bang, followed by Star evolution; this enabled the creation of those chemical elements which can support life. Next came Earth formation, and then the creation of Life itself, followed by biological evolution.

Time scales: (almost incomprehensible!)
Decades for a single life,
   Generations for a family,
      Centuries and millennia for a nation, a culture, a race,
         Hundreds of millions of years for geological evolution,
            Thousands of millions of years for biological evolution,
               Tens of thousands of millions of years for astronomical evolution.

A day, a generation, a life, last as long as the Lord makes them. "With the Lord, a day is like a thousand years, and a thousand years are like a day." (2 Peter 3:8, quoting Psalm 90:4) So we should make further comments on Faith & Science as partners not rivals! Science, as an intelligent description of God's abundant activity, agrees with God's truth about creation and about his relation with human beings.

In the Introduction, I stated that Science has been hijacked by some atheists. Also, the cudgels have been taken up by the Creationists. In Genesis 1 the use of the word "day" does not need to mean 24 hours; it can mean a period of time, an age when something was happening. Genesis is a theological text, not a science journal; it is unfair to load it with this kind of numerical meaning. Similarly 'Evening' and 'Morning' are words which find application outside nightfall and daybreak – we speak of the evening of life, the dawn of intelligence &c.

As with all entrenched positions, so with this gulf between Science and Faith: some Christians brand all scientists as atheists, and some vocal atheists brand all Christians as believing ten impossible things before breakfast! Neither party listens to the other. "Confusion worse confounded."

[For anyone with concerns on Faith and Science, or on Creationism, the book by Francis Collins 'The Language of God' is to be commended. He is a brilliant polymath, with PhDs in Physical Chemistry, then in Medicine, and is head of the successful Human Genome Project in the USA; he continues to work on DNA to bring cures for CF, &c, and he is a humble Christian believer. Now, President Obama has made him Director of the USA's National Institute of Health.]

Returning to the Creation stories and dwelling on Psalm 8, the writer comes before God, the creature before the Creator:

"O LORD, our ruling Sovereign God, how regal is your name ('I AM') everywhere! You have done it! You have put your Glory there! It is painted high above and beyond the universe, right down to weak and insignificant humans who nevertheless praise you with heart and mind." The children praising Jesus, the Son of God, took the religious establishment in the Temple by shock and surprise! Children demolish the pretensions of all sorts of enemies.

"Your creation is vast and marvellous. It cuts mere humans down to size – we wonder 'What is mankind!' Yet you think and care for Ben Adam ('the son of man'). Truly you take loving interest in us, who are poised between the heavenly divine and other earthly living creatures. You have given us glory and honour. You have crowned creation in entrusting this mysterious thing 'Life' into our hands, with oversight of domestic animals, wild animals, birds and fish, small and large. The human creature entrusted with governance by the Governor! It's amazing! "O LORD our Sovereign, how royal is your name everywhere!"

O Lord my God! When I in awesome wonder
Consider all the works thy hand hath made,
I see the stars, I hear the mighty thunder,
Thy power throughout the universe displayed:
Then sings my soul, my Saviour God to Thee,
How great thou art! How great thou art!

[Translated from Russian by S K Hine]

The next chapter turns to consider in more detail the Science description of Creation.

Chapter 2 Cosmological Matters and Planet Earth

> An overall look at the present Scientific understanding of the story of Creation, and of the mystery of Life, moving on to face up to The Anthropic Principle, and some controversies between Faith and Science.

From the standpoint of Psalm 19: "The heavens declare the glory of God…" The Psalm begins with perceptive observations of the heavens, the skies, and the sun's daily travel. These phenomena declare the glory of their Creator and his work. They impress by their permanence and regularity. They impact everywhere, globally.

The Psalm moves forward to deduce from this panoply something of the character or Law of the Creator himself. The Law is perfect and reliable, bright and true. Therefore he is moral Being, pure, sure, and righteous. He communicates wisdom with top value and irresistible qualities, advising and rewarding us as we respond to him. But a sense of our failure intrudes. Nevertheless, the Lord reveals that he is our dependable and gracious rescuer who invests his servant with forgiveness. In right relationship, he empowers me so that lifestyle, speech, and deepest thoughts can please him who is my rock-solid Redeemer.

BIG BANG CREATION

Very Large Numbers.

In UK	In USA	as Longhand numerals	as Powers of 10
Million	Million	1,000,000	10^6
	Billion	1,000,000,000	10^9
Billion	Trillion	1,000,000,000,000	10^{12}
Trillion		1,000,000,000,000,000,000	10^{18}

To express these large numbers unambiguously, this book avoids the word "Billion," and uses "Thousand million" for 1,000,000,000.

Current Science states that The Big Bang is the moment of creation of the universe. At that instant the universe is concentrated into a single point. This moment was some 13,700 million years ago.

Energy in the form of electromagnetic radiation both exerts outward pressure to expand, and also undergoes conversion into matter, as quarks and anti-quarks in very nearly equal numbers. At their high density these annihilate back into radiation; the leftover quarks constitute the existing mass of the universe.

Immediately after the Big Bang (BB), when the universe is much smaller than an Hydrogen nucleus, there is a brief period of accelerated expansion; the evidence for this is still being investigated. This has a critical effect on subsequent expansion, between being Open, and so expanding for ever, and being Closed, and so collapsing into a Big Crunch after a limited time.

BB + one thousandth of a second: the universe is a violently expanding fireball, say of diameter 600km.

BB + 60 seconds: say diameter 30 million km.
The expansion rate decreases as particles fly apart, because gravity slows them down.

BB + a million years: matter is cool enough for Hydrogen atoms to exist.

BB + 1000 million years: irregularities in the dust clouds cause clusters of galaxies to form under gravity. As well, there is radiation, originally from the BB. Today, this is detected as Background Radiation.

BB + 5000 million years: the first stars form.

Star evolution in galaxies

Astronomers today observe what is happening in the stars all the time, and deduce these steps:

1 The gas cloud exists with fluctuations in density, producing fragments.

2 The fragments fall together under gravity, to form the embryo star, releasing thermal energy.

3 The centre temperature rises, and after 50,000 years fusion of Hydrogen nuclei begins, forming Helium nuclei.

4 The star is stable after another 50,000 years, with inward gravity balanced by radiation pressure outwards.

5 After 10 million years, the Hydrogen in the core is used up, so radiation pressure falls and gravity wins; the core contracts and the temperature rises. The outer layers are now hot enough to continue the nuclear fusion of the Hydrogen they contain, so the star expands to become a Red Giant.

6 The core becomes hot enough to fuse Helium nuclei to Carbon nuclei, the nuclei of the all-important element for Life, and also to produce heavier elements, Oxygen, up to Iron. For making nuclei even heavier than Iron, this process of nuclear fusion no longer <u>releases</u> energy, which release would contribute to making the process self-sustaining; so there is a pause in creating elements heavier than Iron. When the Helium in the core of the star runs out, the core collapses dramatically under gravity, and this makes a violent release of radiation energy and causes a supernova explosion. Under these conditions, nuclear fusion does happen, but with <u>absorption</u> of energy, and it generates elements heavier than Iron. The dust and cloud spread outwards, and the old core becomes a neutron star.

7 From the gas cloud a new generation of stars forms, containing these heavier elements.

8 For 1 million years, the cloud contracts under gravity, forming a star.

9 The core heats up; the new star spins and forms a flat disc of dust and gas.

10 The dust and gas form a solar system of planets containing Carbon and the heavy elements needed for generating life. The star – the sun – gets hotter. Now the time is

BB + 8000 million years or more. All this time is needed to produce stars, supernovae, and to generate the life-supporting chemical elements, especially Carbon, and then cooling. For our solar system, our sun is a yellow star, stable, with a core at temperature 15,000,000 K. The outward radiation

pressure from nuclear fusion of Hydrogen to Helium inside the sun balances the gravitational attraction inward. With the time at
BB + 12,600 million years, there is microscopic life on Earth. This time is 1,000 million years before human life appears.

The story of Life

Radioactivity in rocks dates Earth at 4,550 million years old. Data from meteorite rocks and Moon rocks agrees with this figure. Leaving the Time Line above, which started at BB, and running a new Time line, beginning anew at
4,500 million years back from now: in the following 500 million years the rocks show no life down to
4000 million years ago. Then 150 million years later, (though some scientists say 500 million years later)
3,850 million years ago, many types of microbes existed. These one-cell organisms interacted, blending different proteins. [There is no satisfactory hypothesis for the origin of such self-replicating organisms at present. A satisfactory hypothesis may be developed. Collins warns: don't put God in this Gap!]
Moving forward by another 3,300 million years, to
550 million years ago, to the "Cambrian Explosion", a great number of different invertebrates appeared. The fossil record is incomplete, but is being filled. [CAVEAT: not another Gap!] Perhaps this "explosion" reflects a change in geological circumstances so that more fossilization took place than had previously occurred.
400 million years ago plants appeared on land, similar to modern liverworts.
370 million years ago animals appeared on land. There is good evidence for transitional forms from reptiles to birds, and from reptiles to mammals.
230 million years ago dinosaurs dominated.
65 million years ago the last dinosaurs met a catastrophic end, when a large asteroid fell on Earth in the Yucatan peninsula, spreading fine dust all over the Earth cutting off sunlight for a long time. Subsequently, without the dinosaurs, mammals evolved successfully.

Intelligence and humans and first appeared 200,000 years ago.
195,000 years ago   Homo sapiens appeared amongst hominids.
30,000 years ago   The Neanderthals came to their end.

These indigestible times are matched by incomprehensible distances! Our sun is 28,000 light-years from the centre of our galaxy, seen as the Milky Way. (Light travels about 9.5 million million kilometres in a year.) Our galaxy rotates about its central bulge, and our sun takes 200 million years for one rotation round the galaxy.

[Prognosis: After a further 4,000 million years, all Hydrogen in the core of the sun will be used up, so it will become a Red Giant, expanding and engulfing the inner planets and the Earth.
The core then heats up enough to fuse Helium nuclei: this is the "Helium flash".
After Helium is used up, heavier nuclei fuse, blowing out the outer layers of unused Hydrogen to form a ring nebula, with a White Dwarf star at the centre.
The White Dwarf cools and becomes a Black Dwarf, which is invisible.]

Back to Earth! The Earth is special. It has a core of Nickel and Iron and has a magnetic field which deflects the stream of particles from the sun, and so the Earth retains an atmosphere. By contrast, Mars, of half the diameter and one third the surface gravity, has no magnetic field, and virtually no atmosphere.
The Earth has radioactive layers which continue supplying heat, and so it retains fluidity for the tectonic plates to keep moving.
Evolution of our life-supporting atmosphere required an initial phase when Oxygen was released by photo-dissociation of water vapour and by plant photosynthesis. This lasted 2,400 million years.
Our very large Moon's gravity dominates the gravity effects on us of all other bodies in the solar system, and so it controls the

'wobble' rate (precession) of the Earth, keeping the tilt of the Earth's axis at 23° within 0.5°. Without the Moon, the angle would be erratic, and so surface temperatures and seasons, and climate, would all change rapidly compared with the time needed for biological evolution.

The orbit of the Earth round the sun lies within the Life zone; closer to the sun would be too hot for life, as Venus; further away would be too cold, as Mars. Indeed, the Earth is special.

To achieve all this, and more, physical laws and their constants must have certain definite values. They must be "fine tuned." The precise values are needed, for example, to keep the expansion of the universe balanced between too rapid expansion and so cooling, and too slow expansion, so leading to a collapse under gravity into a Big Crunch. Without this knife-edge balance, there would not have been enough time for galaxies and stars for form, and for supernovae to generate the heavy chemical elements needed for life.

Some of these constants are: c, the vacuum Speed of light: G, the Newtonian constant of Gravitation: h, Planck's constant of Action: The Strong nuclear force (which binds nucleons against electric repulsion): The Weak nuclear force (which determines radioactivity): The Mass ratio of proton to electron: The Fine structure constant (referring to spectral lines),

In particular, another example of the Fine tuning is the precise values of the nuclear energy levels of Carbon, and of Oxygen. Slightly different values one way would result in no Carbon being formed, while values the other way would cause all Carbon to become Oxygen. In fact, Carbon is present to form life, and the energy levels are remarkably exact. The significance of the nature of the precise values of these energy levels was first realised by cosmologist Fred Hoyle in 1952. Up till then, only two energy levels of the Carbon nucleus had been observed. Hoyle showed that neither of them gave a stable nucleus. He calculated a value for an intermediate third energy level necessary for Carbon to exist, and this was discovered, having remarkably precise agreement with his value.

It was a turning point for Hoyle, and he wrote "I do not believe that any scientist who examined the evidence would fail to draw the inference that the laws of physics have been deliberately designed with regard to the consequences they produce inside the stars. If this is so, then my apparently random quirks have become part of a deep laid scheme. If not, then we are back again at a monstrous sequence of accidents." (SCM 1959)

The Anthropic Principle
From this Fine tuning, it has emerged that:
(Weak form) There are properties of the universe which are necessary for life to evolve.
(or) Humans exist because physical laws of the universe exhibit special features.
(Strong form) It is a cosmological principle that theories of the universe are constrained by the necessity to allow human existence. [Fred Hoyle]
(or) the universe (and hence the fundamental parameters on which it depends) must be such as to admit the creation of observers within it at some stage. [Carter]

Currently, much Astrophysics is devoted to testing if the 'constants' are indeed constant. The Fine structure constant is being tested from the Red-shift in the Background radiation, the cosmic microwaves originating from the BB and so emitted 13,700 million years ago, thus finding its value soon after the BB, to compare it with its present day value.

Scientists, as others, speculate about the origins. As Fred Hoyle indicated, that the universe and the Earth with its intelligent beings is a fluke, a product of blind 'cause and effect' in the face of total improbability, is a speculation which is completely intellectually unsatisfying. It is more realistic to hold that Life has arisen because some factor has so far not been considered. This is therefore the strongest possibility to pursue.

Determinist Science makes a choice that truth is restricted to what can be verified experimentally.   This Science says that all the features of intelligent life itself can, or hopes will, be explained in terms of biochemical or neurological changes. Thus, for example, determinist Science describes the rain-bow colours of the visible spectrum by frequency, and by human brain neurons involved in the sense of colour. It has also said that human behaviour is determined genetically, or by some related process.

But Scientific Determinism is not absolutely determined, as for one thing the Uncertainty Principle in Quantum Mechanics demonstrates. Scientific truth is restricted truth. But other truth is there to be explored, and the Anthropic Principle urges intelligent beings to consider ascribing purpose to life, deriving from the intelligent force behind the universe.

At minimum, this leads open minds to Theism.

EVOLUTION a Mechanism of biological life.
Darwin proposed, in the Origin of Species (1859):

Each living species is descended from a small set of common ancestors – maybe from one. Variation within species occurs randomly, and survival or extinction depends on the ability to adapt to the environment. (This is Natural Selection.)

Mendel studied Science at Vienna university before becoming an abbot.

His rules of inheritance (1863) were deduced from studies of plants, grown in his Czech monastery experimental garden. The units of inheritance he named Genes, both dominant and recessive. Mendel's rules agree with inheritance rules observed in human disorders seen in medicine.

In 1944, DNA in the nucleus of a cell was identified as the holder of inheritable characters, the genes. Its structure as the double helix was found in 1953.

Evolution comes from natural selection arising from naturally occurring mutations in DNA. A genome is the complete set of all genetic material in an organism. The human genome has over 3000 million letters of the DNA code, but the genes use only 1.5% of the total DNA. A given human has about 60 new mutations not present in either parent; however most of these occur in parts of the genome which are not essential, and so have no effect. Human DNA has 99.9% identity within all members of our species. The major portion of human DNA, not used by the active genes, is most useful in tracing common ancestry across mammalian species.

Collins writes 'Evolution is an established fundamental principle. Nothing in Biology makes sense except in the light of evolution.'

Controversies of Science with Faith

The Argument for God from the observed complexity of life as the designing intelligence goes back to Cicero at least.

Augustine (AD 400) studied Genesis 1 & 2 carefully, and wrote five books with different perspectives. He warned against taking one position or another, thinking that there are many valid interpretations of words written obscurely. This was well before the discovery of geological evidence for the immense age of the Earth, and before Darwin's theory of evolution.

Galileo showed that the Earth revolves round the Sun, not the Sun round the Earth, but the church forced him to recant in 1633 because they were deeply threatened.

Paley (1802) published an influential analogy, in finding a watch and so deducing that it had a designing watchmaker; correspondingly nature has a designing creator. However this correspondence is flawed: Collins considers the proposition that "Electric current is a flow of electrons, and comes from the Power Station. Lightning is also a flow of electrons, so it also comes from the Power Station." This is not so!

As said before, currently there are deep and entrenched positions between Evolution and Faith in a number of quarters. In the USA, Gallup sampled Americans in 2004 to find that only 1/3 believed that the theory of evolution is well supported; 1/3 did not, and 1/3 could not say. Gallup found that 45% of Americans held that God created human beings at one time in the last 10,000 years; 38% held that human beings have developed over millions of years from less advanced forms of life, and that God guided this process; and 13% held that God did not guide any process. In the light of widespread education, this is a surprising result. Of course, problems arise in understanding the extremely long times involved in evolution compared with the experience of human life. And problems arise from misunderstanding sacred texts, despite Augustine's warnings. The Young Earth Creationists hold that Genesis 1 & 2 are to be understood literally in terms of six 24- hour consecutive days and that the Earth was created about 6000 years ago.

<u>Theistic Evolution</u> This is the position of many Hindus, Muslims, Jews and Christians. Collins writes that a typical version rests upon these premises:
1. The universe came into being out of nothingness, about 14 thousand million years ago.
2. Despite massive improbabilities, the properties of the universe appear to have been precisely tuned for life to develop.
3. While the precise mechanism of the origin of life on Earth remains unknown, once life arose, the process of evolution by natural selection over very long periods of time led to the development of biological diversity and complexity.
4. Once evolution got under way, no special supernatural intervention was required.
5. Humans are part of this process, sharing a common ancestor with the great apes.
6. But humans are also unique in ways that defy evolutionary explanation and point to our spiritual nature. Evidence for this includes the existence of the Moral Law (the knowledge of right and wrong) and the Search for God that characterises all human cultures. Not all Christian thinkers are in agreement with this approach.

REVELATION
This has been left out of consideration so far.
For Jews, then Christians, and Muslims too, faith has come from Revelation. The Intelligent Force behind the universe is God, who has disclosed himself to individuals and communities. People need to receive his revelation of himself for themselves. It is a valid experiment for individuals to search for

God through prayer, with the expectation of finding him, and coming to know him, though in humility and without conditions.
<u>Christian Credo!</u>

The Lord has made the universe, and developed the Earth, breathed life here so that humans evolved for his purposes; namely:

To be in his image, to be his agents who operate the systems of nature on Earth, to have intelligence and free-will, and to know him as <u>Lord, Master, and Friend</u>.

In this knowledge, to love and obey him, to be like him, and to be with him. But humans turned from him, and lost knowing him as <u>Lord, Master and Friend</u> – thus they died in spirit.

However, the Lord has intervened. He became human, born to a lowly family and was named Jesus, in an obscure corner of the Roman Empire at a definite place and at a definite time in history. His purpose was, and continues to be, to rescue and restore life to those humans who will receive him, to have spirit life in full, to know him as <u>Lord, Master and Friend</u>. And in this knowledge, to love and obey him, to be like him, and to be with him.

Some critics say that Christians have made God in their own image! This might be justified, except that it ignores the Revelation which God has given to humans. God revealed himself to the Jews in the Old Testament; then in Roman times, Jesus revealed more of the character of God, and he rose miraculously from death; this is clearly attested as historical fact. The Resurrection was no mere resuscitation. Further, if we will but receive him, the Spirit of God witnesses personally to our spirits that we are in his family! After the sleep of human death, we will wake to Resurrection, and then continue to be with God. So, No, we do not make God in our image! Rather, all resemblances are due to the Creator-God making us in his own image.

We may say that Purpose in human life is his purpose in human life.

Back to **Psalm 19.** Observation has brought awe, which has led to my appreciation of the Creator. I am forced to admit my failure, and to my receiving his grace. The Psalm has travelled from the majestic Universe to its Creator and his ordering, and on to my reliable Redeemer.

Final thought in the last verse – it really is possible to please God!

Chapter 3   Tectonic Plates

Geology: Our Dangerous Planet

The next section considers the surface of the Earth around the specific region of the Bible lands, where God chose to work out his global purposes with humanity. Improving Media communications have made us all aware of the hazards of life on planet Earth: Earthquakes and Volcanoes, floods and storms, famines and crop failures. But the Israelites were aware of these things, too.   They feature in **Psalm 46** which was written to lead people's worship:

The God of Jacob, both in battle and in earthquake, is always there to help in trouble, our refuge and resolution.

In the earthquake we will not fear, even when we see land sliding down into the sea – (it was probably into the Dead Sea in the Rift Valley, near Zion.) We will not panic, even when there are earthquakes in the mountains. Zion is secure, with a flow of thirst-quenching water from the Gihon spring; God is there, dwelling permanently in his Holy Place.

In the daybreak attack on Zion, God helps, and the battle is the Lord's. The roar of battle is everywhere, nation rising against nation! The roar of the earthquake is God's voice, and the earth changes shape!

In both battle and earthquake, the Lord is supreme. He is I AM, the covenant making God of Jacob, our refuge and strong fortress: he is with us.

"Come and see…" invites our perception of the LORD, working in earthquake and in battle. The results are ravaged earth, broken bows, shattered weapons, burnt-out chariots or shields. Silence falls! In the stillness, acknowledge God, I AM, to be exalted everywhere, by fighting nations, by quaking earth!

Our Almighty Covenant-making God is our security: HE IS WITH US.   AMEN!

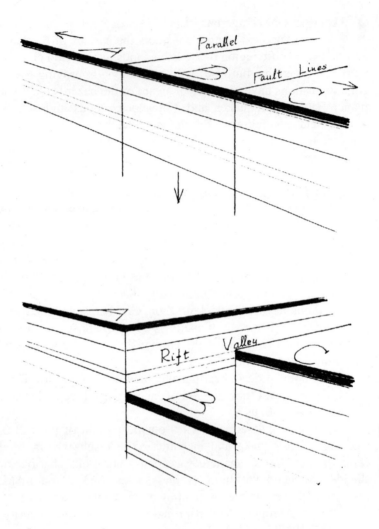

    The land masses on planet earth are composed of <u>Tectonic plates</u> 'floating' on molten rock. Amongst other things, these generate Rift Valleys and Volcanoes.

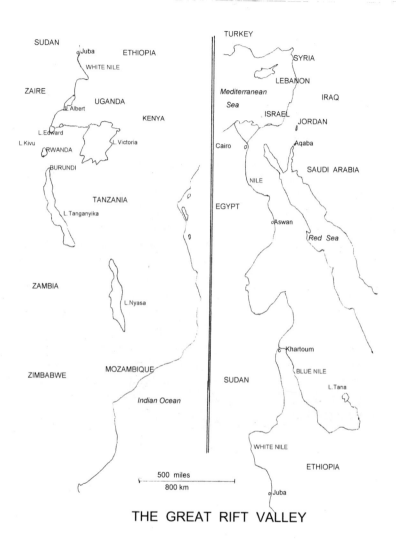

THE GREAT RIFT VALLEY

<u>Rift Valleys</u> develop between parallel faults in the rock strata which then begin to move apart. The piece of land between them drops, leaving nearly vertical walls. This distinguishes them from U-shaped glacier valleys, and V-shaped river valleys.

There is a small rift valley in Wiltshire, running East-West, formed between Salisbury Plain and the Marlborough Downs, making the Vale of Pewsey. The north slope straight down below Martinsell Hill is notably steep. The road runs obliquely down to Oare village, and even that is steep.

Minor earth tremors feature in Bible poetry: Psalm 46, above. Also Psalm 60:2; Amos 1:1; Isaiah 2:19-21, 24:18-20; Haggai 2:6-7 which is quoted in Hebrews 12:26. These all mention the earth shaking. The Israelites were rather more acquainted with tremors than we are. The region of the Holy Land has always been affected by small earthquakes, because it is near the joins of tectonic plates, and these are slowly moving about. The Indo-Australian plate and the African plate movements have generated both volcanoes and the Great Rift Valley.

Referring to the Africa Map, the Great Rift Valley runs north from Mozambique, up the chain of African lakes – Nyassa, Tanganyika, Kivu, Edward, and Albert; then up parts of the Nile, across the Red Sea to the Gulf of Aqaba, the Arabah, the Dead Sea, the Jordan, the Sea of Galilee, and up to Lebanon. In many places the sides form almost vertical cliffs, which can be about 2000 ft (600m) deep in Africa. At the head of the Gulf of Aqaba the drop down the eastward Trade Route from Egypt is about 1500 ft (500m).

Visitors may be surprised to see the cones of many extinct volcanoes on the landscape of Bohemia, Central Europe, between the Alps and the Carpathians. They are evidence that the African plate has moved north into the Eurasian plate; it is this motion that has generated the Alps, and in particular, caused the volcanoes Vesuvius in Italy, Etna in Sicily, and Santorini in the Aegean.

Tectonic plates move slowly. Thus, 200 million years ago, the pebble beds of Woodbury Common in East Devon, and much of southern England, were laid down by a great river when our plate was near the equator. Our average speed north has been 1 inch a year (25mm), though for several thousands of years we seem to have ground to a halt. The geology of Woodbury Common connects with the name of the village nearby, the "new town by the pebble ford" – Newton Poppleford! Edinburgh Castle is perched on the core of an ancient volcano, and Arthur's Seat was a volcano. Killerton House, about 9 miles north of central Exeter, nestles below an old volcano. We live on a dangerous planet!

The geological condition of the Earth which has generated the very slowly moving tectonic plates, with their rift valleys and volcanoes, is also responsible for providing the appropriate environment for evolution of life. Without tectonic plates, there would be no human beings.

There are three volcanoes in north Saudi Arabia, the old land of Midian, and two have been active in the last 4000 years. As well, there are extensive fields of Lava in this area.

Mount Horeb

Below are some recorded Bible observations about Horeb, the mount of God; a quick review picks out 6 different items. Some relevant words are underlined.

Exodus 3:1 Now Moses was tending the flock of Jethro his father-in-law, the priest of Midian, and he led the flock to the far side of the desert and came to Horeb, the mountain of God. There the angel of the LORD appeared to him in <u>flames of fire from within a bush. Moses saw that though the bush was on fire it did not burn up</u>.

Exodus 13:21 <u>By day the LORD went ahead of them in a pillar of cloud to guide them on their way and by night in a pillar of fire to give them light</u>, so that they could travel by day or night. Neither the pillar of cloud by day nor the pillar of fire by night left its place in front of the people.

Exodus 19:16 On the morning of the third day there was <u>thunder and lightning, with a thick cloud over the mountain, and a very loud trumpet blast.</u> Everyone in the camp trembled. Then Moses led the people out of the camp to meet with God, and they stood at the foot of the mountain. <u>Mount Sinai was covered with smoke, because the LORD descended on it in fire. The smoke billowed up from it like smoke from a furnace, the whole</u>

mountain trembled violently, and the sound of the trumpet grew louder and louder. Then Moses spoke and the voice of God answered him.

Exodus 20:18 When the people saw the thunder and lightning and heard the trumpet and saw the mountain in smoke, they trembled with fear. They stayed at a distance... The people remained at a distance, while Moses approached the thick darkness where God was.

Another account is in Deuteronomy:

Deuteronomy 4:15 You saw no form of any kind the day the LORD spoke to you at Horeb out of the fire. Therefore watch yourselves very carefully,

Deuteronomy 4:33 Has any other people heard the voice of God speaking out of fire, as you have, and lived?

Deuteronomy 4:36 From heaven he made you hear his voice to discipline you. On earth he showed you his great fire, and you heard his words from out of the fire.

Deuteronomy 5:4 The LORD spoke to you face to face out of the fire on the mountain.

Deuteronomy 5:22 These are the commandments the LORD proclaimed in a loud voice to your whole assembly there on the mountain from out of the fire, the cloud and the deep darkness; and he added nothing more. Then he wrote them on two stone tablets and gave them to me.

1. (Exodus 3:1) the bush, on fire beside Horeb.
2. (Exodus 13:21) the pillar of cloud by day and pillar of fire by night.
3. (Exodus 19:16) thunder and lightning.
4. Smoke (and darkness 20:18).
5. Earthquake.
6. Trumpet blast.

These physical phenomena imply that Mt Horeb (Sinai) was an erupting volcano.

The mountain of God:

Jebel Musa, in the Sinai Peninsula, marked on the usual maps as Mt Sinai (or Horeb) is made of Red Granite, an igneous rock formed in geological times past, over a hundred million years ago. The common tradition that this is the mountain where Moses and the Israelites met the LORD has been very strongly held for over 1600 years. This was derived as follows:

About 400 AD, Constantine authorised Christianity as the official religion of the Roman empire, and persecutions stopped. Then some early Christians decided that this Jebel Musa was the mountain where Moses and the people had met God, some 1700 years previous to them. From photographs, it is certainly an impressive site. Also they set up the monastery of St Catherine at the foot of the mountain, famous for the discovery there in mid 1800 AD of a 4th Century AD Greek Bible. However, there are many problems with this tradition, not least that the area was under Egyptian control. Pharaoh's men patrolled the region, and Ramses II built a temple in the peninsula. It has too little water to supply thousands of Israelites and their flocks, and there are no volcanoes in this territory which lies between the Gulf of Sinai and the Gulf of Aqaba. Besides these problems, there is no credible place on the way to Jebel Musa for crossing the Red Sea and the overwhelming of Pharaoh's army.

From about 1900 AD other sites have been suggested, but rejected by traditionalists. One distinguished scholar claimed that Mt Sinai was a volcano in Arabia, and as a result was forced to return a gold medal awarded by the prestigious Royal Geographical Society! New research has brought together a coherent alternative. My firm belief is that this modern research is correct, and it makes good sense of the Biblical records as simple unvarnished and accurate observations by one or more persons witnessing and involved in the deliverance from Egypt, and in crossing the Red Sea where Pharaoh's elite army perished. From the Red Sea, the Israelites pressed on into Midian, and then to the sacred volcano, Mt Bedr, the real Horeb, the mount of God.

Paul, writing in Galatians 4:25, mentions Mt Sinai as being in Arabia. (The strongly held tradition forced Victorian map-makers to write 'Arabia' on the Sinai peninsula, and even in Egypt on the west of the Gulf of Suez, in order for Paul to agree with the tradition! Without evidence, they marked the names of the villages on the route to Mt Sinai where they had to be! Some honest ones added question marks!) If the Mountain of God is not Jebel Musa in the Sinai Peninsula, then another site is to be sought. Humphreys most convincingly presents Mt Bedr as the true site of Mt Horeb.

The volcano, Mt Bedr (Hala-'l Bedr in Arabic), has Latitude and Longitude 37 ° 12' E & 27 ° 15' N, and is in the Hadr area of NW Saudi Arabia. This is a volcanic region, to the east of the Great Rift Valley, which runs north up the Nile and then crosses the Red Sea to the Gulf of Aqaba. This area is no longer open to visitors, but it was explored in early 1900 by the Czech archaeologist Musil when he researched ancient Trade Routes. He described the volcano Mt Bedr. Bedr has a Volcanic Explosivity Index (VEI) of at least 2 minimum, so its cloud column is at least 3 miles (5 km) tall, and could be more. As well, with the crater about a mile (1.6km) above sea level, the cloud column would be visible for hundreds of miles. The volcano is conical, black, about 500 ft tall (150m), and sited on top and at one end of a large flat sandstone plateau called Tadra, 6 miles (nearly 10 km) across, forming a large table-mountain. It is 5000 ft (1500m) above sea-level. Being porous, the sandstone holds much rainwater. The surrounding area is fertile and verdant, where the Israelites were able to feed their flocks during the 11 months before they left for the Promised Land.

Volcanic eruptions are described in several Psalms.

Psalm 97. The covenant was first declared to Abraham in an eerie ceremony one evening. [Genesis 15:12. See chapter 4] God made further revelation to Moses for the nation of Israel at the Burning Bush of Exodus 3 (see chapter 6). At that encounter, God gave the sacred name I AM , rendered "the LORD" in many

English translations. Psalm 97 begins with the LORD of the covenant.

[1-6] He reigns, right across the Earth and seas. He reigns, too, at the mountain of God, amid clouds and darkness, fire and lightning, earthquake and flowing lava. The drama of the volcanic eruption proclaims his sovereign righteousness and justice. Foes are overwhelmed and everyone acknowledges his glory.

[7-9] Idolaters are shamed, and the Israelites, secure in the Promised Land, are joyful to know the LORD, who reigns on high and works justice on Earth.

[10-12] The Psalmist exhorts the faithful to live uprightly, under the LORD'S protection, and to worship him with praise.

In the next chapter comes a deadly intrusion of self-will into the Bible story.

Chapter 4   Love forsaken, Paradise lost

> Rebellion, fracture, and shame invade the Human-God scene, but there is mercy. Genesis 3 – 11 touch briefly on prehistoric judgements and rescues. God is not mocked, but works out his purposes.

As we read on from Genesis 2 into the rest of the Bible, and as we know in our own hearts and experiences, humans did rebel, and we continue to rebel. The Bible is God's story – his story whether history, or allegory, or "myth" – of God's continuing loving and providing for rebels, that they may turn from ill and turn to him. He has never given up. When the human pair heard words seemingly verbalised by the serpent, and then chose of their own free will to follow that advice, and turn from the Lord God's known instruction, their guilty consciences forced them to hide. The cry "Where are you?" [Genesis 3:9] is the heart rending cry of God's desolation; he was desperately hurt. It was not only rebellion, but betrayal of God's love and close relationship with Adam and Eve. He had made them in his image, he had been beside them in the Garden, he had given them marvellous reason to live, and they had shared in his life and happiness. He had said it was all very good, "while the morning stars sang together, and the angels shouted for joy." But like Judas Iscariot, they betrayed him. Satan entered Judas, and he kissed Jesus to identify who should be arrested. It was rank betrayal, and so was Adam's action, even if Satan had a finger in it as well. God expelled Adam and Eve from Eden, and things began to go wrong. But God did not abandon them. They had clothed themselves with fig leaves – an act of self justification; but God clothed them with skins which came from animals that had been killed. The animal deaths functioned in effect as substitutes for the human deaths that did not happen. These were the first *vicarious* sacrifices. [Genesis 3:21]

Genesis 4. We read of lies, hate, confusion, murder, worse and worse. Adam and Eve's family began with Cain and

Abel. The boys grew, but it was a dysfunctional family. Abel farmed sheep and brought a meat offering to God. Cain farmed crops and brought a grain offering. God accepted Abel's offering, which involved an animal's death, and rejected Cain's, which did not. Then Cain lost his temper. Despite God warning him to turn from evil, Cain slew Abel. So he had to move off elsewhere. This was a failure of one human family. Later generations of Cain's descendents settled problems with the same kind of violence.

   The Flood We read in Genesis 6:5-14 of "... only evil continually." God's heart was hurt. By now there were many families. One family in particular was led by Noah, who sought to live in right relation with God. So God used him. God reached out graciously to rescue Noah from the violence and depravity of his times (11). The Flood was God's large scale judgement, and the Ark was his rescue plan to take a family through it. The same waters that brought execution to Noah's world also brought safety to the floating Ark and its inhabitants by lifting them above the disaster.

Genesis 6:8-10 God favoured Noah 11-14 Judgement will fall, so Noah was involved in God's rescue plan. 17-22 God gave details of building the Ark, and Noah obeyed.

Genesis 7:11, 17-18 The Flood overwhelmed civilization, and the Ark floated safe.

Genesis 8:1 God thought of Noah and the animals. v.16 God said "Come out!"

Genesis 9 God renewed and extended the Covenant with all humanity.

   The Ark had been an enormous wood construction. If 1 cubit = 18 inches (450 mm), it was exactly the size of Salisbury Cathedral! Genesis 6:14 (AV) "Thou ... shalt pitch it within and without with pitch."

The use of the Hebrew word KAPHAR (or kopher) to describe the sealing of the Ark's timbers against the flood waters adds to the suggestion of rescue from judgement. The gracious preservation of Noah and of all within the floating Ark in mercy, from the universal fate of all outside the Ark, depended on effective waterproofing. Later the same word was used in connection with gracious preservation of offenders against God from the universal condemnation due to those who reject God's rescue. KAPHAR is translated in other places "to make atonement" (70 times) or "to reconcile, forgive" &c (28 times), in particular for the covering of the sacrificial blood on the Ark of the Covenant with Israel made by Moses after the Exodus.

Noah and family and animals lived in the Ark for 375 days: 40 days with the flood rising, 110 days while the waters were subsiding, and then the Ark grounded; 70 days later the first sightings of mountains were seen, and it took 155 days more for full drying out.

Big alluvial deposits have been discovered in Mesopotamia, but they cannot definitely be linked to Noah's story. "The nations spread out over the earth after the flood." [Genesis 10:32] There are legends of a one-time devastating flood in the folklores of primitive peoples, even in mountain tribes such as those in the High Andes.

Genesis 11 and The Tower of Babel. After the Flood, when mankind spread eastwards, they began to build a city with a tower. Perhaps this was the first ziggurat. It was an attempt at independent spirituality by a whole community, making their own religion in defiance of God. It would have led to human beings aspiring to control the Earth and to depose God. But the Lord would not allow this. Just as he had expelled Adam and Eve from the garden to stop them eating from the Tree of Life in defiance, so now he broke the unity of mankind by confusing their languages. This caused them to scatter afar. It was a failure of the human race.

A Time line diagram

The "War of the Kings" is a simplified diagram of the epic story of the Bible. It is a picture; it is not the whole truth. It must be read with discernment. It represents a traditional understanding, helpful at the end of WW2. At that time, the phrases "Resistance Movement," "Enemy Occupied Territory," "Declaration of War," and "Mopping up Operations," were redolent with meaning. One particular defect of the diagram is that it gives too much profile to Satan, almost raising the Accuser of the brethren to a status comparable with God. Satan is a created being, a fallen powerful spirit, one of God's creatures, but rebelling.

The diagram expresses a standpoint taken by the majority of Bible believing Christians.

A sizeable minority see that it is <u>us and our human sin</u>, rather than Satan, that is the key issue. To blame Satan can be a cover for less than our full ownership of guilt before the Lord. [Consider Genesis 3:11-13]

The War of the Kings

God on the throne	reign of the usurper king Satan	Reign of the true King Jesus	God on the throne
1	2 3	4 5 6 7 8	9 10
	BC	AD	

PRE History: Genesis 1 is the breathtaking account of Creation: God created, his Spirit brooded. [Psalm 33:9] God was in complete control, working joyfully with intense interest and loving care. Genesis 2: the Man & the Woman were entrusted with oversight of every living creature: God the King of Creation – Humans his agents.

(These numerals refer to the numerals in the diagram above)
1. <u>Outbreak of Rebellion</u> [Isaiah 14:4-22] Although Isaiah did not write about Satan, this tirade against the king of Babylon can be read as illustrating the *Mystery of Iniquity*: how strange that a perfect angelic creature should defect! However, *free will* must provide a genuine opportunity to rebel. This powerful spirit pushed his own glory above God's, and stole one of God's titles – "the morning star, the son of the dawn, Lucifer." He was

thrown out of heaven and denied God's throne; he set out to usurp God's creation by subtle means. [Revelation 12:7-9]

2. Humanity lost by enticement [Genesis 3]. Rebellion spread [Genesis 4, 6:5-8]. After the Flood, the earth was restocked from the Ark, but rebellion and failure continued.

3. The Resistance movement God called one family to be his in the hostile world, on the basis of trusting obedience. From Abraham, Isaac, and Jacob came the Israelites. But the usurper undermined this [1 Samuel 8:6]. Kings good, weak, bad, led the nation far from God. Nebuchadnezzar swept them into exile. It was a national failure; but there were the faithful remnant [1 Kings 19:18]. God, still king in heaven [Psalm 95:3], sent messengers to the faithful, living in Enemy Occupied Territory [Isaiah 40:3-5]

4. Declaration of War – The First Coming [Luke 1:26-33] Satan attacked – Mary was nearly divorced, the Baby was nearly murdered. But Jesus, though vulnerable, grew up and kept true with his Father. He was forthright [Mark 1:14-15 "The time has come! ..."] and signs followed [Luke 11:20]

5. **BATTLE ROYAL:** the key battle in the whole war – **THE CROSS**. [Colossians 2:13, 2 Cororinthinas 5:21, 1 Corinthians 15:54-57] This single action broke Satan's stranglehold over God's kingdom. [Hebrews 4:9-15]

6. Victory openly proclaimed: The resurrection. [Luke 24:5-8, and later on, Matthew 28:18]

7. Mankind's new role, declared at the Ascension. We are to be witnesses of the True King [Luke 24:46-51].

8. Humanity was empowered at Pentecost [Act 2:1-4], and we now take part in the

9. Mopping up Operation. We are involved in Lifestyle [Matthew 6:25-34], in Life-programme [2 Corinthians 5:11-6:2], and in Life-worship [Philippians 3:12-4:1]. The enemy is doomed, but is still the father of lies [John 8:44], still parading as the angel of light [2 Corinthians 11:14], and still capable of inflicting great damage [Ephesians 6:10-16].

10. The True King will return – The Second coming [Revelation 19:11-16, 20:10] and the end of the usurper. The rightful King will be on the throne in glory [Revelation 21:5-6]

> POST History: God is reigning, the centre of all, renewing all
> [Revelation 21:1-6]

Psalm 32 seems appropriate for us to admit our betrayal of God's love, and to turn to confession of our outrageous rejection of his majesty and his sovereign rights over us. David wrote from his experience of total forgiveness at the instant of turning and confessing. He recorded restoration of access into God's presence, and prayer once more being received, with renewed protection and rescue. The Lord teaches and guides, and surrounds the trusting person with never-failing love. Joy is restored, with humble internal uprightness.

David's confidence depended on the mercy of God, and this was expressed in the OT system of animal sacrifice ministered by the Tabernacle priests. For Christians today, our confidence depends on the Cross, the mercy of God shown to us in the NT.

The next chapter unfolds the setting for Abraham and his family on migration, and the beginning of God's gracious covenant with him and with all mankind.

Chapter 5   God's unilateral grace – the Covenant

Approximate dates: BC 2000 to 1600

> In this chapter, we look at Abram the wandering Aramean (Deuteronomy 26:5) and we note where he travelled, from Ur to Canaan. We consider the Covenant which God made with him, as God revealed himself. We note Abraham's family, Isaac and Jacob, and the descent of the Israelites with a family tree.

Psalm 47. This exuberant Psalm rebounds into praise of God from its recalling his grace and purpose for the three generations of Abraham, Isaac and Jacob. True to the great promise that through Abram's blessing will all the nations on earth be blessed, the call for vigorous worship is a call to every community. 'Joyfully shout to God, the great and gracious covenant-maker God, King Most High of all. For the family of Jacob, he cleared our enemies from the Promised Land, because he chose and loved us.'

God has risen in noisy praise with trumpets. We sing praises to our King. In fact, he is King everywhere, over all peoples, nations and rulers. They all belong to him! They, too, gather to exalt God who is God of Abraham's descendents.

He is greatly exalted!

Middle East Geography   Referring to the Middle East map, the distribution of annual rainfall determines the locations of human settlements and deserts. The Fertile Crescent is the name given to the region curving NW from Ur near the Persian Gulf up the Tigris and Euphrates rivers to Haran and Carchemish, then down the Mediterranean shore and the Orontes and Jordan rivers, and on towards Egypt. The desert region between Mesopotamia and Canaan has less than 4 inches (100mm) of rain per year and does not sustain life. 'Green' Canaan was the bridge for trade between the East, and Egypt and Yemen in the South West. Also Canaan was the land route to

Egypt and Yemen for western invaders, such as the Macedonian, Alexander the Great.

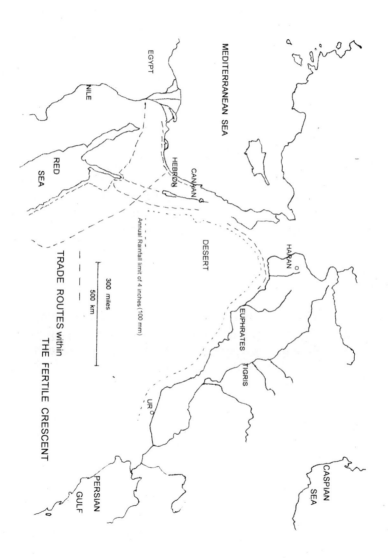

On the Map, <u>Trade Routes</u> in the ancient world followed the Fertile Crescent, into Egypt and into Arabia, down to Yemen. Water supply is vital for travellers and nomads; Trade Routes normally went from well to well, not more than a day's journey, at the most 35 miles (50 to 55km). There was a dry Trade Route eastwards from Egypt to Midian, for which they took water in bags. There was also Trade by boat across the Red Sea from Yemen to Africa. When he left Ur, Abram followed the Fertile Crescent from Ur to Haran, and then eventually down to Canaan, when he also explored as far as Egypt. He got entangled with the Pharaoh and his harem [Genesis 12:10-20]. Perhaps this was the occasion when Sarai acquired Hagar as handmaid.

Genesis chapters 4 to11 links the prehistoric eras to the times of Abram. It contains genealogical lists, and the NIV notes that "father" in Genesis 5 may mean "ancestor". Some significant folk are named, especially Noah and family, though only as participants in the Flood Epic. While not denying they existed, these people do not have serious history.

Genesis 12:1-7

However, Abram is an historical person, meaning that in a dozen chapters we have stories about him in a living world; we read of the places where he lived, and of his person and life-work, and of his relations with people and with God. Much Bible history has been supported by archaeology.

Referring to the Map, Abram came from the city of Ur somewhere near the head of the Persian Gulf. For a long time, it was supposed that the sea came further inland in Abram's day; however, recent studies suggest that was not so. Ur was a prosperous and civilised place, where the mortgage rate was 25%! It has been excavated, and it had a large ziggurat. This was a stepped square building connected with the cult of the Moon-god, for which Ur was one major centre.

Abram's story begins in Genesis 11:31. Abram's father, Terah, moved his family from Ur near the mouth of the Euphrates to Haran, 600 miles NW, nearer its source, where he settled. He may have come from there originally. He shelved the idea of then turning southwards towards Canaan, even though his son wished to respond to the call of God. However, the Lord called Abram to leave his father's home and travel on to Canaan, so after his father's death, he left the Haran property in his brother Nahor's hands and he set off. On his journey south from Haran, he was joined by his nephew Lot. When Abram left Haran, he was renouncing the religious cults of Mesopotamia, and taking on the new vision revealed to him by the Lord. The revelation of God comes amidst the concrete affairs and relationships of ordinary people.

The era was a time of unrest, with some peoples mingling and settling, while others moved from place to place with their families and belongings. The Canaanites, Hittites, Amorites, Perizzites, Hivites and Jebusites, were settled in Canaan, while Abram and his folk wandered from place to place to find pasture in the sparsely peopled hill country. They, amongst many others, belonged to the class called the Habiru (perhaps Old Aramaic – migrant and rootless. Habiru may be HIBRI or 'Hebrew' in the OT); originally it described many more peoples than Abram's family [Genesis 14:13]. They were all wandering Arameans. [Deuteronomy 26:5]

However, the Blessing of God to Abram in Genesis 12:2,3 was specifically for him and his descendents. God promised that he will derive a nation from him, that he will bless him, that he will give the wanderer universal renown, that he will protect him, and that all nations will be blessed through Abram.

Both Abram and Lot were prosperous livestock farmers, and to keep their animals in pasture, they agreed to separate. After the departure of Lot, Abram and his wife Sarai lived amongst the hill peoples at Hebron, the highest point of the Land, about 3000 ft (900m) above the Mediterranean. Lot and his family moved down into the fertile Rift valley, 25-30 miles (40-50km) to the SW of Hebron, and some 4300 ft (1300m) below it. But Lot was vulnerable to foreign raiders. Once, he and his fellow town's people were captured and deported. Then Abram's fighters rescued them 200 miles (300km) from home in a surprise attack in the hills north of Damascus.

COVENANT   Genesis 15:9-21:
This bloodstained experience, scary for Abram, was a solemn enactment of a covenant. It was a standard, well-known procedure. For us, our legal procedures are done before a lawyer, to swear an oath, making an act and deed, signed sealed and delivered. But this covenant was a treaty between two people to go to each other's help, in war and peace, at the cost of life if necessary. The animals were killed and cut in half; the halves were laid out to form an avenue. The two covenant makers, as equals, walked together up the avenue, implying faithfulness to each other, such that any failure would result in the bloodshed and death of that person.   It might be the origin of the English proverb: "blood is thicker than water" – in that the covenant in blood mattered above the family born through the waters of birth. Of course, there are other derivations.

In Abram's experience, he discerned God alone walking the avenue, binding himself to Abram, at the price of blood. Consistently in Genesis, God reveals his deep longing for Abram and family to receive blessing and to respond in faithfulness. God never broke the Covenant. Through and through, God renewed his eternal covenant; it was utterly gracious, entirely one sided: first to Abram, then to Isaac [Genesis 26:2-5], to Jacob [Genesis 28:10-15], and to his children. In the end, Christ died the death which we as covenant breakers, faithless beings, should die; he took upon himself responsibility for our failure, at the price of his own blood. [1 Peter 1:18-21]

All this time, Abram's wife's infertility worried him. He had been promised descendents, but she was barren. Sarai herself saw her Egyptian maid as a possible surrogate mother; she suggested this, and Abram consented. But Sarai regretted it when Hagar began to flaunt her pregnancy, and her anger boiled over. Some years after Ishmael's birth, the Lord met Abram and made more extensive promises to him. He enjoined **male Circumcision**, to be a sign of the Covenant with Abram. At this time, the Lord changed the names of Abram and Sarai.   Abram was renamed Abr<u>ah</u>am, by the addition of 'ah'; Sarai was changed to Sar<u>ah</u>, 'ai' becoming 'ah'; the aspirate letters may refer to Hebrew RU<u>AH</u>, breath, aspirate, the Spirit of God, by whom Abraham was directed, and empowered to make Sarah became pregnant [Genesis 18:10-11; 21:1-2].

Very soon, Abraham and Sarah were surprised to entertain three visitors at Hebron. Quickly it was clear that these were Godly, with a mission to accomplish. First, the Lord made the promise of a son to Abraham in Sarah's hearing; he was 99 and she 89, and so Sarah laughed at this as a ludicrous idea! Then, the Lord revealed his intention of executing judgement on Sodom and the other centres of evil close by. This provoked a remarkable intercession by Abraham for any righteous persons that might be there. He was assured that the Judge of all the Earth would do right, and in the event Lot was spared the volcanic overthrow.

Sarah became pregnant, and could hardly stop laughing. At birth, Abraham named his son 'Isaac,' which means 'he laughs'!

Genesis 22:1-19   God tested Abraham by asking him for the human sacrifice of his only son Isaac. At that time, human sacrifices were not uncommon in Canaan. Abraham was obedient up to the brink! But God stopped him. Then he found a ram caught in a bush, and he sacrificed that in substitution for his son. His faithful obedience was especially commended by God. It is also featured in Hebrews 11:17-19.

Genesis 24 is the long account of how Abraham arranged for a bride for Isaac to be brought from the family at Haran. The mission was soaked in prayer, and God gave full assurance of his purposes in it. Rebekah became Isaac's bride. She did not conceive for 20 years; then after his earnest prayer, she bore twins, Jacob and Esau. [Genesis 25:21] Esau, the eldest, a hunter out in the wild, was father's favourite. Jacob, quiet, subtle, home dwelling, was Rebekah's favourite. He stole Esau's birthright [Genesis 25:29-32]. When Isaac was elderly and going blind, Jacob and mother schemed to deceive Isaac into giving Jacob the formal blessing of inheritance [Genedsis 27]. Esau was disinherited, outraged and threatened murder. So Jacob was packed off to Rebekah's family at Haran, to find a bride in his turn.

At Bethel, on the way to Haran, the Lord graciously revealed himself – the dream of "Jacob's Ladder" [Genesis 28:10-22] – and Jacob responded. [Genesis 29] At Haran, he met his mother's brother Laban and family, and fell deeply in love with cousin Rachel. He became one of Laban's shepherds and served him 7 years in a deal for Rachel. However, at the wedding he had a taste of his own medicine in deceit from Laban, who substituted his elder daughter Leah for Rachel. Then Laban gave him Rachel as well, but in return for a contract of 7 more years of service. Laban meted out devious treatment for all of 20 years, until Jacob could stand it no longer. Then he escaped with his flocks and families, while Laban was away. [Genesis 31] Laban caught up, but after furious exchanges they parted for ever in peace. Then Jacob heard that Esau was approaching with 400 men, so he sent ahead a considerable peace offering. [Genesis 32:22-38] The night before they met, Jacob, alone, found himself wrestling with another person; Jacob's hip was put out, but he refused to let go. Finally he realised that he had been fighting with the Lord! The Lord blessed him, and gave him the new name Israel. Next day, Esau was forgiving and considerate, and they became reconciled. Esau went home to Seir, and Jacob took flocks and families west across the River Jordan, [Genesis 35] to visit Bethel. They moved south to Bethlehem where he had to bury Rachel; she had died in childbirth with Benjamin. Further on, his father Isaac was still alive, living near Hebron. When Isaac died, Jacob inherited the rights of residence, and the family settled there for the next 20 years.

Abraham's Family Tree

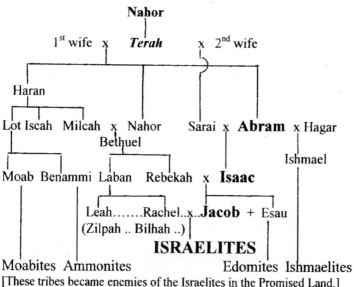

[These tribes became enemies of the Israelites in the Promised Land.]

References for Abram's family tree
    Genesis: 11:26-32; 20:12; 16:1-16; 19:36-38; 22:20-24; 24:24-29; 25:19-26; 29:16-30.

Abram married his half sister; Nahor married his niece; Isaac married his 1st cousin once removed; Jacob married both of his 1st cousins, sisters.

    Their understanding of inheritance was that mothers made no contribution, since they were merely the 'soil' for the 'seed' of the fathers; so in their view, all the Israelites were 100% descended from Abram!

> Abraham is renowned for his faith. [James 2:21-24] He trusted God and acted in obedience to all God told him. [Gen 12:1,4; 13:17-18; 15:4-6; 17:10,23; 22:1-3. Heb 11:8-12,17-19] God handled Abraham so gently and justly, in grace with mercy.
> God's dealings with Abraham are foundational to the rest of the Bible, and so much that we understand about the Lord derives from them. A study of Genesis 11:27 to 25:10 contains:
> Abram's obedient move from Ur to Canaan, and the great promise of 12:2-3
> The experience of Egypt; the separation from Lot, and then his rescue of Lot   Genesis 13 & 14
> The promise of offspring, and the establishment of the Covenant   Genesis 15
> The fathering of Ishmael, and circumcision   Genesis 16 & 17
> The promise to Sarah of parenting, and Abraham's intercession for Lot in Sodom   Genesis 18
> The unhappy experience of life in Negev, and the birth of Isaac   Genesis 21
> Abraham's obedience to the call to sacrifice Isaac, and the outcome   Genesis 22
> The death of Sarah and the purchase of a family burial site   Genesis 23
> The negotiation for Rebekah, as bride for Isaac   Genesis 24
> His death and burial   Genesis 25:1-10

Next is the story of how Jacob came to live in Egypt.

Chapter 6 That "Multicolour Dreamcoat," and an Egyptian story

> The tale of Joseph: a tactless youth sold by his older brothers as a slave and taken into Egypt. Also the challenge of Ethics in natural disasters.

The Psalm 105:1-23 looks outward to the nations beyond Israel. Israel is exhorted to tell of the Lord's wonderful acts, to make known the history so that his name is heard in praise, his glory seen to be honoured, his miracles and his judgements are told with belief, and expectation created that his promises will be fulfilled. For those who seek God's face, becoming aware of his historic actions, cultivated in a worshipful situation is a great way to progress. Believers can feed the seekers' hunger, when they give thanks, sing praise, rejoice in heart, look to God, and remember his deeds. These are the things to attract people to the Lord our God.

God made covenant with Abraham, swore oath with Isaac, and confirmed by decree to Jacob – 'You will have the Land of Canaan.' The Psalm tells of Abram as the wandering stranger in Canaan, and though he was vulnerable the Lord protected him. He was venerable and respected as a prophet amongst the settled population. It was his great grandson Joseph who was enslaved, but when his word from the Lord came true, he was released and made master of Egypt. This brought his father Jacob, with the entire family of Israel, 70 strong, into Egypt, where they were able to flourish.

Genesis 37 begins the stories of Jacob's family from the time of his father Isaac's death, and runs through to the end of Genesis. Most of it centres on Joseph, his child of old age by his beloved Rachel. Later, Rachel had died giving birth to Benjamin, so Joseph, at 17, was Daddy's spoilt brat, wearing a special robe and detested by his 10 half-brothers. The "Coat of many colours" could equally be translated as "a long robe with sleeves." His tactless telling dreams to the family was taken as intolerable arrogance, so the brothers schemed murder; however they disposed of him by selling him as a slave to passing merchants heading for Egypt. The brothers dipped his special robe in goat's blood, which they took home, and grief-stricken Jacob assumed that Joseph had died in the jaws of an animal.

Genesis 39   Joseph became a slave-servant of Potiphar, captain of Pharaoh's guard. The Lord was with him, and Joseph's gifts emerged; he administered Potiphar's household with notable effect. However, Potiphar's wife sought to seduce this handsome Hebrew. He would have none of it, so she falsely accused him of assault and Potiphar put him in prison. In prison, the Lord was with him, and he became the gaoler's trusted administrator. His experiences of hardship were schooling him to live by faith in God. In this situation he correctly interpreted the dreams of two fellow prisoners. These were servants of Pharaoh and had incurred his wrath. Soon one was executed, and the other pardoned, exactly as Joseph had predicted.

Genesis 41   Two long years passed before Pharaoh himself had dreams that none of his staff could interpret. The servant who had met Joseph in prison recommended Joseph to Pharaoh, who sent for him. He was quickly cleaned up and wheeled in, and at once he owned that God would give the answer. Pharaoh spoke of 7 fat cows consumed by 7 withered cows; then again, of 7 good ears of corn consumed by 7 withered ears. Joseph interpreted that 7 years of great abundance were to be followed by 7 years of extreme famine; and the double dream was God's under-lining of the certainty. Joseph spoke with authority, and recommended that Pharaoh appoint an administrator to store up a fifth of the 7 good harvests to be reserved for use in the 7 years of famine. Pharaoh was so impressed with Joseph's plan and vision that he appointed him as governor: "Without your word, no one will lift hand or foot in all Egypt." Joseph stored grain in the cities throughout Egypt, more than could be recorded. He became married to an aristocratic lady, Asenath, and she bore him sons Manasseh and Ephraim before the famine began. His marriage secured his social status, and was no doubt useful in his work.

The volcano Santorini is on the Aegean island of Thira, which is about 70 miles north of Crete. It is quite possible that the 7 years of famine were the result of the extreme volcanic explosion of Santorini. This was even more violent than the famous explosion of Krakatoa, between Java and Sumatra, in 1883AD. Tree rings in Ireland and California show 7 years of restricted growth due to the sun's darkening with the volcanic dust and fumes circling the Earth; the tree rings date the Santorini eruption at 1628BC. So it is reasonable to suggest that Joseph became governor of Egypt in 1635BC.

Genesis 42 'Corn in Egypt'! As the famine began to bite in Canaan, Jacob sent his sons to buy corn in Egypt, but he kept Benjamin at home. When they arrived, they bowed down to Joseph without realising who he was. However, he knew at once who they were. It was a fulfilment of his dreams as a youth in Canaan. He dealt with them harshly, accusing them of being spies, interrogating, and imprisoning them for 3 days. Then he detained Simeon, and sent the others home with corn, demanding that Benjamin come next time. They left, and at a stop on their way, one man discovered that his money had been refunded in his corn-bag. At home with Jacob, their alarm was increased to fear when they found that in each bag the money was refunded. Jacob was distressed: "Joseph is no more, and Simeon is no more, and now you want to take Benjamin. Everything is against me!"

Genesis 43 But the famine continued, so Jacob wanted to send them again. Judah protested that unless Benjamin went with them, they would not be received. Judah argued forcefully with his father that they were facing starvation. Jacob eventually consented. Jacob sent a gift with them, with Benjamin, and with double the money. On arrival they were taken to Joseph's private house, which scared them. Then Simeon rejoined them, and they were treated as respected guests, honoured with a meal. Joseph arrived and again they bowed low and presented their gifts to him. They were astonished to find that they were seated in order of their ages, and that Benjamin was given 5 times the amount of food that was given to the others, a special honour.

Genesis 44 Next morning, they were sent off with full sacks, unaware of Joseph's continuing actions to test their integrity. With his steward's involvement, their sacks now contained not only all their money, but also Benjamin's contained Joseph's silver cup. The steward pursued them; he 'found' the cup and brought them back to Joseph again. Devastated, they threw themselves at his feet to be his slaves. Joseph, however, would send them home to Jacob, and retain Benjamin. Now Judah stood up and pleaded for Benjamin to return, and Judah to become the slave instead, as otherwise father Jacob would surely die. Judah's sincerity and integrity were clear, and Joseph could bear the tension no longer. He told the Egyptian servants to leave, and he revealed who he was to his brothers. It was an amazing and emotional scene. Joseph at once said to them "God sent me ahead of you … to save your lives." Pharaoh heard that Joseph's brothers had come, and he was pleased. So they were all sent back to Jacob, with orders to move from Canaan to live in Goshen, an area in the Nile Delta. (It could be that the previous inhabitants had been overwhelmed by a tsunami following Santorini's explosion. There is evidence of such a major tsunami on the Turkish coast.) All eleven sons now returned to Jacob, with gifts and carts for removal. At first he was stunned and disbelieving, but then he became convinced and deeply delighted at the prospect of seeing Joseph again, after perhaps a dozen years of grieving for him.

Genesis 46 They packed up and set off, probably from near Hebron. At Beersheba on the way, Jacob encountered the Lord once more, and God reassured him that it was right for them all to go to Egypt. The family, with sons and wives, children, and the next generation, now numbered about 70. Joseph met his father at Goshen. He took five of his brothers to present them to Pharaoh, who ratified the settlement in Goshen. Then he presented his father Jacob to Pharaoh. Contrary to protocol, Jacob blessed Pharaoh, who asked him his age. At 120, Pharaoh must have been deeply impressed! All the time Joseph was maintaining the business of selling corn to sustain life. If the date of the Santorini eruption is correctly taken to as the date of the onset of the famine, then Jacob entered Egypt 2 or 3 years after, 1626BC or so.

Genesis 49,50 Before Jacob died, he blessed Joseph's two sons, and then all 12 of his own sons. Jacob was embalmed in Egypt, but Joseph petitioned Pharaoh, and they held an impressive burial back in Canaan, in the cave of Machpelah where Sarah, Abraham and Isaac had been buried previously. On return to Egypt, the old fears broke out, and Joseph needed to reassure his brothers that he would not turn on them in a vendetta. He repeated that God had used him to save life at the time of famine. Before he died he made them swear an oath to bury him in the Promised Land. It was generations later that Moses took Joseph's remains out of Egypt at the Exodus, [Exodus 13:19] to be buried at Shechem in Joshua's day. [Joshua 24:32]

Genesis ends with the death of Joseph... Note that Genesis starts in a Garden, and ends in a coffin in Egypt! What an epitaph for the fallen human race!

<u>Some parallel probable history of Egypt</u>: the Hyksos were invaders of Egypt from the north who had carefully supplanted earlier Egyptian dynasties. They moved the capital, from Thebes down the Nile, to the Delta. It was there that Joseph became Governor of Egypt, and where Jacob had brought his family in time of famine. The Hyksos were prepared to trade with Mesopotamia and the land of Midian, and they accepted Semitic peoples in times of drought; it was good business! Within some 10 Israelite generations from Jacob's day, the Hyksos had been swept out by Ahmose from further south, and he restored the capital to Thebes. Later, another dynasty came to power and moved its centre back to the Delta. There, the new rulers made slaves of the resident Israelites and others, to rebuild the area with forced labour. Pharaoh Ramses I was succeeded by Seti I (or Sethos) who was in power when Moses was born. Seti I maintained the oppressive regime for many years, until he was succeeded by Seti II. This Pharaoh ruled only for one year, and then Ramses II became Pharaoh.

Arising from volcanoes and earthquakes, it is appropriate to consider

Ethics in Natural Disasters
There are two kinds of disasters, the natural and the unnatural.
Unnatural disasters derive from human aggression of one person or a group against another. Be it murder or warfare, it is man's inhumanity to man. This kind of disaster can be attributed to human folly, and such events keep on happening.

But natural disasters, with loss of human life, also happen all the time. Those recorded in the Bible include the Flood [Genesis 6,7,8], the destruction of Sodom and nearby habitations [Genesis 19], the death of the Egyptian firstborn [Exodus 11,12], the elimination of Pharaoh's army in the Red Sea [Exodus 14], the engulfing of rebels [Numbers 16], and the collapse of Jericho's walls, so that Joshua's forces were victorious [Joshua 6]. These disasters were assigned as judgements on the victims. But when Jesus spoke about the fall of the tower of Siloam, killing 18, he removed that event from specific judgement [Luke 13:4].

Our planet is a risky place to be. Volcanoes erupt, such as Vesuvius destroying Pompeii, Herculaneum and Stabiae in 79AD. Earthquakes cause buildings to fall on people: San Francisco 1906, Tokyo 1923, San Francisco 1989, Haiti and China 2010. They cause mudslides which engulf villages, and Tsunami, as recently in Indonesia.

Precipitation, rain or snow, causes destructive floods, as Lynmouth 1952, Prague 2002, Bangladesh frequently, English Lakes 2009, in the Andes 2010. Snow avalanches kill the unwary. Big storms break structures – hurricanes in the Caribbean, and typhoons in the China Seas.

Lack of rain causes famines, leading to starvation and death. Plagues also kill thousands.

We may well ask:
1. Should not people choose to live away from volcanoes and known fault lines, and also from flood areas, and from storm smitten zones? But volcanoes deposit minerals which make the

land fertile. They are a source of prosperous farming, bringing in wealth; people choose food and money, not poverty and famine.

2. Are these large-scale disasters, which bring much loss of life or injury, compatible with the Creator of humans, the God of love, whose Son died to rescue all human beings? But if we think of God as arbitrary and callous, we should question whether it is our view of what God should and should not do that is at fault.

[Romans 9:14-23] "Aslan is not a time lion." [CS Lewis – The Lion, the Witch, and the Wardrobe.]

3. Some ask: Is it all the result of the Fall? But others would judge this to be simplistic.

4. Can we live close to the Lord and be guided out of harm [Psalm 91]? But that depends on his purposes for our lives [Job 13:15; Luke 22:42].

It may be that we cannot reconcile our understanding of his concern for humanity [2Peter 3:9] with our understanding of events. What do we think?

Reverting to **Psalm 46**, from chapter 2, the refrain:

In both battle and earthquake, the LORD is supreme. He is I AM, the covenant making God of Jacob, our refuge and strong fortress: HE IS WITH US.

Next, some dozen generations later, enter Moses to bring God's rescue.

Chapter 7   Exodus at Moses' Hand

> We look at God's deliverance of the Israelites from slavery in Egypt. They were a nation at this time, descended from the families of Jacob's 12 sons. The Bible establishes the reality of the escape of the Israelites from Egyptian oppression by the Exodus and Red Sea events, and of their travel on to Horeb, the mountain of God. This epic story is full of amazing coincidences and answered prayers – all truly miraculous – as their covenant Lord worked for the Israelites by grace even when there was mass fear rather than faith.

In Chapter 6, there is a short history of the Pharaohs. It was Seti I (or Sethos) who held Israel in slavery when Moses was born and reared, and from whom he escaped to Midian. Seti's grandson (or son) was Ramses II, a meglomaniac who had plans to build an immense palace complex at Rameses, in the Nile delta. The ruins of this palace at modern Quantir are 4 square miles (1000 hectares) in area. This man was the Pharaoh of the Exodus. In the absence of supporting archaeology, for which there is good reason, some scholarly suspicions have been supposed of myth in the tradition, and of embellishment by the later Hebrew editors. Then, also the record needs rescue from what has obscured the story for the past 1600 years when an error, made in about 400 AD, gave rise to a mistaken belief, still strongly held. Nevertheless, these things truly happened as recorded in the book of Exodus.

The book Exodus wastes no words. One by-product of this chapter is to discover that this economy of expression does not disguise the truth and accuracy of the details which it does record. Some have dismissed as 'poetic license' the words they cannot reconcile with the mistaken strong belief. So much the worse for that belief! The sequence of the events, perfectly balancing the moves of the people led by Moses, was truly miraculous.

Exodus 1

For all peoples in the ancient world, the first-born son was the most important member of the family, upon whose survival depended family continuity. He was treated with extra care and attention in an age with no medical facilities. The first-born son was always fed double rations, even in time of famine, when the youngest could well starve and die. In Egyptian religion, Pharaoh was divine, the first-born son of an Egyptian god, with the gift of life and death. In trying to deal with the Israelites, Pharaoh presumed to the right to kill their firstborns – he ordered the midwives to kill baby boys, and they frustrated this; and he ordered the Israelites themselves to throw male babies into the Nile to drown. So he usurped the role of the real God, the Lord of the Israelites. He had acted in defiance of the Creator, the Creator of the life of both mankind and animals.

So Moses was born under sentence of death. His sister, Miriam, and his brother Aaron were born before him. Moses was perhaps the third healthy child born to Amram and Jochebed. They were of the tribe of Levi [Exodus 6:16-20]. To begin with, he was hidden by his mother, and then at 3 months old she placed him in a basket in the papyrus rushes on the banks of the Nile where he was discovered by Pharaoh Seti's daughter. The princess paid his real mother to bring him up! As a young child he would have absorbed his mother's faith and heritage. Then he entered the Egyptian court, adopted by the princess; he was therefore highly educated, perhaps to be the next Pharaoh. The adult Moses was intelligent and educated in all the wisdom of ancient Egypt. As a Royal, he had access to their libraries and records, and no doubt had ability with languages, Egyptian, Hebrew and Aramaic (the universal basic, and diplomatic language from East to West in the Middle East). As well, he was probably able to read the Hieroglyphics. And he was aware of the formidable army. He saw the temples built for worship of the Nile-god, and of the Sun-god, and maybe others. But he also knew, from his mother's knee, the faith of Abraham, Isaac, and Jacob, and knew their covenant with the Lord.

At this time, the other Israelites were viciously enslaved. Young man Moses visited his native people and was horrified at their mistreatment, so much so that he slew a slave master who was beating a slave, possibly to death. As a result he incurred the wrath of Pharaoh, and he had to fly for his life; so all this outstanding education was wasted - apparently. He fled along the trade route east, most likely by horse, taking bags of water as it was a dry route for 180 miles (290km), from Egypt to the head of the Gulf of Aqaba. Crossing to the East side of the gulf, he turned south, along the trade route which took him into the land of Midian; this is the top NW corner of Arabia. Here he met Jethro, priest of the land, who lived at Madian, a village on one of several Trade routes from Yemen along the Fertile Crescent to Babylon.

Midian Here, Moses met a very different culture from that of Egypt, with its pastoral business in livestock, and its religion in the Moon-god. He married and settled as Jethro's shepherd, and became familiar with the district. It is a volcanic region, to the East of the Great Rift Valley. He and the other local shepherds took their flocks up the mountains in the summers to escape the intense heat below by the Red Sea. The sacred volcano, Mt Bedr, was there, black and conical, on the side of a vast plain of porous sandstone rock. This nourished good pastures for flocks. Jethro, priest of Midian, would have come to the mountain for sacrifices many times, as it was a centre of the Moon-god cult which extended round the Fertile Crescent from Yemen to Babylon and beyond to Ur. Jethro knew about the pastures. He sent his shepherd son-in-law Moses there in the hot summers to provide for his flocks. Consequently Moses learned all about the region.

The sketches show two faces of a stone cube with edges about 15 inches (38cm), from Tayma, to the east of Mt Bedr. The cube is dated 6th Century BC. The horned bull reflected the horned Moon, also shown in one sketch, and the disk between the bull's horns is perhaps the full

Moon. The winged figure might be some hovering spirit or even a Sun-god.

From two faces of a stone cube 6th Century BC from Tayma

THE HORNED MOON AND THE HORNED BULL-CALF

Exodus 3:1-15

Abruptly, Moses met the true Lord God who had a great commission for him. Just beside this sacred mountain Bedr, he saw a bush burning brightly, yet not being consumed. The burning bush could well have been the result of an intensely hot volcanic gas issue under a local species of acacia which forms hard charcoal, such as was used for smelting in the metal industries in the region. Here, the Lord showed Moses that he is God, right at the heart of the territory of the Moon-god: he proclaimed **I AM THAT I AM**. God told Moses that he was very concerned for the suffering Israelites, under the lash of slavery, and that Moses was to go back to Egypt and demand that they be released. Moses had many questions, but in the end he obeyed God. He met his brother Aaron, and together they came to Pharaoh.

Ramses II, a year or so after he became Pharaoh, was organising his major building project, when two Israelites suddenly arrived in his court, and demanded that he release the Israelite slaves for a week – 'to go 3 days into the desert for a religious festival'!

"No Way! How dare you! Who's Pharaoh round here?!"

Ramses tightened the slavery, and so began the epic struggle between Moses and Pharaoh, lasting several months. "The Plagues of Egypt" struck at their gods, including the Sun-god and the Nile-god.

The Plagues of Egypt

1. The Nile was turned into 'blood' by an abnormally high flood. The river flooded every August to October, with peak levels in September. This exceptional one brought red silt and bacteria &c. (So the Nile-god brought ruin, not prosperity, and sacred fish died.)
2. Frogs – (regarded as sacred and the source of life. But they died.)
3. Maggots or mosquitos.
4. Flies – (sacred to the Sun-god.)
5. Cattle sickness and death, maybe due to anthrax. (The bull was sacred)

6. Human sickness, septic boils. (in January)
7. Prolonged hail storms with thunder and lightning (in February)
8. Locusts (in March)
9. 3 days of darkness – (blotting out the Sun-god)

These were forms of natural disaster which afflicted Egypt from time to time. But these were extreme and happened one after another over several months. The Israelites could see that the Egyptian gods were being exposed as worthless. The timing, intensity, and duration of the Plagues were miraculous. The whole series of events was both natural and supernatural, a miraculous demonstration of God's power and purposes with humanity. It seems that some Plagues follow on obviously as a consequence of the previous ones.

10. The death of the firstborn (in March)

With regard to the last catastrophe, the Lord God had sent Moses to Pharaoh with this stark warning: "Israel is my firstborn son, and I told you 'Let my son go, so he may worship me.' But you refused to let him go; so I will kill your firstborn son." [Exodus 4:22,f] The 10th Plague fulfilled this threat and broke the proud stranglehold of Pharaoh.

Exodus 12:1-13   The Passover

At the start of Exodus 12, there are the Lord's instructions to Moses and Aaron, to prepare the Israelites for the 10th Plague and for their immediate escape, their Exodus from slavery. It was the Lord who the one in charge. Months began with the New Moon, so Full moon was on the 14th day. This was important for the Israelites' journey across the desert. The Lord said 'Take a good Lamb on the 10th day.' They were to feed it well to the 14th day, and then slaughter it at twilight, just as the full moon was rising. The lamb's blood was painted on the sides and tops of the doorways, a sign of death, as much to the Israelites as to the Lord. They roasted and ate the lamb, which was their last meat-meal for a least a week, and they were to be ready for a quick getaway. All Egyptian firstborn sons died, animals as well, while Israel's were spared. In fact there was a death in every household in Egypt, but in Israel it was a lamb that died and not a son. The Egyptians in horror threw the Israelites out. Even Pharaoh told Moses to go! Egypt howled when the Lord <u>passed through</u> them, while Israel was safe when the Lord spared them, or <u>passed over</u> them.

In Exodus 12 & 13, there are instructions for the later annual celebrations of the Passover, and for the once-in-a-lifetime redemption of the first-born Israelites. There are 44 verses for these directions, while the action-story takes up 39 verses for the facts of the Exodus from Egypt, and then the Red Sea triumph over Pharaoh and his powerful army. This points up the greatest importance to Israel in recalling the history and the significance of the redemption act by the Lord God of Israel, and therefore the value of consciously celebrating all this. Many songs proclaimed this miracle of deliverance. Because the Israelites had had no time to use yeast to leaven their bread, the Passover became part of the Feast of Unleavened Bread.

The Passover became an annual celebration, when they were to remember for ever the terrible means by which they were rescued, and to honour the Creator's right to the lives of the firstborn. Jesus celebrated Passover with his disciples. He altered the final Passover in the Upper Room so that Christians remember the Cross, the terrible means by which we have been rescued.

Exodus 13:20-14:31   The Red Sea
(This follows Professor Colin Humphreys whose recent researches and on-site investigations are presented in his book "The Miracles of Exodus" – Continuum, 2008.)

The Israelites took with them their herds, many Egyptian valuables, and food and water for the 7 days. Moses led them along the Trade route east to the head of the Gulf of Aqaba, along which he had once fled, seeing the cloud by day and the fire by night ascending from the volcano Mt Bedr which itself was below their horizon. The distance from Succoth to the gulf is 180 miles (290km), and marching desperately 30 to 35 miles (48-56km) a day, they would have reached it in perhaps 6 days. They went down the steep track over the edge of the Rift valley.

Pharaoh's permission extended to 7 days, but he soon learned that they had no intention of coming back. So now they were pursued by the Egyptians. The infantry followed the track over the edge of the Rift Valley, but it was too steep for the Egyptian crack corps of 600 chariots. These went with Pharaoh himself a 100 miles (160km) longer path to descend into the Rift valley further north.

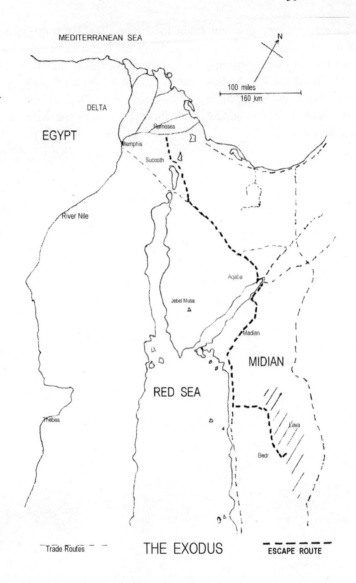

    The Israelites camped by the Red Sea for the night, but soon they were trapped by the valley wall on the west, the water of the gulf on the east, the Egyptian infantry on the south, and the chariots on the north.

Pharaoh thought that he had set a perfect trap, to capture and recover these rebelling slaves. But his plan was delayed by a great dust storm that night, with the wind roaring down the Rift Valley from the north-east. The air was clear in the Israelite camp, but the Egyptians were blinded by the dust. The wind increased, the water parted ("set-down"), and the wind dried out the sandy sea bed. In the early morning with moonlight the Israelites started to stream across. At dawn the Egyptians began to see, and they started to chase them; but now the heavy chariots became stuck in clay, perhaps delaying the infantry. As the last Israelites got over, the wind abruptly stopped, and a great wall of water swept the Egyptian army away. It overshot, and then swept back again.

The Covenant God of Israel had used the terrified Israelites as bait, to draw Pharaoh's men into an even better trap than Pharaoh's, where they were annihilated by an extreme event of nature! Pharaoh, watching in his chariot, at last acknowledged that the God of Israel was no longer to be challenged. He lived until he was 92; for the next 60 years Egypt never attacked Israel in the Promised Land, although it was relatively near.

After possibly refilling their water-bottles from fresh water coming down the Arabah, Moses led the Israelites on. There was much grumbling and squabbling. From Madian, where Moses cured the polluted water with a piece of wood, the Israelites journeyed to the shore of the Red Sea, and then turned inland to reach the mountains and valleys. Here were mineral workings and small furnaces for extracting metals. In about three months out from Egypt, now high summer, they neared Mt Horeb, (Hala-'l Bedr,) but they were opposed by armed Amalekites, Moon-god worshippers, who were no doubt anxious to have their summer celebrations by the sacred volcano. The young Joshua led the untried Isrealite forces to victory, supported by the praying of Moses, attended by Aaron and Hur. Thereafter, Joshua became Moses personal assistant. In time of need, Moses obeyed the Lord and struck the sandstone, so that the covering broke and a generous stream of water flowed out.

Exodus 20:1-17

Soon, with all the Israelites settling in the Desert of Sin (Sin = Moon), the Lord called Moses apart and gave him the Ten Commandments. There was much more to come; however the Lord dealt at once with both the spiritual and social order for the community. They were instructed to acknowledge their covenant Lord as deliverer from Egypt and slavery, to have no other gods, and they received a total ban on any idol or material to represent God. God said No! to presuming to his authority, and Yes! to cooperating with his blessing the Sabbath. The remaining 6 commandments set forth pure and basic principles for community lifestyle.

Later, the Lord showed the way to come to him, and worship with sacrifices for right relation with him and with fellow Israelites, and for happy festive thanksgivings.

Psalm 105 Continuing from v.24, the poetry dwells on a summary of the wonder-working events of the Exodus. The Israelites had grown from Jacob's family into a prospering ethnic group which became an embarrassment to their host nation of Egypt and a hated people. The Egyptian pharaohs with force of arms enslaved them and put them to heavy manual work. Then the Lord sent Moses and Aaron to Pharaoh to demand "Let my people go!" Pharaoh refused, and they contested this with a miraculous and escalating series of wonders – darkness, the Nile waters turned to blood, infected so the fish died; there were frogs everywhere, swarms of flies, and gnats. Heavy hail and thunder ruined the Egyptian vineyards and fig trees, which were all shattered. Locusts stripped every green plant and crop. Lastly the firstborn of man and beast were struck. It was then that Israel left, taking Egypt's riches with them.

The Lord provided for Israel, in food and water, as they travelled. In the end, they received what the Lord had promised to their ancestor Abraham, centuries earlier; they possessed the Land of that promise, taking over what others had cultivated.

The final verse, v.45, declares the Lord's intention behind all this gracious work: Israel was to keep his commands, and so become a nation devoted to a living faith and a prospering lifestyle, focussed entirely differently from the previous inhabitants of the Promised Land.

As with Israel, so for Christ's followers: entirely out of God's grace, we have been rescued from spiritual slavery to powerful worldly forces, miraculously through the Cross. We are to remember this by the adapted Passover given by Jesus. We may have worldly provisions, though in our land of life and faith we receive all we will ever need, by grace and favour of the Lord. His intention is that the Christian community of faith is to keep his commands and live a lifestyle focussed for ever on the Kingdom of God, a focus which is entirely different from the world in which we live. The world is in the clutches of the wicked one, while the Good Shepherd will ever prevent his sheep being rustled.

Next come details of the foundation of Israel's worship system.

Chapter 8   How to worship God!

> The Name of God. The Ten Commandments. The golden calf. The artefacts of worship - the Ark of the Covenant that brilliantly eliminated material idolatry, the Tabernacle, Holiness, the courtyard, the surrounding Israelite camp.   Sacrifices. The priestly blessing   Psalm 67.

At the Burning Bush Moses had asked for a name for God: [Exodus 3:19] - Moses said to God, "Suppose I go to the Israelites and say to them 'The God of your fathers has sent me to you,' and they ask me, 'What is his name?' Then what shall I tell them?" Now, to name somebody was more than to identify. It was to define or put a boundary or limit round them; it was even to claim an authority over them; this is what the man Adam did to the animals (Genesis 2:20), and to his wife (Genesis 3:20). So God replied to Moses, "**I AM WHO I AM.**" Or you might think that God was saying emphatically "I'M ME!" It was not a name, in the sense that the various false gods had names – Ra in Egypt, Baal and Ashtaroth in Canaan, Asshur in Assyria, Bel, Marduk, Gog, &c in Babylon and Persia. We must hold this sacred word I AM in respect, JHVH in Hebrew (no vowels), Jehovah, Yahweh. Scribes reading the Scriptures in Synagogue would pronounce 'Adonai' (means Sir, or Lord) rather than read the sacred name out loud.

Exodus 19. As soon as the Israelites arrived and set up camp in the desert of Sinai (ie in Moon country) near the erupting volcano Horeb, Moses made them come no further while he negotiated with God. Moses went up to the Lord and down again several times, giving the Israelites the Lord's instructions. Then he went up again with Aaron to receive the Ten Commandments. Right at the start of their time there, God gave the Ten Commandments [Exodus 20] by spoken word, which was then relayed and taught to the Israelites by Moses.

Exodus 20: v.1 Moses reported to the people God's words.
ONE   v.2   I AM THE I AM who extracted you from slavery in Egypt. You shall relate to me only. No synergies, blending me with superstitions, not even for luck. No syncretism.
TWO   v.4   Make no material representation of me, and give no veneration to any artifact – do you hate me or love me? Any error here infects coming generations.
THREE v.7   Watch your language. Do not presume to my authority. Speak to others about me with respect. Be real not religious, be uplifting never casual. They hear every idle word you speak, and so do I.
FOUR v.8   I settled the pattern of weekly work, 6 days on, 1 day off. I created mankind to devote 1 day in 7 to be holy to me. Keep to this. It's the way life works.
FIVE v.12 I created families, so respect parents: relate to them, listen to them, learn from them, love them, be patient with them, support them, honour them. This is the foundation of a practical society, of a prospering community lifestyle.
SIX   v.13 Life is sacred, full of mystery. Do not assassinate character, do not murder.
SEVEN v.14 Sex is my creation, built into your life. Hold the powerful attraction in faithful respect for your opposite sex. Do not deceive yourself into crossing the boundary. Stay faithful to your relationship.
EIGHT v.15 No stealing, whether it is from your workplace, or from other peoples' belongings, or identity, or money, or reputation. Take care to build people up. Restore what you find that they have lost.
NINE v.16 Speak the truth about other people. Truth frees up and creates respect. Have integrity.
TEN   v.17 Other people rightfully have their own folk and property, and they are allowed to be different from you. Do not envy them, nor covet what is theirs.

The Golden Calf

There was trouble, as not all accepted Moses. Once, shortly after arrival at Horeb, he was meeting the Lord, away up the volcano with Joshua; then the rebels bullied Aaron who made them a golden idol, the calf with its horns symbolising the regional Moon deity. Constructing the golden calf was an expression of installing the local Moon-god and its cult in Israel in place of the Lord God of Abraham, Isaac and Jacob. Moses' fury is understandable. Perhaps it was a defining moment, a first step towards the Lord overcoming their idolatry, defying and rubbishing the pervasive hold of the Moon-god in the whole region. Moses struck at those who had misbehaved. He forced everyone to take note by involving the water supply, because he dumped the dust of the pulverised gold image in the water supply. This is recorded in Exodus 32 and 33.

The Ark and the Tabernacle

The Lord had already given instructions about making the artefacts for worship. They are written in Exodus 25 to 31, and these are summarised in Hebrews 9:1-10. After emphatically settling the perversion expressed in the Golden Calf, construction work on the Ark and the Tabernacle started.

The Lord told Moses to make a big tent, the Tabernacle, which was placed in a curtained off Courtyard. (See 2 diagrams.) Between the gate and the Tabernacle was an Altar of sacrifice, and a Laver for the priests to wash. Inside the Tabernacle was a Table, a 7 branched candlestick and lamps, and a small Altar of incense, all in the first room, called the Holy Place. This was roughly a double cube 15 X 30 ft (4.5m X 9m) and 15 ft (4.5m) tall. Adjoining and curtained off was the second room, roughly a single cube 15 X 15 X 15 ft, (4.5m X 4.5m X 4.5m) called the Most Holy Place, where the Ark of the Covenant was to be placed.

The Ark of the Covenant was the centrepiece of the system. This wooden chest was sheathed in gold, and was about 3'9" x 2'3 x 2'3 (110 x 70 x 70 cm). There were 4 gold rings at the corners and two gold covered poles through them for carrying. Inside the Ark were the stones engraved with the Ten Commandments. On top of the Ark was a plate of gold, having a pair of gold figures of cherubim, one at each end. Their spread wings and the gold plate together formed a seat on top of the Ark where God promised to sit, to meet man. *"The Lord reigns, let the nations tremble; he sits enthroned between the cherubim, let the earth shake."*[Psalm 99:1] The structure of the Ark of the Covenant with the two cherubim facing across the seat, gazing at the empty space, was a brilliant device, a remarkable demonstration of there being no material object for veneration. The two stones inscribed with the Ten Commandments were placed in the Ark, so they underlay the Mercy Seat. This arrangement taught people of the holiness of the Lord, and of the holy lifestyles needed for associating with him.

THE TENT OF MEETING
[Scale about 1:57]

The Holiest Place of All
15 ft x 15 ft x 15 ft
(4.5m x 4.5m x 4.5m)

The <u>Ark</u> of the Covenant
and
<u>The Mercyseat</u>
between two cherubim

The thick <u>Inner</u> Curtain

<u>The Altar of Incense</u>

The Holy Place
30 ft x 15 ft x 15 ft
(9m x 4.5m x 4.5m)

<u>The Table</u> with
The Bread of the Presence

<u>The Lamp</u> with
The seven lights

<u>The hanging Curtains</u> on poles with the
four layered roof <u>Covering</u>

<u>The Outer Curtain</u>

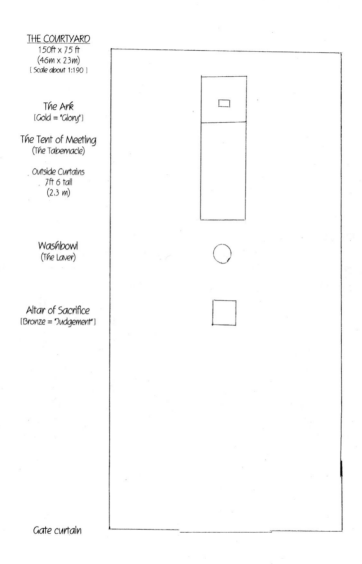

THE COURTYARD
150ft x 75 ft
(46m x 23m)
[Scale about 1:190]

The Ark
[Gold = "Glory"]

The Tent of Meeting
(The Tabernacle)

Outside Curtains
7ft 6 tall
(2.3 m)

Washbowl
(The Laver)

Altar of Sacrifice
[Bronze = "Judgement"]

Gate curtain

<u>The Tabernacle</u> was the portable sanctuary, the big tent divided into the Holy Place and the Most Holy Place, by a thick curtain. Daily worship was conducted by the Priests in the Holy Place.

But the Ark alone stood in the Most Holy Place; only once a year, the High Priest conducted worship there.

The Courtyard was the precinct for this, enclosed by a 7'6" (2.3 m) wall of curtains on poles. This system was designed to teach people how to approach God. Coming from outside, and making towards the Ark, you must step towards:

The Gate, the only entrance. There was no other way into God's presence. Israelites could enter the courtyard through the gate, and they were required to bring sacrifices. At that time, you needed to be an Israelite to be allowed to enter. You would next meet

The Brass Altar, brass symbolising judgement – atonement requires sacrifice. Then

The Laver, or bowl for washing – cleanliness is necessary. Next,

The Holy Place, for priests only – worship requires separation from ordinary things. Only priests, after sacrificing and washing, could enter the Holy Place of the Tabernacle, to perform their daily duties and maintain the lamps and incense, and supply the Bread of the Presence on the Table. These were symbols of light and worship and prayer and the presence of God. Then,

The Altar of Incense – representing spiritual communication of worship and prayer. Next,

The Curtain – Only the High priest, once a year on the day of Atonement, with blood of sacrifice, could pass the Curtain to enter the Most Holy Place. This showed that the way into God's presence was there, but it was not yet open to all. Finally, once within the Most Holy Place, and coming before

the Ark of the Covenant, containing the Ten Commandments, where

upon the Ark was the Mercy Seat, the throne of God's gracious presence; and

upon the Mercy Seat, was the sprinkled life-blood from the sacrifice, its covering making the atonement, then might you be in God's awesome presence.

In summary, by stages, into
The Courtyard: graciously, (ie, for the Chosen People alone)
The first room of the Tent of Meeting God: HOLY
The second room of the Tent: HOLY HOLY
And the LORD of the Covenant himself: HOLY HOLY HOLY
[Isaiah 6:3   Revelation 4:8]

Moses ordered the construction of the Tabernacle or Tent of Meeting. God called his brother to be the high priest, so Moses prepared magnificent robes, and he consecrated Aaron with special anointing oil. The Tabernacle within its curtained off compound was set up on the extensive table-top mountain before the volcano Horeb. The Israelite tribes were assigned positions in the camp round it, and so gave it protection from intruders. The worship was at the centre of their community life. The Levites were encamped around the Courtyard, focussed on their assigned duties, both in daily worship and in portage on the march.

The Israelite Camp on the table mountain by Horeb, and when halted on the march

The North camp, with the camp of Dan to be set out last:

| DAN | ASHER | NAPHTALI |

The West Camp, with the camp of Ephraim to be set out third:	The Centre Camp of the **LEVITES**	The East Camp, with the camp of Judah to be set out first:
BENJAMIN	Merarites	**JUDAH**
MANASSEH	Gershonites [Courtyard] Moses Aaron Eleazar Ithamar	**ISSACHAR**
EPHRAIM	Kohathites	**ZEBULUN**

The South Camp, with the camp of Reuben to be set out second:

| GAD | SIMEON | REUBEN |

They were there for nearly a year, in which time they had constructed their worship centre, and learned new forms of worship and sacrifices. Aaron's ministry, supported by the Levites, and maintained for several months alongside Horeb, established the LORD, the Most High God of Abraham, Isaac and

Jacob, over the previous traditional deity of the Moon at that place.

Sacrifices

The Israelites had to eat! They were livestock farmers who regularly ate from their flocks and herds. Moses set up the Altar of Sacrifice to centralise slaughtering and to replace bloodshed at random. In this, God told them to value and respect the lifeblood of animals, and they learned much more too. It all prepared for an understanding of the life of Jesus laid down at the cross.

Some sacrifices are enjoined in the book Exodus, including the two lambs daily, morning and evening [Exodus 29:38-43]. The next book, Leviticus, gives details of the several varieties of sacrifices: the burnt offering, the grain offering, the fellowship offering, the sin offering, the guilt offering. The principle behind every sacrifice is that life is sacred: the worshipper or penitent identifies with the animal by laying his hand on the animal's head and its death is taken to be in place of his death [eg Leviticus 4:32-35]. Therefore his life is preserved for a worshipping relation with the LORD. The sacrifices were for personal sin, for family worship, for thanksgiving, for annual atonement for the whole community, and for the annual Passover remembrance of deliverance from Egypt's slavery.

Both OT and NT emphasise that all this correct religious activity is worthless without people living the life and lifestyle of obedience to God, receiving God's grace to do so in faith. Jesus at the well of Sychar told the Samaritan woman "God is Spirit, and his worshippers must worship in spirit and in truth." [John 4:24]

The OT system was temporary and symbolic; when Jesus died, the way into heaven's Most Holy Place was opened for all time, for all people. This opening at the time of the crucifixion was given drama and emphasis when the thick curtain in the Temple between the Holy Place and the Most Holy Place was torn in two from top to bottom. [Mark 15:38] The writer of Hebrews was a Christian Jew who used the symbolism of the OT

Israelite Tabernacle system of worship to show in detail how much better the New Covenant (NT) Christian way is over the Old Covenant (OT) system. He says 'God has got something better for us!' [Hebrews 11:40] All the requirements for mankind to rejoin God have been fulfilled by Jesus at the time of his Cross. 'Put our trust in Jesus, and we have a better hope, a more certain, future [7:19], a better deal [covenant, 7:22], with better promises [8:6].' Hebrews is a great book, though it takes much work to penetrate what the original Jewish Christian readers would have understood straight off. Hebrews 10:19-25 urges people to come to God by entering God's Most Holy Place in heaven, since this is now wide open. Its call is clear: [22] let us draw near to God in faith, [23] let us hold unswervingly to the (forward looking) hope in God's reliability, [24] let us think how to help one another grow in life and love, [25] let us value our meeting together, and let us encourage one another.

The story of The Ark and the Tabernacle
The Ark and the Tabernacle were carried with the Israelites from Horeb to Kadesh Barnea, and then after the rebellion at Kadesh, they went with them during their wanderings. When Joshua had led the Israelites across the Jordan into the Promised Land, they set up the Tabernacle with the Ark at Shiloh [Joshua 18:1]. Here they remained through the time of the Judges, until Samuel's day under Eli. The Ark was lost to the Philistines [1 Samuel 4:10,11], who quickly returned it, and it remained at Kiriath Jearim for 20 years [1 Samuel 7:2]. The Tabernacle and Brass Altar were still at Shiloh in Saul's reign [1 Samuel 14:3]. At some time they were removed to the high place at Gibeon in Benjamin. David, when at first king of all Israel (about 1003 BC), fetched the Ark to his newly established Jerusalem and he put it in a tent of his own. He set up worship here, and also maintained worship at Gibeon [1 Chronicles 16:37-42]. It could have been impolitic to move this shrine to Jerusalem at that time.

A generation later, the Ark was incorporated into Solomon's Temple, the more permanent stone building replacing the Tabernacle. Solomon visited the Tabernacle and Altar at

Gibeon [2 Chronicles 1:1-6], while Shiloh remained a prophetic centre for many more years [1 Kings 14:2]. Shiloh was devastated some time, perhaps by the invading Assyrians, and its destruction became a byword for Jeremiah's prophecies about Jerusalem in the last years before it was sacked by Nebuchadnezzar. The Ark was probably destroyed with Solomon's Temple in 587BC. The Tabernacle fabric either wore out at Gibeon through neglect or was destroyed by invaders or by the weather. The Ark and the Tabernacle appear to have survived some 700 years.

The Blessing The priests pronounced the blessing of Numbers 6:22-27 on the people in a formula which ministers still use today. They put the covenant name of God, I AM, on the Israelites.

Later, the Temple musicians composed Psalm 67, a prayerful anthem based on the Blessing. It also recalls the Blessing of Abraham [Genesis 12:2-3]. The Psalm prays for God's grace and blessing, and for an awareness of his face-to-face radiance; then for this light to become known to others near and far. "May there be praise, justice and joy, with gladness and singing." They looked forward to a productive land, blessed with milk and honey. God's blessing Israel will bring awe of God to the ends of the earth.

Through Jesus Christ, may it be so for us in our time.

Chapter 9   The Power of Doubt

> The Israelites travelled from Horeb to Kadesh Barnea, and prepared to enter the Promised Land. But a positive march ended in a sorry wandering.

Moving on   [Numbers 10:11-13, 32-36]   When the time came to possess the Land, promised by the LORD to Abraham, Isaac and Jacob, the Israelites packed up their tents and the Levites folded up the Tabernacle. It was all carefully organised. When packing up, first Aaron and his sons covered the Ark with the inner curtain, and with other sheets they covered the gold altar, the table, the lamps, the brass altar, and all the utensils. Then the Kohathites carried all these covered holy things. The Gershonites carried all the other curtains, and the Merarites carried all the frames, posts, bases and ropes.

Starting on the march, the East Camp under Nashon, leader of Judah, set out first, to be followed by those Levites carrying the curtains and poles &c of the Tabernacle. The South Camp tribes went next, and were followed by the Levites carrying the Ark and holy things; this placed the Ark in the centre of the whole Israelite column. The West camp followed the Ark, and Dan's North camp came last, forming the rear guard. Details are in Numbers 10:14-27. On arrival, while the Levites unpacked, the rest of the column arrived in order and set up camp round them.

Order of March
(North camp) → (West Camp) → (Levites with) →
(led by Dan)   (led by Ephraim)   (**The Ark**)

(South camp) → (Levites &) → (East camp) →
(led by Reuben)   (Tabernacle)   (led by Judah)

Moses had invited Jethro, Moses' father-in-law, and priest of Midian, to come with them as guide. He seems to have acknowledged the LORD. [Exodus 28:11] No doubt he gave

Moses some advice, but he declined to go with them [Numbers 10:29-32]. They left Mt Horeb and travelled a day's journey east across to the Trade route which would take them north to the Promised Land. Eventually they crossed the Arabah to arrive at Kadesh Barnea. (See the Map)

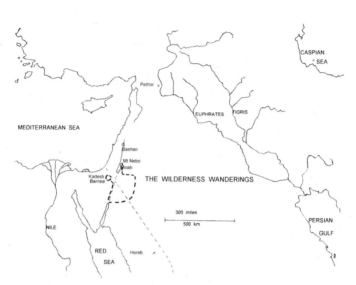

Altogether, it was an 11 day journey [Deuteronomy 1:2]. This is a statement of distance, at an average of about 32 miles (52km) a day. It does not say that the Israelites achieved all 358 miles (575km) in 11 days.

Half-hearted following. So far, so good. From the camp at Kadesh, some 16 months after their deliverance from Egypt, Moses sent twelve leading men, one from each tribe to spy out the Promised Land; [Numbers 13:1-2,17-21, 25-14:9]. Six weeks later, these men brought back a good report about the Land, indeed flowing with milk and honey. But of the twelve, only Caleb of Judah, and Joshua of Ephraim were bold, confident, and stood firm, while the other ten were weak and brought complete discouragement to the Israelites by claiming that the Canaanites were too strong for them to overcome. Fear spread, and everyone said that they wanted to go back to Egypt, with all its horrific slavery! Instead, the LORD sent them wandering in the Wilderness for a generation, until 'natural wastage' had claimed the lives of all the fighting men who had been the faithless rebels. It was to be their children who were to enter the Promised Land, under Joshua who would lead them victoriously. The wanderings were a fruitful time, even if a whole generation was wasted. The book Numbers continues the story of education by experiences and of training by Moses.

Numbers has this English name from the Greek OT, the Septuagint. It records two major censuses taken by Moses of the Israelite fighting men. That in Numbers 1 was held at Mt Horeb shortly before they left for the Promised Land, listing the names of able-bodied men 20 years old or more. The fighting force was listed and identified, in preparation for active service against the Canaanites. The census in Numbers 26 was of the same kind as that in Numbers 1, and was taken a generation later, when the Israelites were soon to cross the Jordan under Joshua and begin the fight to claim the Land. In Numbers 4, Moses and Aaron took a separate census of the Levites, of their branches the Kohathites, the Gershonites, and the Merarites. The Levites were listed and excluded from fighting, as they had care of the Tabernacle and its belongings.

All through Numbers, Moses, and often Aaron, were hard pressed by the Israelites whose actions ranged from grumbling to out-right rebellion and disobedience.
Numbers 11: the grumbles about food brought the LORD'S fiery judgement; then the community leaders received vision and blessing so that they were trusted again, and all were fed on quail until they were sick of that diet!
Numbers 12: Moses' brother Aaron and sister Miriam rebelled against him, and the LORD needed to intervene, with humbling drama.
Numbers 13,14: at Kadesh Barnea, the response to the report of the mission of the spies whom Moses sent to explore the Promised Land was almost universal fear and rebellion.

Numbers 16: records a serious rebellion at high social level. This took fire and an earthquake, and a sign of authority given to Aaron by the LORD, to restore a right fear and respect for Moses and Aaron.

Numbers 20: the quarrelling Israelites demanded water at Kadesh Barnea. This touched a raw nerve in Moses. They so outraged him that he failed to obey the LORD in public. He was told to speak to a rock, but he smote it with his staff, twice, and the water issued. But he had offended the Lord.

Numbers 21 records making the Bronze Snake: The camp was on the march to avoid Edom, and was passing through a remote dry region to its east. The grumbles started again, and desert venomous snakes came in. People were dying, and they begged Moses to pray for help. At the LORD'S instruction, Moses made a replica snake out of bronze, which he lifted up on a tall pole in the camp, so that those who looked at it, lived. [Jesus spoke to Nicodemus of this event, with respect to his eventual death by 'lifting up' (viz by crucifixion), such that those who put their faith in him on the cross for their rescue will receive eternal life. John 3:14] Moses and Aaron's prayers for the LORD to forgive in each situation, and to bring glory to himself and blessing to his rescued people, were answered, sometimes dramatically.

Sihon, Og, Balak and Balaam

The Israelites moved on to lands east of the Jordan. Under direction from the Lord, they scored great military victories over Sihon king of the Amorites and Og king of Bashan. Then, Numbers 22 – 25 recount the events of a spiritual attack while they were camped on the plains of Moab, across from Jericho. Balak, king of Moab, sent for Balaam who was a psychic living far to the north at Pethor close to the Euphrates. He paid Balaam's fee and demanded that he come and curse the Israelite invaders. The LORD intervened and told Balaam not to go, as the Israelites were blessed. The later messengers from Balak were more important, and promised handsome rewards. Next day, Balaam complied and set out for Moab. On the way, the LORD rebuked him soundly by speaking through his trusty donkey, and with direction from a visible angel. Twice the LORD spoke to Balaam: "Do only what I tell you," and "Speak only what I tell you." [Numbers 22:20,35] So Balak offered sacrifices, and Balaam, with and without sorcery, pronounced seven oracles. These were blessings on Israel, and not the curses that Balak had paid for. He was furious, and Balaam turned to go home. However, from Numbers 31:16, Balaam visited people in Moab, and recommended that their women seduce the Israelites. The fabric of family life was in peril. This led to the events in Numbers 25, with Phinehas, the High Priest's son, taking violent action against such flagrant and public disobedience. This brought him renown in Israel. [Psalm 106:24-31]

In between all such events, Moses was receiving regulations for the life of the Israelite communities from the LORD, and teaching them God's unchanging love and faithfulness. His holiness and uncompromising wrath against rebellion is clear. Indeed, Miriam, Aaron, and Moses himself, never entered the Land. God provided remedy for doubts and disobedience, and he gave deliverance from their enemies. This book is full of the LORD'S grace.

Paul [1 Corinthians 10] urged Christians to learn spiritual lessons from Numbers. The spiritual rock – ie Christ – accompanied the Israelites. Our hearts must not be set on evil things, - idolatry, pagan revelry, sexual immorality, challenging the LORD, grumbling against him. Rather we should participate in Christ , and seek the good of others over our own, so that they too may be rescued. Follow Christ's example, said Paul!

Moses' last words: In the book <u>Deuteronomy</u>, there is recorded a landmark conference for the new generation. It was held on the plains of Moab below Mt Nebo. The aged Moses, still dynamic, addressed the tribes shortly before his death, preparing them for possessing the Land under the next leader, Joshua. The conference lasted many days.

Deuteronomy begins with a recapitulation of their story from the time of going from Horeb, and the march to Kadesh Barnea, where the previous generation had rebelled. After an abortive attack on the Amorites who repelled them, they had stayed at Kadesh for a long time. Then they retired south along the Arabah to go slowly round the hills of Seir, which was territory belonging to the descendents of Esau. The 38 years of wasting in the wanderings eventually led them back north, but further east than before. They had defeated kings to the east of the Jordan and the Arabah, and now here they were, listening to Moses on the plains below the heights of Mt Nebo. In a score of packed chapters, Moses taught them practical rules and regulations for living as a new community in open and exclusive relation with God. Compromise and blending with the existing inhabitants and their religion and customs were absolutely forbidden as utterly unacceptable, and fatally dangerous. The book ends with Moses' impassioned prophetic preaching. Moses pleaded with them and warned them, with the blessings for obedience and the curses for disobedience. He wound up: "This day I call heaven and earth as witnesses against you that I have set before you life and death, blessings and curses. Now choose life, so that you and your children may live and that you may love the LORD your God, listen to his voice, and hold fast to him. For the LORD is your life..." [Deuteronomy 30:19,20] He appointed Joshua to lead them into the Promised Land. But Moses, in his Psalm of Numbers 32, had no illusions that the Israelites would stay faithful to the LORD for ever. However, he blessed the conference, and then each of the Twelve tribes. Finally, he climbed to the summit of Mt Nebo for a preview of the Promised Land, from North to South, and he died there. The last three verses of the book are a glowing epitaph of Moses.

A summary to present the wonder-working achievements of the LORD, through Moses his servant.
In the course of one year, the LORD:
Struck down the false gods and idols of Egypt by the Plagues
Delivered a nation of slaves from serious oppression
Annihilated an imperial army in the Red Sea that had held them secure from escape
Through the Golden Calf incident, struck down the idolatrous worship of the false Moon-god of a whole region

Took over its sacred site for 11 months to be Horeb, the mountain of the LORD Most High God of Abraham, Isaac, and Jacob
Established the idol-free system of worship, through the Ark and the Tabernacle
Affirmed God's gracious covenant and taught the people a detailed pure and upright community life-style
Raised a potentially effective army.

Through the next three decades, the LORD refined his chosen but flawed people, through Moses' teaching, rebuking and encouraging them; Moses continuously organised the discipline of the rebellious people, getting them ready to posses the Promised Land.

Very few groups, and fewer still individuals, bring to pass a complete change of life and faith of a people in a territory, anywhere in the world. Moses, servant of the LORD, was one such individual.

Psalm 81 encapsulates the Lord's workings through Moses. It was composed some three centuries later for worship in the Temple, maybe at Passover:
1-4 recounts in song God's gracious actions and his longings for Israel.
5-6 He rescued them from the heavy manual slavery of Egypt, which had caused such distress,
7-12 He taught them with wonders, and tested their loyalty. He spoke the Ten Commandments, but again and again his people would not take heed, nor submit.
13-14 Even now, the Psalm concludes, if his people would change mind and heart and actions, then their foes would be vanquished, and the Promised Land's abundance would provide all they could desire.
What of us his people today?

After Moses' day, Joshua led the Israelites into the Promised Land – the next chapter.

Chapter 10   The Promised Land

> The Promised Land was verdant indeed, after the Israelites' desert experiences. It was promised to be a land flowing with milk and honey: milk derived from cattle and flocks, honey derived from plants and bees. The Israelite communities were agricultural, and were aware of the goodness of the Lord in their Land. After Joshua, then Judges, and the world of the Women within the patriarchal society.

Psalm 65 radiates praise of the Lord. It begins in the Temple, with worshipful converse with its Resident. "Praise to you, our vows fulfilled, prayer, all people come to you, Lord. You rescue from enslaving sin, you atone, you choose and bless and you bring us to live near to you. Good things are there in your presence, and we have everything! You meet with us and we are overwhelmed, awestruck that you rescue us and relate to us in righteousness, God our rescuer!"

Now the Psalm moves its praise outwards from the Temple to the natural world beyond. "You are the reliable one to whom all can turn, from distant lands and seas; you created mountains and control wild seas; nations, too, are under your power, from east to west; we worship you in joyful singing. Our lovely Land, the Promised Land, is abundantly productive under your care. Streams flow, corn grows, showers fall, crops flourish, farm carts stagger home with harvest. The desert places sprout wild flowers, everything looks wonderful, and nature sings joyfully to you."

Joshua A generation earlier, as the Israelites had approached Mt Horeb, 2 or 3 months after crossing the Red Sea, Moses had sent the young Joshua to lead untried men victoriously against the attacking Amalekites [Exodus 17:8-14]. The LORD had brought him to Moses' notice, and he became Moses' right hand man. Joshua helped Moses going up the mountain [Exodus 24:12-18]. Joshua was there in the original tent which Moses used for meeting the Lord, before the

Tabernacle was made [Exodus 33:7-11]. A year later, Joshua with Caleb and 10 more leaders were sent to explore the Land of Canaan, in preparation for entering it [Numbers 13:1-16]. Of the 12 men, Caleb and Joshua alone were confident of success [Numbers 13:30, 14:6-9], while the Israelites were fearful and refused to advance. Joshua was Moses' faithful shadow through the next years of wandering, gaining the experiences of the leadership of Israel, and the purposes and faithfulness of the Lord. Shortly before Moses died he commissioned Joshua to take his place [Numbers 27:15-33, Deuteronomy 34:8,9].

Joshua, the new leader, now on his own, found the Lord resourcing him, and the people's chiefs encouraging him, as he prepared them all for the big event: possessing the Promised Land [Joshua 1]. There was the Jordan to cross, now in flood-time spate, and Jericho, a formidable fortress double ringed by walls, to overcome. He sent two trusted men to reconnoitre and come back with up-to-the-minute data [Joshua 2:21-24]. They encountered Rahab, who ran a B & B on top of the walls, and who co-operated. When they returned to Joshua, they reported that the whole country was scared stiff by the Israelites who had conquered the land of the Amorites and Bashan on the other side of the Jordan.

Crossing the Jordan was another miracle, like crossing the Red Sea a generation earlier [Joshua 3:14-17; 4:23]. Parting the water was in response to obedience to the Lord's word to Joshua, and probably geologically facilitated by a tremor in the Rift Valley precipitating a heavy landslide at Adam, a place higher up the river. The river was blocked and the river bed dried up, even though it was in flood at the time. There was long enough to get the Israelites across the Jordan. When the soil damming it gave way, and it flowed back again, there was no going back for the Israelites. But imagine the horror in Jericho when they realised that the invaders, who one moment were the other side of the flooding Jordan, were now about to advance the five miles (8km) up to their doorstep! The Israelites set up camp at Gilgal beside the Jordan, and prepared themselves for the fight. They enjoyed different food from desert fare, and they sought purity before the Lord. They circumcised all their men, symbolising the community's commitment to the Covenant, and they celebrated the Passover, reflecting the Lord's grace upon Israel in the past, and at their present time.

Jericho Joshua 5:13-15. As Joshua began to think about attacking Jericho, he met an armed warrior with drawn sword: "Who goes there? Friend or Foe?...." Instantly, he recognised the Lord's voice, and he submitted to the Commander-in-Chief. So he did not need to make plans, but rather, to obey orders.

Joshua 6:8-23 Joshua sent the priests with trumpets and the Ark, and the army, round the town each day for 6 days. On the seventh day they went round seven times silently, then they gave a great shout; the walls fell outwards and the army rushed in to slaughter, set fire to the town, and destroy everything. Only Rahab and her family survived and were protected.

Next came Ai. Joshua didn't consult the Lord, and was taught a lesson. At first Ai's men defeated the Israelites. This devastated Joshua, who sought the Lord for some time; he learned that Achan had seen, desired, and stolen a goodly garment in Jericho, with silver and gold; so Joshua had to purge this offence by the destruction of Achan and family and the property which should have been destroyed in the first place. That done, it needed a stratagem to draw the defending fighters of Ai out of their security, and then a hidden part of the Israelite army ran into Ai and fired it before coming out to attack the men of Ai from behind.

In time, Joshua led his forces to conquer the villages in the hills to the south of Gilgal, before turning to deal with those in the north of the Land.

The Israelites pitched camp and Tabernacle in the middle of the Land, at Shiloh, and Joshua allocated by lots which tribe was to possess each part of the Land. Joshua sent the fighters of Gad, Reuben and half Manasseh home to their families to live in the Land to the east of Jordan, allocated to them by Moses. The fighting went on, small scale and less effectively. But there remained much of the Land still to possess. [Joshua 13] In fact, calculating by area, they only occupied about 40% of what had been promised to them by the Lord.

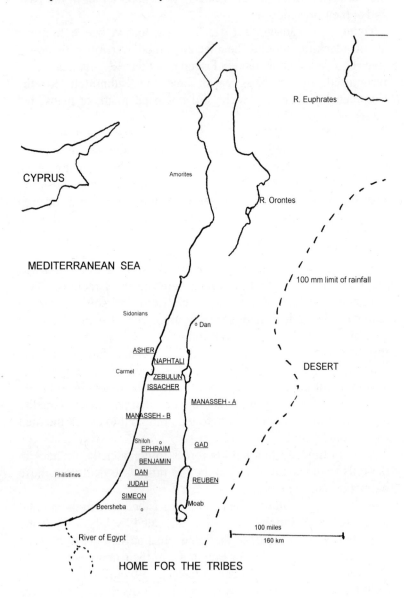

HOME FOR THE TRIBES

Joshua 24 tells how the aged Joshua spoke a big challenge to the Israelites before he died. They protested their faithfulness to the Lord. In the event, this affirmation lasted about 2 more generations. While the book Joshua records much bloodshed and conquest, the next book Judges is a sorry tale of failures and of disunity. The tribes began to separate, and there were fights between brothers, and indeed some ethnic cleansing.

The Judges were leaders that the Lord raised up when the Israelites cried out from their oppression under the local enemy tribes. The leaders summoned the tribes by trumpet and led them to victory. From then on, the leader held court to administer justice in Israel. The Israelites were safe for a generation, until their leader died, but after that they reverted to compromise with evils and idolatry, and they suffered oppression all over again. Such cycles of events were going on concurrently in different regions of the Promised Land.

In Hebrews 11, four leaders are celebrated for their faith: Gideon, Barak, Samson, and Jephthah.

[Judges 4, 5] Barak, encouraged by the prophetess Deborah, defeated the Canaanite king Jabin in the north. His commander, Sisera, was killed by Jael the wife of Heber. This considerable victory was celebrated in Deborah's song.

[Judges 6,7,8] Gideon delivered the Israelites from the hoards of Midianites coming in from the east and rifling the Promised Land east and west of the river Jordan. The Israelites cried out to the Lord who sent a prophet to tell them that the Land was being ravaged because they were faithless and disobedient to him. Gideon was a farmer's son with faith in the Lord. He encountered the Lord, and although amazed he responded in faith. His confidence steadily grew, and emboldened, he led a surprise night-time attack with but 3 companies of 100 men each on the Midianite camp in the valley below. Gideon's men carried trumpets and empty jars with flaming torches inside. They moved to positions round the camp, and then all together they smashed the jars, waved the torches, blew the trumpets, and yelled "The sword of the Lord and of

Gideon!" They stood their ground while panic reigned in the camp below. It was the start of a great rout of the invaders.

[Judges 13-16]   <u>Samson</u> was a man of enormous strength, endowed by the Spirit of the Lord. He lived in the southern hill country near the Philistine lands on the coastal plains below. He knew that he was a Nazirite, set apart to the Lord, and never to shave off his hair. He had a weakness for a Philistine girl, whom he married but who was disloyal. This brought conflict into the open, and from then on he harassed the Philistines effectively. After some time, he let himself fancy other Philistine women. One of these, Delilah, wheedled out of him that his great strength would be lost if his hair was cut. She set a trap, had his hair shaved off while he slept, and delivered him into the hands of the Philistines. Now he was weak and helpless, and they put out his eyes and made him a slave grinding corn. Soon they all came together in their large temple to celebrate their conquest of Samson. They sent for him to dance before them. But his hair was growing again, and he prayed earnestly to the Lord for a return of his great strength. He heaved with all his might on the two main pillars of the building which collapsed; it killed Samson and more Philistines than he had killed in his entire life-time.

<u>VIOLENCE</u>

It is appropriate to consider <u>the Issue of Violence:</u> Unredeemed humanity is violent. We live in a violent society.
The extermination by the Israelites of the previous inhabitants of the Promised Land.
Joshua met the Lord as an armed warrior (Joshua 5:13-15). The Israelites knew God had commanded the conquest. So Joshua slaughtered all in the villages of Canaan. It was total killing, men, women and children, and sometimes the animals.
Later, Samuel ordered king Saul to eliminate the Amalekites and their king (1 Samuel 15:1-3)
David and his fighters annihilated many villages who were enemies of Judah. (1 Sam 27:8-11).
How should we view ethnic cleansing?

Military Service. Israel's army was disciplined by Moses: Deuteronomy 20:1-4.

Nations have Armed Forces. Isn't commitment to Queen and Country at War part of "render unto Caesar..."? We have both personal and community responsibility. "Your country needs you!" It is a time for Just War! But is there ever a Just War? When should we defend ourselves? Or a weaker person? Or our family? [Matthew 5:39 Do not resist an evil person... turn the other cheek]. "It is necessary for the good man to do nothing for evil to triumph" [misquoted from E. Burke].

Allied to considering the violence of Moses, Joshua and David, the violence of today is to be faced:

Should we back today's Israel against its enemies? Has not God promised the Land to Israel for all time, and has he not ordered their raging enemies to be killed? Should we presume to hold back from what he has ordained? But is this not to confuse today's political Israelis with biblical Israelites? Is the Promise to Israel, which is sworn and cannot be broken, really about physical and geographical topography? Or, since Jesus' time, is it about a heavenly kingdom?

How do we view radical Islam and its Jihad? We have lived in an officially Christian society since AD 600 (Augustine's day), but now Britain tolerates everything, including active Islam; some Islamists want to campaign for Sharia Law, angrily and violently. Active Christianity is condemned as Racist, because of intolerance of other ethnic traditions. Indeed, the Christian claim that Rescue from God's wrath is only by Jesus promotes strife, so Christians have been dubbed Terrorists!

Christian Action "Christians are to be counter-cultural. In efforts to live peacefully with all folk, as much as lies within us, too often Christians blend indistinguishably from the non-Christian crowd. We hesitate to rock the boat, so we pose with inoffensive blandness, and end up with terminal niceness. But we need to be positive and attractive to non-Christians by our lack of religiosity, with a willingness to forgive, and a trust in God to provide; we should not take advantage of others, and we need to have a genuine respect for authority. And our life-style is to be a counter-cultural model that other Christians can copy."

Balance this with the dilemma:-

God wants all to be saved, and none to perish [2 Peter 3.9]. God is love [1 John 4:16]. Love your enemies and pray for those who persecute you…[Matthew 5:44] However, Jesus also said: Do not suppose that I have come to bring peace to the earth. I did not come to bring peace, but a sword… Anyone who does not take his cross and follow me is not worthy of me. [Matthew 10:34-38] Would Jesus have killed? No! Not during his First Coming. But he will, at his Second Coming: Paul wrote [2 Thessalonians 1:6-9] "God is just. He will pay back trouble to those who trouble you, and give relief to you who are troubled, and to us as well. This will happen when the Lord Jesus is revealed from heaven in blazing fire with his with his powerful angels. He will punish those who do not know God and do not obey the gospel of our Lord Jesus. They will be punished with everlasting destruction and shut out from the presence of the Lord and from the majesty of his power on the day he comes…"

Inconclusively, devout Christians hold opposite views on all these matters, which might be the product of over-individualistic protestantism, against a catholic unity of the community of faith.

<u>Suggestions for further work</u>: Christian pacificity and political persecution, Islamic aggressiveness and Christian assertiveness. Propagation of the Christian gospel by love and peace, and in contrast propagation, for example, of Hinduism or Islam, by hate and holy war.

"Women at the Well"

So far, the Bible story has been an account of men's activity. But now, women's initiatives break into the scene with the stories of Ruth and Hannah.

Most of the O.T. stories are records of politics, the wars, and the law in action. This is the world of the men: it is 'androcentric'. There were few mentions of women leaders in the first 7 books: just Miriam, sister of Moses and Aaron, and Deborah who, with Barak, led the Israelites at one season in the time of the Judges.

Ruth The next book, the 8th, is a great story of Ruth and her mother-in-law Naomi, whose loving faithfulness brought rescue to them both from being in the class of "widows, aliens and poor." It is one of a few 'gynocentric' stories, meaning that it centres on women. Ruth became the mother of Obed, the grandfather of king David, and so she was also the great x 43 grandmother of Jesus [Luke 3:23-32].

Importantly, the other spin-off of Ruth is that it empowers all readers of the O.T. to engage with the invisible actions of the women within the essentially patriarchal society of the 2000 years of O.T. story.

<u>Chapter 1.</u> Sets the scene: v.2 reads: *"They were Ephrathites from Bethlehem, Judah"* almost as if "They were Devonians from Exeter, West Country..." (Ephron was the Hittite landowner who sold a field to Abraham for burying Sarah. [Genesis 25.] In Jacob's time, Ephratha was the district in which Bethlehem was situated.)

This Bethlehemite family was hard hit by the famine. Elimelech had land but not crops nor money to pay for food for his family. He knew that Moab had mines and salt, and that kind of business is not dependent on weather, so he emigrated there. It was not far, about 2 days journey; Moab had a similar language, they were Semitic people, though Moon-worshipers, and employment was better than starving. Elimelech soon died, but in the next 10 years his sons Kilion and Mahlon grew up and supported their mother Naomi; they found nice girls and married. But then, almost at once, alas for Naomi, both her sons died, (was it a mining accident?) and so there were now three widows at home. News came to them that Bethlehem had abundance again, so Naomi decided to go back there. They packed up and left, but suddenly Naomi realised what she was asking of Orpah and Ruth. She released them to go back to their Moabite homes.

They all cried together; Orpah left, but Ruth committed to stay with Naomi. She made this extremely strong pledge: Ruth 1:16-18 Ruth replied, "Don't urge me to leave you or to turn back from you. Where you go I will go, and where you stay I will stay. Your people will be my people and your God my God. Where you die I will die, and there I will be buried. May the LORD deal with me, be it ever so severely, if anything but death separates you and me." It was a form of covenant vow, used all round the Near East. Thereafter Ruth never left Naomi.

They arrived in Bethlehem and news flashed round the grapevine in minutes. But the old sights and scenes brought all the trouble back to Naomi and she became very depressed, and despaired of the Lord's treatment of her.

Chapter 2. Naomi's depression made her exhausted; but Ruth loved her and soon took action. Ruth found a possible field, approached the foreman, and started working, gleaning after the harvesters. It was Boaz' field, and Boaz was a close relative of Naomi ! Boaz spoke to the foreman when he arrived, for he had spotted the stranger at work. Boaz had heard about Naomi and Ruth, so he welcomed Ruth and signed her on. Ruth was amazed! Then she renewed her request for this work, and she was drawn into the family team. At the end of the day she threshed out the grain and took home much barley, and the leftovers of her lunch. That Boaz had been so kind and supportive turned Naomi from despair to hope.

Chapter 3. Naomi and Ruth grew closer in love and respect as the summer passed while Ruth worked for Boaz. One day, as the harvesting was ending and Ruth's work was going to run out, Naomi felt it was time to claim the right of redemption for them as widows. In those days, throughout the Near and Middle East, only men owned property – fields, houses, animals, wives, and children. Moses had added a responsibility to the men: they were to respect the widows who had no sons who could look after them. [Deuteronomy 25:5,6 refers.] Naomi could have claimed for herself; however she knew that Ruth would then have no hope of marriage in Bethlehem. So she primed Ruth on the local customs and sent her instead. Ruth bathed and perfumed and dressed in her best clothes. She walked down to the threshing floor in the evening, where Boaz was working. She let him eat and drink and settle down to sleep, and then she crept in and lay down at his feet.

Later that night, he woke with a start and saw a woman there ! Ruth made her family claim with respect, and once more Boaz was impressed by Ruth's integrity: "You are showing more family loyalty than ever by not running after younger men." [3:10 NLT] To do that would have taken Ruth out of Elimelech's family. In fact, Ruth did not belong, and nothing she did could gain her any rights in Bethlehem. Although she was respected for her commitment and her practical hard wok and caring for Naomi, all she obtained was by favour and grace. Boaz responded to Ruth's claim with warmth and generosity. He was indeed willing to be her kinsman-redeemer (Goel). Both of them took great care to keep secret this very personal private family encounter. Ruth returned to Naomi who was bursting to know!

Chapter 4. They settled down to wait for Boaz to negotiate with another possible kinsman-redeemer, to do a legal property deal, and to fix the wedding. All Bethlehem knew the news by mid morning! The appeal "You are witnesses" and the reply "We are witnesses" were the community ratification of the legal deal, after the customary shoe action, explained in 4:7: "... For the redemption and transfer of property to become final, one party took off his sandal and gave it to the other. This was the method of legalising transactions in Israel." It was followed by a united male blessing: this is androcentric, male-centred, that Boaz is going to provide an heir for Elimelech. There is almost no mention of women!

When Ruth and Boaz married, the LORD enabled Ruth, for she had not conceived from Mahlon. This was followed by the excited delight of the women when the son was born! The women's gynocentric blessing, women-centred, was that Naomi has been redeemed from poverty. Ruth had toiled so hard to support Naomi, like 7 sons! It was the duty of sons to support their womenfolk. But now Obed will grow up to take over. "Naomi has a son!!" It is ecstatic! There is almost no mention of men! Of course it was the men who named the baby at the circumcision on the 8th day.

Israelite family trees trace the male line of descent, by generations and not by dates. From Perez, rather than from Judah, Boaz occupies the significant and important 7th position. David is 10th, also important. For us in NT days, the genealogy goes on from David by another 40 generations to Jesus. All androcentric stuff! In Matthew's corresponding list, women are included.

Some Conclusions
    a) <u>JUDGES</u> is a book of disaster as God's people turn away from him. But
    <u>RUTH</u> is a book of blessing when a foreigner turns towards the LORD God of Israel.
    b) Ruth's wholehearted involvement rescued her and Naomi from the status of the poor, resulting in their redemption from the class of "alien, fatherless and widows."
    c) The book Ruth empowers readers of patriarchal writings to see the vital role of women in their society: courageous, committed, devout, caring, teaching, &c. Ruth is one of the few gynocentric pieces in the Scriptures. Ruth in the Bible reveals the ever present women's world, making us aware of the lack of women's perspectives elsewhere. It authorises us to bring this important aspect into stories written mostly from a male mind-set. There are only a few other similar pieces: Jael [Judges 4], Hannah [Samuel 1, especially 2:1-10, her song], Esther, (Judith – not a nice story in OT apocrypha), and Mary [Luke 1 & 2, especially her song 1:46-55].

The book Ruth makes visible the invisible work of women in the Bible. Men at the Gate talk status, politics, government, law, property, war and fighting. Women at the Well talk water and food, men, marriage, babies and families, birth and death.

Samuel   The book <u>Samuel</u> starts with the story of Hannah. It is another gynocentric piece.

1 Samuel 1:1-20 Hannah, after much grief over her infertility, had her prayer answered and became the mother of Samuel. Hannah dedicated her young son to the Lord, and brought him to Eli, so that Samuel grew up in close association with the Tabernacle at Shiloh under the priest. Her prayer of 1 Samuel 2:1-10 foreruns Mary's Magnificat in Luke 2:46-55.

Fast Forward to the New Testament:

Jesus' respect for Women   There are over 30 references in the gospels to this matter. Men normally ignored women. They had no legal standing in Jewish life, nor indeed in Roman life. They were in submission to their menfolk, to their fathers, or husbands, or sons. But within the system, Jesus treated them equally with men. He upheld marriage, he healed them and received their ministry and support. He spoke at length with a Samaritan woman at Jacob's Well. They were there in the listening crowd, he replied to their questions, he defended an adulteress against public injustice. He loved the family at Bethany, and returned at a time of personal danger to restore their Lazarus to the sisters. On the way to crucifixion he paused to exhort and explain to the lamenting women, and from the Cross he arranged care for his mother.

He responded to the faith of the women who came to the tomb on Resurrection Day, and it was to Mary Magdalene and then the other women that he first appeared, to lift their spirits and bring new meaning to their lives. Jesus clearly valued women as the people they were, regardless of their assigned role as home-makers and mothers of the day.

A New Testament Addendum: Women in Public Ministry today

While on the topic of the world of Women, it is appropriate to insist that women and men equally have minds and wills and gifts for today's communities and churches. This section is derived from an article by Don Ronsa, Pastor in Edmonton, Alberta, in "Fire" from TACF Oct 97.

The church has based doctrine and practice on 1 Timothy 2:11-14 (amongst other scriptures) for many years. However there is evidence that the Greek has been mistranslated and misunderstood.

v 11,12

γυνη εν ησυχια μανθανετῶ εν παση υποταγη
A woman in silence   let learn   in   all   subjection
GUN**E** EN **E**SUCHIA MANTHANET**O** EN PASE UPOTAG**E**

διδασκειν δε γυναικι ουκ επιτρεπῶ ουδε
but to teach   a woman   I do not permit   nor
DIDASKEIN DE GUNAIKI OUK EPITREP**O**   OUDE

αυθεντειν   ανδροσ αλλ ειναι εν ησυχια.
to exercise authority of a man   but   to be   in   silence.
AUTHENTEIN   ANDROS   ALL EINAI EN **E**SUCHIA
(from RSV Interlinear NT)

AUTHENTEIN: This word occurs just once, here, in the Greek NT and not at all in the LXX. So there is need to find its use in contemporary literature.

In the 6thC BC it meant to initiate or be responsible for murder.

In the 3rdC AD it meant to claim ownership of property, or to usurp power.

Between these two,

In the 1stC AD it meant to claim to be the author or originator of something.

<u>Cultural context</u>: Timothy was the leader of the Christian Church in Ephesus, which was a great centre of paganism, with the <u>cult of Artemis</u>. Feminist doctrine made the female superior and dominating; Artemis was a goddess able to procreate without men. So this led to perversion, fertility rites, magic, and demonic activity. Also at Ephesus there were <u>Jewish Gnostics,</u> who set out to be spirit guides. They made a syncretistic combination of the OT with Artemis: eg. from Genesis 3, they thought that Eve was the illuminator since she received true knowledge from the Serpent which they represented as Saviour. They alleged that Eve was the mother of Adam, and that Yahwey was a lesser god. Physical matter was evil, but the spirit world was good; &c.

Paul tells Timothy to confront false doctrines. Timothy was to forbid certain people speaking false teaching in church, and to warn about myths and endless genealogies. [1 Timothy 1:3,4] He was to oppose those who spoke falsely about the living God, to rebuke doctrines of demons, and silly controversies, old wives' tales (eg corrupted Genesis 3). [1 Timothy 4:7] He was to use the Scriptures as antidote, as they are there "for sound teaching, reproof, correction, training righteousness." [2 Timothy 3:16]

So for 1 Timothy 2:12 read: "I am not at all allowing (present tense, for that situation) a woman to teach or to proclaim herself the originator (AUTHENTEIN) of man." Next, ESUCHIA means silence or harmony, peace, conformity, agreement. So Paul says "she must be in agreement (ie with the Scriptures and sound apostolic teaching.)" "Adam was formed first, then Eve," as against Eve as progenitor. "Adam was not deceived; it was Eve," so Eve was not the illuminator.

This translation and understanding fit the social context of Ephesus, and is true to the Greek text. It speaks to that troubled situation, and lines up with Paul's other teaching about women.

Paul worked with Priscilla and Aquila; Paul encouraged Timothy to trust his mother and grandmother. He commended Phoebe (Romans 16) as deacon, so to line up with Stephen and Philip; he greeted Junia as prominent among the apostles. Paul insisted women be trained to teach the truth of Scripture – to "put them on the payroll" on equal footing as in Galatians 3:27,28.

Besides Paul's emphatic refutation of such error in Ephesus with its Gnostic menace, his pastoral letters to Timothy contained much more that is positive, with encouraging exhortation supporting his younger colleague.

All this supports women in ministry down the centuries. Ronsa, as pastor, was writing in the face of the hard doctrine of the Righteous Right, that 'Good women submit to men, and that is what the Bible teaches, of course.'

We turn again to the Psalms.

Psalm 68 comes from a time after Ruth and Hannah, maybe when David's son Solomon was king. It is the confident song of the community of women and men on the march into Jerusalem for a big festival, as a large column heads towards the Temple. They praise the Lord, and the Psalm recalls their story. They pray and prophesy. Other nations are involved. Enemies are dispersed, the vulnerable defended, and the wicked perish. The earth shakes under God's footfall. [1] They pray, "may God arise, scatter enemies, and make foes flee; as smoke, blow them away, melt them like wax. May the wicked perish, and may the righteous be glad and happy, and rejoice.
[4] They praise, "Sing to God, praise and extol him. God rides high; he is the I AM, so we rejoice!
[5] As Father for the fatherless, the widow, the lonely, and the prisoners, he sets them in families; rebels find it too hot for them!"
[7] They recall, "You led us from slavery, you marched us through deserts; you are the God of Sinai, the God of Israel. You refreshed us with showers, and you provided for the poor. Your people settled in the Promised Land." The Lord spoke, and the great company proclaimed his word, with kings and armies taking flight; spoil is divided amongst us.
[15] The mountains of Bashan gaze in envy on God's chosen mount, where he dwells for ever. The Lord has come with his massive army of chariots, from Sinai to Zion's sanctuary. "You ascended (Zion's hill), leading captives, receiving gifts, to dwell there.
[19] Praise: he bears our burdens daily; he rescues, he is Sovereign over death, he crushes enemies.
[24] The procession comes into view. The band has men and women, the column has princes of each tribe. The singers, musicians, and maidens playing tambourines, lead the throng from Benjamin and Judah, the two southern tribes; and last are princes of Zebulun and Naphtali, two tribes from the north.
[28] They pray, "Reveal your power; then kings will bring gifts, the mythological beasts will bring silver, Egypt and Cush will submit to you; all come in humility."

Now that the procession has reached the Temple courtyard, praise rises in crescendo, "Sing praise! Worldwide powers, kings, the ancient skies, with thunder and majesty and power in the skies! There is awe in your sanctuary; God gives power and strength to Israel!"

This resplendent worship has all the power of the big occasion, where the many women and men are joyfully blended into unity of heart and soul, with humble amazement before the Lord, the God of Israel.

Praise be to God!!

Ruth and Hannah were deeply spiritual and practical people. They gave their lives to the LORD, and through their prayers God richly blessed their descendents, Samuel and David.

Chapter 11   Samuel, Saul, David, and Solomon.

> God works out his purposes for the Israelites through selected people. David's experiences as a godly Bethlehemite, a shepherd, a courtier to Saul, and then an outlaw, were the LORD'S training him for becoming a godly king of all Israel. He was succeeded by his son Solomon.

A "possible" time chart:
BC
1240   Joshua led the Israelites over the Jordan
1235   Salmon m. Rahab
1200   Joshua died |
       Judges |
                    Boaz m. Ruth
                           |
       Eli at Shiloh |
                    Obed
1110   Samuel born |
                    Jesse
1050   Samuel anointed Saul as King
1045   David born
1028   David defeated Goliath
       Samuel anointed David to be King
1010   David made King of Judah
1003   David made King of Israel

Samuel
Israelite worship was at a low, reduced to superstition, but Samuel became acknowledged as the Lord's prophet [1 Samuel 3:19-4:1a]. He spent his life ministering and teaching on a circuit of towns in the middle of the Land. Samuel was the last of the Judges, or leaders, over some or all of the Tribes. Also he was the first of the Prophets of Israel, after Moses [1 Samuel 7:15-17]. At this time, the Philistines menaced Israel; they were the Phoenician settlers on the coastal plains of

the Mediterranean. As Samuel aged, the Israelite chieftans rejected his leadership, centred on the Lord, and they demanded that he appoint them a king. They wanted a warrior who would march an army against other enemies, and who would be the final authority in politics and trade. Samuel sought the Lord, who directed him to make <u>Saul</u> their king. Saul started well, but eventually went his own way. Samuel was openly angry with Saul, yet inwardly he grieved for him and for Israel. Saul was the Lord's anointed king, but he failed to obey God. Once, Samuel himself needed to execute an enemy king that Samuel had been told to slay, but had spared.

Secretly, Samuel anointed <u>David</u> to succeed Saul [1 Samuel 16:1-13].

David

In David's great grandparents' day, Bethlehem was a place where people of faith dwelt. Boaz and the elders of the town had farmed with blessing and lived uprightly, and they respected the God of Israel. Three generations later, David continued in their faith. He grew up with six older brothers and at least one sister. They left him the chores they did not like. Nobody wanted to look after sheep; shepherds were despised. It was thus that David helped his family's business by taking over the flock. The shepherd needed to find good pastures for his sheep and to defend them against both human sheep-stealers and against wild animal predators. He learned to use sword and sling accurately. Also he learned survival skills and the wilderness tracks. Being by himself with the flock, David developed his talents for poetry, music and song. He made music on the hillsides, and composed songs of faith and worship, and later developed these into the Psalms.

Psalm 23. [1] In simple meditation, David places the covenant God of Israel, I AM, as his Shepherd and himself as a vulnerable needy lamb, sublimely confident of his needs being completely met in the Shepherd. The pastures are fresh and green, and the water supply is calm. Inwardly he is refreshed, and guided in right living, all for the sake of the Lord. Right through dark times and places, he sings "I will fear no evil, for you are with me." The Shepherd's rod for enemies and his crook for rescuing sheep give assurance and strength.

[5] His song rises to worship, rejoicing in a feast provided under the noses of his enemies, aware of being chosen for God's purpose, with a delightful draught of wine! The Lord's goodness and love will be his all his life, and one day he will dwell in the Lord's house for ever.

This was the confident faith that propelled David to fearless outrage against Goliath, defiant of the Lord, and to knock him down by slingshot.

Saul

David, this young musician-shepherd, was brought in to King Saul's service, to play the harp and sing, to soothe the king from time to time when he was afflicted with his increasing mental illness; he was given a court appointment, but was not required to live there [1 Samuel 16:22].

From home, Jesse sent him with supplies for his three eldest brothers, soldiers in Saul's army facing the Philistines [1 Samuel 17]. The two armies were on opposite sides of a valley with its stream between them. While there with the soldiers, David heard the challenge of Goliath, the 9-foot monster, so he offered his services to Saul, to overcome him in the Lord's name, just as he had dealt with wild animals attacking his sheep. After consultation, Saul approved [v. 37]. David probably used stones about 1 lb (about 450gramme), slinging at nearly 50 mph (80kph), so were lethal with practised accuracy. He felled the giant and dispatched him with his own sword. Even if Saul could not remember who he was, David was now a national hero, and he became friend of Jonathan, Saul's son and heir [1 Samuel 18:1-4].

"Saul has slain his thousands, and David his tens of thousands!" The women's song [v.7] created extreme jealousy in Saul and it provoked his mental illness again; so David played him music, but Saul threw his spear at him, twice, and David dodged [18:15-16]. David became a successful soldier against the Philistines. Saul, thinking to use Philistine swords to kill him, set 100 dead Philistines as the bride price of his daughter Michal. David killed 200, and he and Michal were married [v.20-27]. Michal

foiled her father's attempted assassination over one night, and David went on the run. He spent time with Samuel, where he was safe from Saul. Saul sent posses to bring David out, but they were overpowered by the spirit of prophecy; so Saul went himself, and he also was overpowered [19:24, as 10:12]. David asked Jonathan to find out what his father's real intention was; Jonathan was deeply angered to discover Saul's determination to kill David [20:1-24]. David fled, first to Ahimelech, priest at Nob, who gave him food and the sword of Goliath. Ahimelech paid for this with his life; one of Saul's men had been present, and so Saul slew the priest and his family, though Abiathar, one son, escaped to join David. David and his men took to the hills and quartered in the cave at Adullam. He placed his elderly parents in safety with the king of Moab, for the Moabites were the people of Jesse's grandmother Ruth [22:1-5]. David now moved to Judah. He trained his men, and they delivered the town of Keilah from the Philistines. But the Keilahites informed Saul, so David and his men moved to Ziphite country. They, too, told Saul who brought out forces to find the outlaws; at a tense moment, a fresh Philistine invasion diverted Saul in the nick of time [23:26-28]. In the mountains, Saul inadvertently put himself into David's hands, but David refused to harm him, because he was the Lord's anointed King. He spoke deferentially to Saul who conceded David's integrity and returned home [1 Samuel 24]. Then Samuel died and was deeply mourned in Israel. After Samuel's funeral, David moved his men north to Carmel where he encountered a rich farmer, Nabal. Nabal, with insults, churlishly refused a polite and civil request. His wife, Abigail, intercepted David's vengeance party with wisdom and gifts. When Nabal heard the full story he had a heart attack and died 10 days later. David soon married Abigail.

Later, Saul hunted David and his 600 men with 3000 crack troops. One night David, with Abishai, came down the hills and crept into Saul's camp, all asleep, spread in the valley below. Again he spared Saul's life; he took his spear and his water pot by his head and they went back up the hills. At first light David called out from a safe place; Saul acknowledged his wrong in pursuing David, and again he returned home. But by now, David was disheartened and sought refuge amongst the Philistines. Achish, king of Gath, received him, and let him settle in Ziklag, in the south. It became home for the families of his men and for their belongings. From here David raided the southern enemies of Judah. But the other Philistine commanders would not let him join a major attack on Israel in the north [1 Samuel 29]. When he and his 600 returned to Ziklag, they found it destroyed and deserted! He enquired of the Lord, who promised him success and full recovery. He took the raiding Amalakites by surprise, rescued the families, and as a bonus gained all the Amalakite plunder.

At the same time, further north, Israel was threatened by the Philistines. Saul, now without Samuel, was unable to find the Lord's counsel, so he consulted a medium, the witch of Endor. The spirit message was macabre: "This time tomorrow, you and your sons will be dead, and Israel's army will fall to the Philistines." Indeed, Saul died, with Jonathan and his brothers.

King David

David was now guided by the Lord to move to Hebron, in Judah, together with his men and their families who then settled in the neighbourhood. The people made him King of Judah, and he governed there in the south for the next seven years, increasing his influence towards Israel in the north.

David, with gifts of poetry and music, composed many songs, the Psalms, throughout his life. David's Psalms were often his personal prayers before the Lord. The Psalms draw people in to a worshiping relation before God, however they feel at the time. The OT Jews became a music loving people, famous for their songs (Psalm 137:3). Songs were nearly always accompanied by instruments, which it would seem existed for the sole purpose of worship. A common feature of the poetry is 'parallelism' in a couplet:

Eg. Psalm 59:1 Deliver me from my enemies, O God;
  Protect me from those who rise up against me.
- the second line restates what had been expressed in the first.

Psalm 55:6 I said 'O that I had the wings of a dove!
   I would fly away and be at rest' –
– the second line amplifies or compliments the first.

Psalm 1:6 For the Lord watches over the way of the righteous,
   But the way of the wicked will perish
– the second line expresses a contrast.

Another feature is the use of acrostics in some Psalms, where each verse begins with successive letters of the alphabet. In Psalm 119, it is the eight verses in each stanza that begin with the letters of the alphabet.

Although we have lost any rhythm in the translation, we can feel the reinforcement of ideas. Also we have no idea of the music they sang as a community, so to make some engagement with song, we can read antiphonally. As we read, we should think on the Lord, and "sing" in our hearts.

Psalm 27   has David passionately seeking to encounter God while being in an adversarial situation.
[1] The LORD'S light and rescue, and the LORD being his fortress, it is these that counter all fear. Evil men intend destruction, they attack, they lay siege, and they make war. Yet David will keep confident. He earnestly longs for the steady inward awareness of God in his life, for being enthralled by the vision of the shining beauty of the face of God. "He will protect me, he will be my rock-solid foothold. I shall stand head and shoulders above the enemies, and my praise of God will be voluble!"
[7] In calmer vein, David still earnestly seeks after God's face, in the radiance of the priestly blessing, that God will bless and keep him, will shine graciously, and will turn towards him with peace. He clings to the LORD as rescuer, mindful of experiencing rejection by others, and of unjust accusations.
[13] He declares faith in the goodness of the LORD, so he resolves to be encouraged and, in the long haul, "to wait for the LORD."

The Lord continued to build the Israelites into a great kingdom ruled by David. His diplomacy won the day. David, as king of Judah in Hebron, had a well-trained army who fought victoriously. While in Hebron for 7 years, he negotiated with Abner for the loyalty of the other Israelite tribes. Abner, Saul's cousin, had been his commander, and he co-operated with David; but he was murdered by Joab, David's commander, as a result of a blood feud. David handled the fraught situation with sincerity and tact, and in the end, the Israelite tribes made him their king, too [2 Samuel 5:1-5]. [On the Map page 123 – find Jerusalem, and note the regions of Judah and Israel.]

David, King of all Israel

He conquered the fortress of Zion, on the south ridge of Old Jerusalem, throwing out the entrenched Jebusites. Diplomatically, he moved his court and capital here, to neutral territory between Judah in the south and the ten tribes of the north. The citadel of Zion became the City of David, although the site was too small to bring in civilians. Immediately he had to vanquish the Philistines [2 Samuel 5]. Then he sent men to bring the Ark of the Covenant into Jerusalem. It had been 8 miles (13km) away west, for 20 years at Kiriath Jearim. Contrary to Moses' instructions, they put it on a cart which wobbled, and one of the carters, Uzzah, put a hand on the Ark to prevent it toppling off. He was struck dead, so the project was abandoned for 3 months. Then with better respect, for the remaining 2 miles (3km), David himself came, dressed humbly, and the Ark was carried by its poles – as originally intended – with many sacrifices on the way, with shouts and trumpets and praise, and David dancing in worship. His wife Michal, Saul's daughter and so a princess, and apparently a snob, saw all this from the upper floor of David's palace. She complained, and then in effect David shamed and disinherited her. [2 Samuel 6:12-23]

David knew that the Ark, with central worship of the LORD, would be a strong unifying force for Israel. He restored the LORD'S worship with music, singing Psalms, and he reinstated Levites, Priests and Prophets.

He continued military campaigns, and defeated the Philistines to the west, Moab and Edom to the east, and he fought enemies to the north, the Arameans and the Ammonites, all the way up to the Euphrates. He established a sound national administration [2 Samuel 8:15-18], and he made his united kingdom strong and prosperous.

David had a great yen to build a Temple for the Ark, a house for the LORD'S presence. The Ark was now in a tent on the hill-top site immediately north of Zion. David had restored regular worship, reinstating Priests and Levites, and bestowing his personal gifts of Music and Song (the Psalms). But to Temple-building the LORD said 'No!' Instead he made David gracious and personal promises. [2 Samuel 7:8-16] David was deeply humbled, and the prayer of the next dozen verses is his response [18-29]. He had a real heart for God. God is amazingly generous, and involves us in his plans and purposes. The Lord continued to build the Israelites into a great kingdom ruled by David. But flagrant private sin broke his authority.

His first wife was Saul's daughter, Michal. She had loved him originally [1 Samuel 18:20]. He married others, including Abigail who had been married to a churlish husband who died. One of the hallmarks of a successful king at that time was the number of wives he possessed [2 Samuel 3:2-5].

One spring-time, David for once stayed at home, working, while he sent his army commander Joab to deal with enemies in the east, at Rabbah. The Philistines in the west had already been fixed. One evening, relaxed, he strolled on the roof of his palace, which was the highest building in the city, housing all his families. Nearby, Bathsheba took a bath on the roof-top of her house, where no one could see, except from the palace. David saw beautiful Bathsheba, naked; his lust was roused. He found out that she was the wife of one of his soldiers. He sent for her and he slept with her. She became pregnant, so he got her husband Uriah home on leave; but the plan misfired; so he sent him back to the battle, with a letter telling Joab to fix it that Uriah was killed by the enemy. Then he married Bathsheba. "But the thing David had done displeased the LORD"[2 Samuel

11:27]. Nathan the prophet spoke to him 9 or 10 months after the event; Bathsheba's baby died, and David at last deeply repented. The LORD forgave him, but desperate damage had been done. The virus of lust infected his family, and Amnon, his eldest son and heir, raped David's daughter Tamar; family pride and resentment provoked Amnon's murder by Tamar's brother Absalon; and David's loss of grip brought national disaster through two attempted coups – first Absalon's, then later Adonijah's. We know that sin can be forgiven, but its consequences are still devastating – damaging personal relationships, disrupting the local community, causing national disaster, and impacting God's purposes and even forcing him to achieve things by another way. David's moral authority over his family was reduced; his misuse of love left him too hesitant to stop others following his example. However, the LORD really had forgiven him, and later Bathsheba had a son, Solomon, who became the next king; furthermore, Solomon was an ancestor of Jesus.

Psalm 51 is David's agony of repentance, set in verse after Nathan's word to him, in 2 Samuel 12. He made full admission and owned entire responsibility. He pleaded for complete cleansing. Hyssop was the small herb used by the priests to sprinkle the blood of the sacrifices on penitent sinners; the life of the animal was taken in substitution for taking the life of the sinner. Then came washing to snow-whiteness, and David prayed for restoration of relationship with God, with joy, a pure heart, and with a renewed commitment of spirit. He asked for grace to worship God again, to declare publicly God's righteousness, and for protection and prosperity for Zion, which was David's allotted responsibility as king.

David's heart for God	
1	As shepherd Psalm 23 ['The LORD is <u>my</u> shepherd…"]
2	When anointed by Samuel as future king 1 Samuel 16:13

3	His uncomplicated faith in the LORD of his nation about Goliath 1 Samuel 17:32-37, 45-47
4	He spent time, learning from Samuel 1 Samuel 19:18-24
5	He placed his parents in Moab for safety 1 Samuel 22:3
6	He listened to the prophet Gad 1 Samuel 22:5; 2 Samuel 24:11-19
7	He sought guidance over action for Keilah 1 Samuel 23:1-6
8	He respected Saul as anointed by God as king 1 Samuel 24 and 26
9	He sought guidance over action for Ziklag 1 Samuel 30:1-8
10	and again over dealing with Philistines 2 Samuel 5:17-25
11	He led worship when bringing the Ark into Jerusalem 2 Samuel 6:1-19
12	His humble response to God's No! over building the Temple, and to God's gracious promises given to him 2 Samuel 7
13	His response to the gifts given for the Temple building project 1 Chronicles 29:1-20
14	His repentance over Bathsheba Psalm 51

Psalm 110, composed by David, contains prophetic words about the Messiah.

[1] God of the Covenant, I AM, speaks to David's Lord, who is the Messiah. "You are to sit enthroned as God's right-hand executive; all enemies will be subdued under your feet. God will empower your reign, spreading out from Zion. Your loyal troops will burst forth victoriously, like morning dew falling on the battlefield."

[4] God, I AM, continues with asseveration, "You, David's Lord, are sworn to be an eternal priest like Melchizedek."

[5] Judgement day will fall on kings, and rulers and nations of the whole world, on the day of wrath. God is supreme; David's Lord will be paramount.

     In Jesus' day, Israel expected that the Messiah would indeed be God's enforcing ruler, rather than the priest mediating blessing, and than the prince of peace. For sure, the Messiah will come in wrath and judgement at the Last Day.

Solomon

The next king after David, his son Solomon, certainly became an enforcing ruler, as well as having the gift from God of outstanding discernment and practical wisdom. Power works. Solomon, unlike his father, was not a soldier, but was an extremely astute and powerful king. [1 Kings 3:29-36] He held Judah with little Benjamin and the 10 northern tribes together by clever use of force, but made enemies, notably Jeroboam who had been an able army officer, and who removed himself to Egypt for his own safety.

David had grown rich indeed, but Solomon became fabulously rich. Solomon secured his throne during the 4 years after David's death and then in 966 BC he started to build. He built the Temple of the LORD in Jerusalem, on the Rock perhaps where, generations before, Abraham had nearly sacrificed his young son Isaac [2 Chronicles 3:1]. The Temple incorporated the Ark of the Covenant, and replaced the original portable structures with big wood and stone buildings, reflecting the original design of 300 years previously under Moses, but about double the size [1Kings 8:1-11]. This took 7 years, so it was commissioned and consecrated about 960 BC. Then he spent 11 years building his colossal palace for his wives; it overshadowed the Temple!

At that time Egypt was in eclipse and the peoples in the north were not yet united. The 'kings of the north' meant all who would tramp down the western limb of the Fertile Crescent, both from Turkey (originally Hittites) and from Mesopotamia (Assyrians, Babylonians, Persians &c), and from those literally north of Israel (Arameans). Those in the south meant both Egypt and the desert peoples of Arabia.

Solomon's wisdom became known internationally. Solomon built ships at the head of the Gulf of Aqaba, and traded making big profits. Israel prospered. He had a well-equipped army, and numerous slaves from subject peoples, and he received a visit from the Queen of Sheba who was ruler of lands at the south end of the Red Sea. She was vastly impressed! [1 Kings 10] Solomon had hundreds of royal wives, in fact more wives and concubines than any other king. But the verdict was that they led him astray from his worship of the LORD [1 Kings 11:1-6].

Psalm 84 While the Jerusalem leadership varied in its depth of personal devotion to the Lord, Temple worship was led by the director of music of the day. Asaph, for one, had been David's devout musician. This Psalm, sung by the Korahites, uplifts everyone in the Temple courtyard.
[1] 'The LORD dwells in this lovely building, and my whole being yearns for the living God. Birds fly in to nest inside; blest are all like them who dwell where you dwell.
[5] Blessing is for determined pilgrims who overcome troubles on the way to reach God in Zion. I pray for the LORD God Almighty to bless our sovereign.
[10] To spend a day here is better than spending a thousand anywhere else. Being a Temple doorkeeper is for me, over any living with wickedness, because the LORD shines on and protects me, giving favour and honour and good things to those who walk with him.'
"O LORD Almighty, blessed is the one who trusts in you!"

The story moves on. But first, the next chapter looks more deeply at Old Testament Wisdom.

Chapter 12   Wisdom

> Old Testament Wisdom, including understanding, insight and prudence, was a serious art.

Old Testament Wisdom led to right plans and success. It dwelt in the heart of man, the centre of moral and intellectual decision. It included technical skills, for shipwrights, navigators, even mourners. It was a necessity for official leaders. God owns the fullest wisdom in his plan and execution of the Universe [Proverbs 3:19] and of man [Psalm 137]. The fear of the LORD brings insight into God's ways, and requires a daily obedient walk in life [Proverbs 9:10].   Wisdom turns people to live so that the name of God is honoured.

Wisdom Books

Wisdom Literature was international. In Israel, the prophets brought revelation from the Lord. "Wisdom taught the application of prophetic truth to individual life in the light of experience." (H Wheeler Robinson) Wisdom is more practical than philosophical. God is Wisdom, and he reveals wisdom if people will but receive it and fear him.

There are two types of Wisdom books: Proverbial, with short pithy rules for happiness and welfare; and Speculative, delving into the meaning of existence and the relationship of God and man.   This wisdom, too, is practical and based on experience, not detached and theoretical.

The OT Wisdom Books are the poetry of Job, some Psalms, Proverbs, Ecclesiastes, Song, and some other passages. Some of this was written in Solomon's time.

In summary:

<u>Job</u> contains many dialogues exploring the relations of God and Mankind, and raising the issues of undeserved suffering, sinfulness, and hurtful criticism. The book presents a godly, God-fearing man of substance devastated by loss of wealth and family and health. In deep suffering he is "comforted" by three or four friends whose theology tells them that all this disaster has to be result of sin and evil in Job's life.

Job knows this is not true. They criticise remorselessly, while Job cries out for a hearing before God. Towards the end of the book, God himself addresses Job, and Job is completely overwhelmed with his encounter with God.

Proverbs is a collection of short powerful sayings to teach practical success in social and religious life in the community. The book has many wise sayings. Wisdom is personified in female form [Proverbs 8,9] and contrasted with the woman Folly. The last chapter, 31, contains The Wife of noble character, [31:10-end] setting an impossible standard! Clearly, wisdom starts by respect and awe and fear of the Lord.

Ecclesiastes is a monologue. The Preacher/Teacher (Heb. QOHELETH) finds no secular activity in itself has any value or meaning. After looking into work and life and death, he concludes "Fear God and keep his commandments… God will [judge] …everything." Ecclesiastes 11:7 – 12:14. Perhaps QOHELETH was Solomon himself; it was one who researched many things from the vantage point of freedom from daily work.

Song is a love poem, explicitly romantic and sexy. He and she encounter, and react in love with exquisite delicacy, extolling one another's glorious physicality and having intimacy at several points in the poem. The wisdom here is the portrayal of a practical respect for human love, for the human body and for love-making.

Psalm 37 is ascribed to David. It is the wisdom of an experienced older person of faith, addressed to fellow followers of the LORD, I AM.

He begins with warning: Don't fret about evildoers; refrain from anger. Then his warm heart overflows with counsel for the righteous; Trust in the LORD, Do good, Dwell in the Land, Delight yourself in the LORD, Commit your way to the LORD, Be still before him, Wait patiently for him, (James 5:11 refers to the "patience of Job"), Wait for the LORD, Keep his way, Consider the upright.

In contrast he catalogues the acts of evildoers: they are wrongdoers, they plot against and attack the righteous, they victimise the poor and needy, they borrow and do not repay. The Lord repays these people at some point, even as they flourish.

David (or the person of faith) has great memories of the acts of the LORD for the upright; he gives, he makes righteousness shine, he upholds and blesses, he delights in our path, and loves the just; he will not leave the righteous in the power of the wicked; he exalts him to possess the Land, he is the stronghold, he helps, delivers, and rescues the righteous.

Out of this loving wisdom of God, so active on our behalf, comes the Character of the Just: such a person hopes in the LORD, he inherits the Promised Land, he is meek and enjoys great peace. He gives generously, he is upheld, is generous and lends freely. He lives securely, under protection; he inherits and dwells in the Land; he utters wisdom, with the law of God in his heart; he has a future and posterity, and he takes refuge in the LORD.

A fuller look at Job

Chapter 1 In the Introduction, Job is presented as blameless and upright, one who feared God and shunned evil. He was the greatest man among the peoples of the East, who greatly respected him.

He is accused before God by Satan. Satan implies that Job's devotion to God is self-seeking. God permits him to face trials. In the first disaster, he is brought to ruin by loss of animals, servants, property and family. In the event, Job worshiped and praised God, because 'God gives and now he takes away, and that's all right.'

Chapter 2 He is accused again. Satan's charge is that Job's loyalty to God is less than his love of his own life; remove that security and he will curse God. In this event, Job suffers affliction – loss of health and of a wife's support. However, Job responds that God directs both good and trouble.

Then three friends arrive, to share his grief and to give comfort. They seek to be real friends, spending time with Job. Clearly, things are far worse than they thought.

Chapter 3 After a week of silence, Job moans that God is his problem. Job is overwhelmed, and he would find peace in death. This crystallisation of Job's thinking is the start of his resurgence from rock bottom.

Chapters 4,5   The first friend to speak is Eliphaz, who is supportive and caring. He advises 'Let God be God, for you cannot be more pure than God. Our world can be hazardous physically, and also as a result of our rebellion, by battle and lash of tongue. Blessing comes from God's correction.' Much that he says is worthy.

Chapters 6,7   Job replies, more to God than to Eliphaz. He thinks of God being active in his suffering; he clings to his afflicting God for his need, as Jacob clung to his divine assailant. [Genesis 32]   Job is growing, but the others do not budge from Cause & Effect, simply that Good behaviour brings prosperity and Bad living brings suffering.

Chapter 8   Next to speak is Bildad. He does not understand, and remains with the received wisdom of the aged. He states that God does not pervert justice, and does not reject the blameless man. These are the rules. It is Law, not Grace.

Chapters 9,10   Job knows their wisdom, but it only drives him to rage again at the God who made him tenderly, but is not now there, other than to accuse him. Job wants out – yet, 'if only there were someone to arbitrate between us.' [9.33]

Chapter 11   The third friend wades in. Zophar tries a firm approach: To him, God is beyond our limited wisdom; 'sin is in your hand, so put it away,' and then all will be restored.

Chapters 12, 13, 14   Job is angry that God is being defamed by his friends. He replies 'I know all this. You smear me with lies.' He knows that God is total; he is there in disaster as much as in prosperity. Power and understanding are his. 'I trust him, even though he slay me.'

Chapter 15   Now Eliphaz is upset. He raises a dozen questions! He believes that suffering is for the wicked alone. Job's raging only condemns himself.

Chapters 16,17   In reply, Job asks 'Are we no-hopers?' He wants their encouragement, not their misery! Job is experiencing God's violence, his overwhelming, and his judging. And yet he speaks of a witness in heaven, an advocate on high, an intercessor and friend who pleads with God [16:19-21]. To his visitors Job says 'Try again!' [17:10]

Chapter 18   Without referring to God, Bildad says that it is the fate of the wicked to be driven from light into darkness, marched off to terror, as the lot of one who knows not God. All that is <u>not</u> God's doing, whatever you say. To every action there is a reaction upon the doer; that's the rule.

Chapter 19   Job replies that you torment me, you all reject me with total alienation. 'Have pity on me!' It is God who has besieged me, struck me down. Yet I know that my kinsman-redeemer (Goel) lives; I will see him. [19:25-27]

Chapter 20   Zophar is getting upset by Job. He states that wicked man will perish. He implies that Job has oppressed the poor; misery and terror are the traditional fate of the wicked. He is aware of a chasm of understanding between him and Job. He is right, and Job is wrong.

Chapter 21   But Job asks 'Why do the wicked live on prosperously? The evil man is spared from the day of calamity [v.30]. This is true worldwide. You speak nonsense!'

Chapter 22   Eliphaz is still simplistic. He concludes 'Your wickedness is great; return to the Lord.' He says many good things: Choose life [21ff] and then you will pray with great power [27ff]

Chapters 23,24   Job replies 'I cannot find him, he is aloof. I am in fear of him. He is the refiner, taking time to purify Job in the furnace of suffering (and was in there himself, too – suffering the cross). Finally God will judge, bringing mercy and justice for the widows, the poor, the orphans, and the needy.'

Chapter 25   But for Bildad, God is remote; he puts God at the distant top of Creation, in regal awesomeness. 'You cannot make yourself righteous; man is just a maggot, a worm.'

Chapters 26 to 31   But Job's reply cuts him short, and does not give Zophar a chance! Job speaks to all three, [26:1 – 27:12] maintaining the greatness of God's creating work, his justice and his own integrity, despite all that his 'comforters' say. Then he soliloquises over the fate of the wicked. [27:13ff] Job speaks a great poem to exalt practical wisdom [chapter 28] It starts with the miner and smelter of metals, who have great practical knowledge[1-11]. 'Where is wisdom? God understands the way to it, [12ff] and he directs man.' "The fear of the Lord is the beginning of wisdom."[27,28]

In Chapter 29, Job states what he used to be before the disasters, and it echoes God's concern for the powerless [12-17]

In Chapter 30, he turns and says 'now they mock me. I am reduced to nothing, and God doesn't answer me.'

In Chapter 31, sixteen times he pleads 'If I have … done evil things, then may … disaster come on me.' He ends with a passionate cry to the Almighty (31:35).

<u>Elihu</u>   The poem inserts another character, a younger person than Job and the three sages.

Chapter 32   Elihu is angry with Job for justifying himself rather than God. He is also angry with the other three for not being able to refute Job, and yet they have condemned him. "I'm exploding with things to say!"

Chapter 33   To Job, he says: 'You say that you are without sin; but God has found fault and become my enemy. You are wrong! God is greater than man, he speaks, maybe in dreams, to turn man from doing wrong, from being proud, to preserve his physical life. Or he uses pain and brings near death; then he is the mediator, graciously to spare and to restore. Therefore admit sin, find favour and be restored! (QED!)'

Chapter 34   Elihu turns to the three: 'You three wise men, Job says "I am innocent, but God denies me justice." God does not do wrong, but repays man what he deserves. If God withdrew his spirit, all would perish. God sees everything and all people. He punishes the wicked. Job is answering like a wicked man who is rebelling.'

Chapter 35   Elihu now speaks to all four, to Job and his three friends: 'You cannot give righteousness to God, and sin has no effect on God. Arrogance is not answered; you say that his anger never punishes, he ignores wickedness;

Chapter 36   'but my Maker is just, mighty, firm of purpose, and gives rights to the afflicted; he observes the righteous and lifts them up. But those bound with affliction – God is telling them of their acts and arrogance, and commands that they repent. If they do so, they will have prosperity; but if not they will perish. He is wooing you from the jaws of distress.

Chapter 37 'God commands thunder and he has uncontrollable power. God's golden splendour is seen in the brilliant sun. The Almighty is beyond our reach.' [v.23]

All this has been said before, a bit more calmly! Perhaps Elihu was put into the poem to show that both seniors and failed younger sages do not have answers for Job; and also to give a summary so far.

God speaks

Chapter 38 The LORD now addresses Job directly, ignoring both the three older sages and the young upstart. God speaks out of a storm which is beyond control. He speaks with a completely different focus from all five men. He questions Job about his role in Nature: the creation of land and sea, light, death, weather, and stars; 'are you concerned with the supply of food for lions and ravens?'

Chapter 39 'Do you know about the birth of wild animals, the mountain goat, the fawn, the donkey, the ox, the independent ostrich, the strength of the horse, the life cycle of the eagle?

Chapter 40 'Job, can you correct me?' Job: 'I am not worthy to reply.' 'Can you exercise judgement? Consider Behemoth (Hippo) and

Chapter 41 'Leviathan (crocodile) (fearsome and untameable big animals, primeval monsters of chaos.)'

Chapter 42 Finally, Job responds: 'I have been groping with things I have not understood. I heard of you, and now I have seen you. I admit my limits: I repent.'

God now speaks to the three: 'You have not spoken aright of me. Come now with sacrifice and with Job's prayer for you.' God restores Job, doubles his original property, and restores his family; Job then lives on to a ripe old age.

Denis Lennnon writes that Satan's accusations have been demolished, and Job also has become silent before God. God saw in Job's heart his submission and truth, so he told the others that Job has spoken what is right. He had faith to tell God his complaint. But the others, unhelpfully, had rigidly stuck to their wisdom tradition. That Job was wonderfully restored implies that the old tradition still stands, but that 'suffering' does not mean 'you have sinned.'

Encounter with God

This meeting of God with Job, one-on-one, and its person-shattering effect on Job is the reason for this poetic book. As soon as God spoke, Job was quickly overwhelmed. God's presence broke over him, tsunami-like. God had been there all the time! Job was dumb-founded as God in Creator-Majesty spoke directly to him, about the vast enterprise of the universe, and of our sun and moon and earth. God's panorama of Living things in the waters, on the land, and in the air above, is redolent of his involvement and joy, excitement and strength, and of his delicate care and passion and experience in the human world. Job reeled from the infinite, the majestic, the loveliness, the transcendence. He was overpowered by the mystery that is God. Suddenly God is encountered; he is revealed; the nagging questions and doubts are silenced; and the heart is almost stopped. Job in awe knows that God is beyond him in every respect. He becomes totally abandoned to God; he experiences heaven for a time. He receives God's deep love of him.

Further wisdom from Denis Lennon: We do not control God, yet we take part in what he is doing. God parades Creation before us, so we should look as it reveals the Creator; we can see his purposes in the designs: order not disorder, with freedom, beauty, humour and joy. The impossible times and forces and distances reflect the impossible redemption given to us. In his engagement with us, Jesus took our humanness, and transformed physical life by his resurrection. Like Job, we may be made aware of the inexpressible, the infinite, the majesty, and the mystery. He is there all the time, but suddenly he is revealed, and we are silenced in awe: 'The King of kings and Lord of lords, who alone is immortal and who lives in unapproachable light, whom no-one can see or has seen.' [1 Timothy 6:15-16] It is the inexpressible wonder and loveliness of God, entirely different from a natural person's experience. The Cross is part of this breathtaking exposure, for never are we worthy and his holy worth wrings out that deep shattering upon us, so that we fall at his feet.

Besides Job, other OT believers received personal encounters with the overwhelming holiness of God: Moses the shepherd, at the Burning Bush beside Horeb: Exodus 3:1-6. Isaiah in the Temple: 6:1-8. Young Jeremiah: 1:4-9. Ezekiel, freshly exiled to Babylon: 1:1 – 2:2. Daniel in Persia: 8:15-18, and again 10:4-9. These men were permanently changed by such encounters, and commissioned for God's purposes.

Other thoughts: Job's friends came and spent time with him [2:11-13]. Jesus came and spent time with us, by being one of us. Then he acted on our behalf as our kinsman-redeemer at his own expense and suffering [1 Peter 1:18,19]. Once redeemed, Christians need to act with practical wisdom [James 1:22-27].

Also: Elihu may have spoken out of turn, embarrassing his seniors. He said some good things, and at least he spoke! Denis Lennon asks if today's broadminded tolerance cloaks a loss of nerve and conviction.

Wisdom for Today

As foreseen in Isaiah 9:6, the Son of Man is our wise and wonderful counsellor. Jesus' wisdom amazed people. (Luke 2:40,47,52 Mark 1:22,27 6:2) He claimed wisdom himself. (Matthew 12:42)

Jesus, Son of God, who is our Wisdom, in his obedience to the Father God completely justified God's wisdom in creation, in particular in his making human beings. He lived and suffered, and in the resurrection he changed human life and revealed God's huge love for us all.

Paul's declaration of God's wisdom in Christ (1 Corinthians 1:17-2:16) lifts perceptions from human wisdom ("sophistry") to God's power on the cross, by preaching and belief. Jesus is the wisdom of God - in righteousness, holiness, and redemption, in demonstration of the Spirit in power. He is revealed to believers who have received the Spirit, so that we may have understanding, given free of charge, in Spiritual words expressing Spiritual truth – we have the mind of Christ. God's wisdom is supremely revealed to all in his action in the cross, in redemption; this confounds all human wisdom, which seeks to sort out the problems of life without reference to God.

In NT times, as well as all who received the Holy Spirit with his gifts at Pentecost and later, some had shattering experiences of being met by God. Paul testified to this on the Damascus Road (Act 9). John wrote of meeting the sovereign Lord Jesus himself [Revelation 1:9-18], as well as of his vision of the victorious King of Kings and Lord of Lords. [Revelation 19:11-16]

NT wisdom has the same strongly practical nature as OT wisdom. Wisdom is for everyday life, and in persecution, to speak worthily. It is given that we may understand God's revelation, to perceive God's purposes for both leaders and the led. It is for instruction to walk worthily of God, and discreetly before unbelievers. It matures in faith and life, so Christians may teach others.

We do not command God to appear. But, by unreservedly casting ourselves upon him, we may prepare to take part in his action in our day. When we truthfully come to the end of ourselves and cry out to him, then we may well be surprised by his revelation to us.

Psalms

These three Psalms are part of the Wisdom writings:

<u>Psalm 133</u> speaks of a living unity amongst fellow Israelites. Such community life has sweet agreement. It is like the fragrant anointing oil poured so liberally upon Aaron. It is a precious spiritual accord.
Also, it is as if the dew of Mt Hermon, over 100 miles (160km) to the north, were to bathe Mt Zion in its moisture, and be the place of the LORD'S life giving blessing.

Psalm 128 focuses on the wise individual and his family. He fears the LORD, and this is the beginning of wisdom, for he chooses to live accordingly. This brings satisfaction and prosperity, and a thriving wife and children. "May you live long and experience Jerusalem's good things and Israel's peace."

Psalm 127, attributed to Solomon's era, is a wise assessment; for the builders of the Temple and for the City guards, all is in vain unless the LORD acts. The same is true in their farms. Indeed, family is a gift from the LORD. A quiver held five arrows, and a quiverful of sons would grow and triumph in the fight for the City gate. This blessing comes from the LORD.

The next chapter covers the rise to power of Assyria, Egypt, and Babylon, with the failure of Israel and Judah.

Chapter 13   Military Powers in Motion

> Soldiers had fought in small tribal groups; but now, in a new concept, vast armies swept across the Land in unstoppable might. A chart of the Kings of all Israel, and a Time line from Solomon to Nehemiah's work.

The Military Powers

Egypt was concentrated along the banks of the Nile. A succession of invaders brought different dynasties of pharaohs to rule the peoples. Some used Thebes (Luxor) as capital, some Memphis (by today's Cairo). In Abraham's day it was the 12th dynasty in power, and in his great grandson Joseph's day it was a later Hyksos dynasty whose pharaoh ruled Egypt. Then the powerful 19th dynasty enslaved non-ethnic Egyptians, including the Hebrews originally from Canaan. So Egypt had become formidable about the time of Moses, while the peoples of the areas to the north and east of the Fertile Crescent were not then organised into powerful nations. Ramses II was intent on building a great palace complex in the Delta, but the Israelites under Moses escaped his clutches. Also his elite army perished while in pursuit of them. A generation later he allowed Israel to occupy the Promised Land unchallenged, although it was close to Egypt. Later, David, then Solomon, built the Israelites into a strong nation, powerful from about 1000 BC for 70 years.

The two kingdoms

After Solomon, his son was hopeless! But whoever succeeded Solomon would have had an impossible task. His son Rehoboam took over when Solomon died, and forthwith Jeroboam, Solomon's enemy, arrived from Egypt. Rehoboam completely mishandled the challenge, and the 10 Tribes of the north, seceded under Jeroboam. They made a unilateral declaration of independence. Now the united kingdom became split: Judah in the south with little Benjamin, capital Jerusalem, ruled by Rehoboam, and the much larger Israel in the north, capital Shechem at first, then Samaria, ruled by Jeroboam.

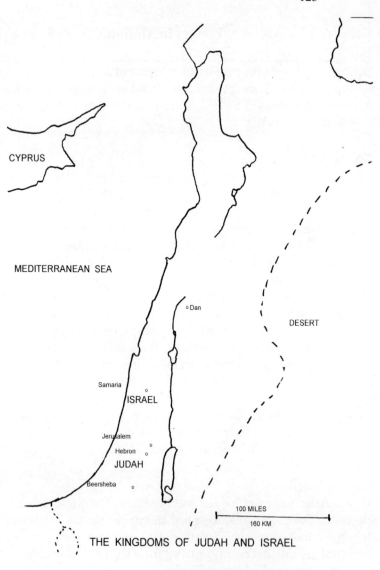

THE KINGDOMS OF JUDAH AND ISRAEL

Rehoboam's lack of perception had lost the northern 10 Tribes. Jeroboam prevented the Ten Israelite Tribes from returning to Jerusalem, and so to Rehoboam, for attending obligatory Temple feasts. He set up two idols, one in Bethel near the boarder with Judah, and one in the north at the town of Dan. [1 Kings 12:25-

32] These idols were a reversion to the golden calf of the Moon-god worship, the nominal religion of many other nations of the Fertile Crescent. Such false worship had been incipient within the Israelites all though the OT up to the Exile, from Rachel stealing her father Laban's idols, to the golden calf that Moses destroyed, to the idols that the aged Joshua spoke of [Joshua 24:14], to the idols of Solomon's many wives.

Assyria So the power of Solomon's reign was whittled away. Meanwhile a force in Mesopotamia was growing strong with very large numbers of men compared to the smaller groups elsewhere. This army was from Assyria, with capital Nineveh, conquering westwards, before turning south to Israel. Samaria fell to Shalmaneser in 722 BC. Later, when ruled by good king Hezekiah, Judah survived the approach of Sennacherib, a succeeding king of Assyria.

The Assyrians under Ashurnarsirpal rose to overwhelming strength through sheer numbers, and with skilful propaganda. The lust for conquest took possession of the Assyrian kings. Their armies began to move forward with aims which grew more ambitious year by year. Their god Ashur must reign over a world empire; and any tribe which challenged his claim must be ruthlessly overthrown. Ashurnarsirpal struck with the utmost brutality at every Aramaean group which might conceivable become a power of any importance. His son and successor Shalmaneser, with incredible energy extended the god Ashur's domain both to the west and to the south. He overran Cilicia and seized all its natural wealth, the silver mines of the Taurus and the great supplies of timber. He recorded a battle between his troops and the armies of twelve allied kings at Qarqar on the Orontes. He mentions Hadadezer of Damascus, with the king of Hamath, and Ahab king of Israel. According to this report, Shalmaneser naturally carried the day. 'I dammed the Orontes with their dead!' Assyrian kings were always victorious! The divided kingdoms of Israel and Judah, now small beer, were completely out-gunned. Israel was overthrown by Shalmaneser. They were slaughtered and dispersed, and never reappeared again.

2 Kings 18 [v 13-15]: Hezekiah's attempt to buy off the Assyrian Sennacherib failed: [v 28-36]. Isaiah encouraged Hezekiah to stand firm: [19:5-7]. Bullying and propaganda continued, and Hezekiah resorted to desperate prayer: [14-19]. Isaiah received words from the LORD about Sennacherib: [21-22, 32-34]. Indeed, he retreated home where he perished. Then Assyrian power declined and Babylon defeated them. At the same time a new Egyptian dynasty, the 20th, arose.

Josiah

Elderly Isaiah died, and Hezekiah too. His successors were bad news, until good king Josiah was crowned. He was a spiritual and energetic king whose Temple rebuilding unearthed the "Book of the Law": [2 Kings 22:8-11, 23:1-3]. In Josiah's reign, Jeremiah was called to be prophet in Jerusalem. [Jeremiah 1:1] Babylon to the east, and Egypt in the south, were growing strong; Pharaoh Neco marched north to support the Assyrians and attack the Babylonians. Little Judah, in between, was ruled by Josiah; unwisely he led his forces against the Egyptian incursion along the coast road, and he was slain in battle at Megiddo in 609 BC. [2 Kings 23:29] Judah was defeated, and Pharaoh replaced Josiah with a puppet king.

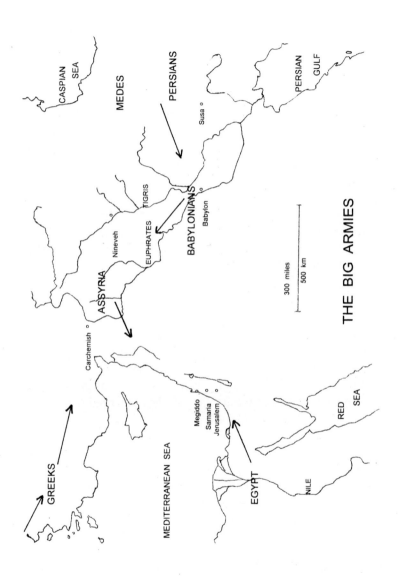

Babylonians 4 years later, in 605 BC, the Egyptians fought the Babylonians led by Nebuchadnezzar in the battle of Carchemish, in the far north west of the Fertile Crescent; Pharaoh was defeated, so the power of Egypt was broken.

Nebuchadnezzar was crown prince of Babylon, and a brilliant soldier. That same year, when still in the west limb of the Fertile Crescent, he heard of his father's death, so he took men and rode direct across the desert back to Babylon – which was a formidable feat – and he was made king before anyone else could claim the throne. Then he returned to demolish Egypt and possess all the territory from Egypt to the top of the Fertile Crescent. At that time (597BC) he picked off Jerusalem without firing a shot – Jehoiakin surrendered. Nebuchadnezzar deported 10,000 men plus families, to camps outside Babylon. Jeremiah was left behind under the new puppet king Zedekiah, while the prophet Ezekiel who was a devout and visionary priest, and four young men, Daniel, Hananiah, Mishael, and Azariah, travelled to Babylon with the captives.

The king recognised the four as having unusual potential. They were schooled in Babylonian ways and law, and yet they all retained and practised their faith. [Daniel 1,2] When they were faced with a Catch 22 situation, Shadrach, Meshach, and Abednego (their Babylonian names) stood their ground and were thrown into the Fiery Furnace, but they emerged unscathed. This story is in Daniel 3. Nebuchadnezzar, a superstitious man, seems to have come to acknowledge the Lord [Daniel 4:34-37].

While Jerusalem was still standing, Jeremiah wrote a letter to the captives in Babylon, to encourage them to settle in for 70 years of exile. Then there would be prospect of a return to Jerusalem [Jeremiah 29:1-14]. After 7 years Zedekiah rebelled, so Nebuchadnezzar returned to sack Jerusalem. Zedekiah had broken his oath to Nebuchadnezzar; he had rejected Jeremiah's words, and he drew down Ezekiel's condemnation, and a prophecy that Nebuchadnezzar would destroy Jerusalem and the Temple. At the time, the Scribes, both in the exile and in the Temple, rejected Ezekiel's prophecy, as they believed the

Temple was sacrosanct. In fact Jerusalem and the Temple were devastated in 587BC. [2 Chronicles 36:15-21]

Psalm 137 expresses grief and horror amongst the exiles when freshly deported from the Promised Land. Jerusalem had been demolished and its people savaged. The survivors are shocked and weeping in the camps beside the rivers at Babylon. They are taunted by the guards – 'Sing us a song of Zion!' Their response comes from between gritted teeth: 'The LORD is not here! We have to be in Jerusalem to sing to God.' They swear to remember their city as the focus of their beings, and this sparks prayers of imprecation against neighbouring Edom who had sided with the destroying invaders, and against the Babylonians themselves. The exiles recall the terrible treatment of families, which happens in all violent conflicts, down to today.

As a result of Nebuchadnezzar's assaults on Jerusalem, many were slaughtered, and some escaped to Moab, Edom, or Egypt; only about 10% of the original population of Judah were marched to Babylon where they were held in concentration camps until released. Then they settled and prospered.

ISRAELITE KINGS The assessment of good or bad was determined by the sovereign's practice of seeking the Lord, or otherwise. These figures for the lengths of reigns are those in 1 & 2 Kings, and are repeated in 2 Chronicles.

United Israel

Saul	40 yrs	bad	killed in battle
David	40 yrs	good	natural death
Solomon	40 yrs	good	natural death

Judah divided from *Israel*

Judah				Israel			
Rehoboam	17 yrs	bad	natural death				
				Jeroboam I	22 yrs	bad	natural death
Abijah	3 yrs	bad	natural				
				Nadab	2 yrs	bad	murdered
Asa	41 yrs	good	natural				
				Baasha	24 yrs	bad	natural
				Elah	2 yrs	bad	murdered
				Zimri	7 days	bad	suicide

Jehoshaphat	25 yrs	good	natural death
Omri	12 yrs	bad	natural
Jehoram	8 yrs	bad	natural
Ahab	22 yrs	bad	in battle
Ahaziah	2 yrs	bad	accident
Ahaziah	1 yr	bad	by wounds
Joram	12 yrs	bad	killed
Athaliah	7 yrs	bad	executed
Jehu	28 yrs	bad	natural
Joash	40 yrs	good	murdered
Joahaz	17 yrs	bad	natural
Jehoash	16 yrs	bad	natural
Amaziah	29 yrs	good	murdered
Jeroboam II	41 yrs	bad	natural
Azariah (= Uzziah)	52 yrs	good	natural
Zechariah	6 mths	bad	murdered
Shallum	1 mth	bad	killed
Menahem	10 yrs	bad	natural
Jotham	16 yrs	good	natural
Pekahiah	2 yrs	bad	murdered
Ahaz	16 yrs	bad	natural
Pekah	20 yrs	bad	murdered
Hezekiah	29 yrs	good	natural
Hoshea	9 yrs	bad	in exile
Manasseh	55 yrs	bad	natural
Amon	2 yrs	bad	murdered
Josiah	31 yrs	good	killed in battle
Jehoahaz	3 mths	bad	died in Egypt
Jehoiakim	11 yrs	bad	natural
Jehoiakin	3 mths	bad	died in Babylon
Zedekiah	11 yrs	bad	died captive in Babylon

(The figures in Kings do not agree with each other. As example, 2 Kings 17:1 Hoshea began in 12th year of Ahaz, 2 Kings 15:30 Hoshea began in 20th year of Jotham; but Jotham reigned for only 16 years!

Adding back the reigns of the kings of Judah to the fall of Jerusalem in 587BC, it follows that Rehoboam became king after Solomon in 956BC.

Adding back the reigns of the kings of Israel to the fall of Samaria in 722BC, then Jeroboam seized power in 949BC. Yet Solomon reigned 40 years from 970BC, founding the Temple in 966BC, so Rehoboam and Jereboam began their reigns in 930BC.
Clearly we are not understanding the written numerical data correctly!)

An accepted approximate time line BC:

Solomon reigned	961 – 922	(or	970 – 930)
Solomon's Temple completed	950	(or	959)
Judah and Israel divided	922	(or	930)
Uzziah's death	742	(or	740)
Isaiah's ministry			742 – 700
Hezekiah reigned			715 – 687
The northern kingdom, Israel, overrun			722
Josiah reigned			640 – 609
Jeremiah's ministry			626 – 587
Battle of Megiddo			609
Battle of Carchemish			605
Jerusalem surrendered to Nebuchadnezzar			597
(Ezekiel, Daniel, and his 3 friends deported)			
Nebuchadnezzar demolishes Jerusalem			587
Return from Exile begins			537
(Zerubabbel, Jeshua)			
The Jerusalem Temple is rebuilt			515
(70 years after its destruction)			
The Wall of Jerusalem is rebuilt			445
(Nehemiah as Governor)			

There were enemies of the Jews, both locally around the Land, and within the Persian empire. One of Nebuchadnezzar's successors was Belshazzar whose defiance of the God of Israel brought "the writing on the wall"; Daniel was wheeled in to interpret, and that night the kingdom was overthrown by Darius the Mede [Daniel 5]. Daniel prospered under the new regime;

later, however, he was trapped by rivals and so was thrown to the lions; and yet he survived. We may read this story in Daniel 6.

<u>Esther</u> is the story of one woman's life commitment, within the Persian king's harem, to save the Jews in his empire from being ethnically cleansed. Although there is no explicit mention of God in Esther, Jews hold the book in much esteem. Esther's faithful persistence for her people is celebrated by the festival of Purim.

Psalms reflect the destruction of Jerusalem.

Psalms 74 & 79 are ascribed to Asaph, who was perhaps a descendent of David's Director of Music for worship. In Psalm 74, the defilement and destruction of Solomon's Temple was the cause of his personal woe. He was very upset. God is mocked; God is his king, the deliverer in the world. Asaph remembers the powerful Exodus events, and thinks back to the works of the creation. He pleads that the LORD of the Covenant will defend his own cause, while the enemy uproar rises in crescendo.

In Psalm 79, the Temple and Jerusalem are in rubble, and dead bodies lie unburied as carrion. Neighbouring tribes sneer: "Where is their God?" Clearly to Asaph, the LORD is angry, and he spreads out the appalling scene before God. It is the only and rightful action he can do. The reproach has been thrown at God. But God is also the Shepherd of his flock; he is the God of glory, the rescuer. Asaph can look forward to God's people again bringing him praise.

All through these times, Prophets emerged, and they brought the LORD's words to Kings and peoples. This is the substance of the next chapter.

Chapter 14   Men of Conviction

> A summary of and guide towards reading the OT Prophets, and so through their messages encountering God in our time.

The Prophetic Voice

God called Prophets for different ministries, to be his voice to various peoples.

<u>Moses'</u> call came at the Burning Bush in Midian by Horeb [Exodus 3:1-10]. His ministry was for the Exodus, for training Israel at Horeb in worship and purity of community life, and for preparing them for readiness to occupy the Promised Land. Before he died he spoke of another Prophet like himself that would come [Deuteronomy 18:14-22]. This was fulfilled in Jesus.

<u>Samuel</u> received God's call as a young boy [1 Samuel 3:1-11]. His ministry continued Moses' work, in speaking the word of the Lord to Israel [3:19-20] in difficult days of low-ebb spirituality [7:2-17]. He trained others in prophetic ministry [10:1-13, 19:18-24].

<u>Gad</u> prophesied with David, from his outlaw days to the time of David's misguided census of his army   [1 Samuel 22:5, 2 Samuel 24:18].

<u>Nathan</u> ministered in David's court in Jerusalem, through to his anointing Solomon (with the priest Zadok) in succession as king [2 Samuel 7:2, 12:1, 1 Kings 1:34].

As the kingdoms fell apart, prophets arose to call both Israel and Judah to turn from their idols back to the Lord, to repent from evil and "to act justly, to love mercy, and to walk humbly with their God." [Micah 6:8] The prophets demanded a change of heart, of lifestyle, and for real faith in the Lord.

<u>Elijah</u> challenged Ahab king of Israel [1 Kings 17] and held contest with the prophets of Baal on Carmel. He fled from Ahab's wife Jezebel to Horeb [1 Kings 19]. On his return he inducted Elisha to succeed him. Before long, he was taken up to heaven in the whirlwind [2 Kings 2:1-12].

Elisha ministered with miracles [2 K 2:19 – 7:2], including healing Naaman the Syrian.

Some other non-writing prophets:
Ahijah to Jeroboam
An old prophet in 1 Kings 13:11
Jehu (not the king of Israel) in 1 Kings 16:7
Young man in 2 Kings 9:4
Shemiah in 2 Chronicles 12:5
Iddo in 2 Chronicles 13:22
Oded in 2 Chronicles 15:8
Hanani to Asa 2 Chronicles 16:7

The Prophetic Word
Of the written OT prophets, the books of Isaiah, Jeremiah, Ezekiel, Daniel, are the longest and are called the "major" prophets. The other 12 are shorter and so are called "minor", by no means, however, implying of lesser importance.

THE 16 WRITTEN PROPHETS, in a suggested chronological order; a measure of agreement exists for these dates, but a "?" indicates uncertainty.
Possible ministry Dates BC

---------------------- **ministry before the Exile** ---------------------
Joel 9th C ?
To Judah, using a towering plague of locusts to urge repentance [1:4-7, 2:1-11], and speaking of glorious hope to come [2:21-32].
Hosea   760-700
To Israel, pleading for right living, speaking in terms of married love, tenderly [1,2,3, 11:1-11]. Glimmers of hope [14:4-9].
Amos   760-740
To Israel, acerbic! And with power [3:11 – 4:1]. He pleaded for right living. There is hope in 9:11-15.
Isaiah   750-690
To Judah and Jerusalem. He was called in the Temple [Isaiah 6:1-8]. Chapters 1-35 speak in powerful and extended poetry about the destruction of Jerusalem, with restoration in view [2:6

– 3:26; chapter 5; 9:8 – 10:4; 28:9 – 19. Then hope comes in 4:2-6; 7:13 – 16; 9:1-7; 11:1-9]   Some 120 years before the destruction of Jerusalem Isaiah wrote of captives returning. Chapters 36-39 copy a piece from 2 Kings 18-20, inserted by an editor as it tells of Isaiah's ministry during Sennacherib's threats against Jerusalem under Hezekiah.   Chapters 40-66 prophesy restoration of Jerusalem, of Cyrus' benevolence [44:24-45:7], of dead idols and the death of the Servant of the Lord, and of future judgement, life and glory. [See below]

Micah   740-690
To Israel and Judah, pleading for right living [1:3-6,9,12. 6:1-8]   There is hope in 4:1-8, 7:11-20.

Nahum   640
To Nineveh, capital of Assyria; [1:9-14, 2:4-13]
        Look for hope in 1:7, 15, and 2:2

Zephaniah   640-610
To Judah and neighbours. [1:2-6]   Some hope 3:14-20.

Jeremiah   630-585
To Israel [2:1-4:2], then to Judah and Jerusalem [4:3 to end]. His call is written in 1:4-10. As well as speaking prophecies in Jerusalem, he wrote to the exiles in Babylon [chapter 29] to encourage them for restoration in some 70 years [chapters 30-31], and he prophesied about the New Covenant.

Jonah   620 ??
It is a story told against Jonah and against the uncaring Israelite attitude to outsiders. Hope in 4:11.

Habakkuk   600
To Judah ? [1:5-11, 2:5-8]   For hope, see 2:4.

---------------------- **ministry during the Exile** ----------------------
Ezekiel from the 5th year of the Exile to the 25th
To the captives in Babylonia. His call came after the first vision: 2:1-3:1. He was given visions, especially that in chapter 1, that God is with them in Babylon, chapter 2. Between 597 and 587, the Jerusalem priests reckoned that they were secure in the Temple, even if Zedekiah and Jeremiah were under duress in the town and the palace. So they assumed that they could reject Ezekiel's ministry. He told them that, according to the vision he

had seen, the Lord had withdrawn from the Jerusalem Temple. When the Temple was demolished, as Ezekiel had prophesied, the priests of the exile at last agreed that he was a true prophet. Chapter 37 has the vision of the valley of dry bones and the restoration of the nation. In chapter 40, he sees the new Temple, and in chapter 43, God returns to his Temple. In chapter 47, there is the river from the Temple, and in chapter 48, the new Land allocation, with the new City. He prophesied total cleaning, a new heart, and a new spirit [36:22-38].

Daniel   597-530*

He was not strictly a prophet, but an interpreter of dreams and visions, as was Joseph in Genesis. Chapters 1-6 appear historical, when he was taken from Jerusalem to Babylon and became a court administrator. Chapters 7-12 are his dreams and visions which reveal conflicts in his day and in the End times in the heavenly realms. (*Many academics dispute the date of Daniel and its interpretation; but credible arguments exist for regarding the book's history as reliable.)

Obadiah   585 ?

To Edom, judged because Edom (Esau) gloated over the destruction of Jerusalem in 587. See vv 19-21.

--------------------- **ministry after the Exile** ------------------------

Haggai 520

To those rebuilding the Temple at Jerusalem [1:2-11]. He was very encouraging [2:4-9]

Zechariah   520

Also to those rebuilding the Temple [1:2-4; 4:1-10]. There was positive news – [1:17; 2:3-5; 3:6-10; 8:1-8; 9:9-11; chapters 12-14].

Malachi   450 ?

To Judah, especially the Levites. [3:1-5, 4:1] Encouragements – 3:16-18; 4:2-6.

Isaiah, the man and the book

Isaiah as a young person developed faith in the Lord through the Temple, although he lived in an age of luxury and nominal religion. He had gifts of prophecy which he expressed in profound poetry. This is lofty and very cultured. He married a person who also had a gift of prophecy. If Isaiah lived into Manasseh's evil reign, he would then have been over 75. He had grown up in Jerusalem during the later years of the good strong king Azariah (Uzziah). Uzziah's son Jotham functioned as regent because the king was confined at home by 'leprosy.'

The king, in the ancient world, was the centre of the soul of the people. From his "person, blessing and strength went out to the nation, like life-giving sap through the branches of a tree." (BW Anderson) When Uzziah died and Jotham was showing that he was not up to the job as king, Isaiah went to the Temple. His account of his overwhelming experience of meeting the Lord begins: "I saw the Lord seated on a throne…" making clear that the people were not dependent on a king enthroned in Jerusalem, but on the real King, the Lord of Hosts. That vision commissioned Isaiah, already known for his prophecies, to speak messages of judgement to people who at heart were deaf and blind, too far gone to respond. In distress Isaiah asked "For how long, O Lord?" He was told of houses and towns sacked and desolate, of fields ruined and the Land of Promise completely forsaken. The Land would be devastated a second time, but like tree stumps which remain after timber is felled, "so the holy seed will be the stump in the Lord." [6:13] A faint hope of restoration!

After 16 years of Jotham as king, Ahaz succeeded to the throne, and was faced by foes all round. Isaiah took his young son with him (the boy's name meant "A remnant will return") to give Ahaz a challenge to trust the Lord for defence, and not to cobble up alliance with any other king. Ahaz rejected this call, and turned away from seeking a sign from the Lord. Isaiah, thus bruised, declaimed to all present the sign of "Immanuel," God with us, a child born of a maiden, and he spoke of Assyrian invasions and ravage of the Land.

Isaiah withdrew from public ministry for a spell at that time, perhaps gathering round him a group of like-minded disciples. He was blessed with a second son (whose name frighteningly meant 'Quick to the plunder, swift to the spoil'), and he wrote more prophecies about Immanuel. He declared "Here am I and the children the Lord has given me. We are signs and symbols in Israel from the Lord Almighty, who dwells on

Mount Zion." [8:18] While out of public eyes, he continued to deliver prophecies. Assyria had overpowered the lands of Zebulun and Naphtali, but Isaiah spoke of the great light to dawn on Galilee, then the land of darkness and the shadow of death, and of the child who would become the Prince of Peace. He continued to prophesy specific judgements, mixed in with songs of praise and promises of a return from exile and of restoration.

Ahaz was succeeded by godly Hezekiah who energetically set about removing idols in Judah, and restoring the Temple and its worship. But the Assyrians overwhelmed the last traces of Israel in the north, and began to threaten Jerusalem. Isaiah emerged to encourage Hezekiah and to prophesy the enemy's withdrawal. Indeed Sennacherib went back to Nineveh and was murdered. Then Hezekiah fell seriously ill, and he prayed fervently. Isaiah brought both a promise of life to him, and of deliverance from Assyria; also he brought a sign from the Lord. Hezekiah received this in faith, in contrast to his father Ahaz who had rejected any sign some 20 years before. Later, Isaiah prophesied that Babylonians would obliterate Jerusalem and take Hezekiah's descendents into exile. This becomes a bridge to the prophecies from chapter 40 onwards. These spoke from the future vantage point – or 'disadvantage point' – of the captives in exile in Babylon, with Jerusalem and the Temple devastated, prophecies applying some 175 years after Hezekiah and Isaiah, and later still to the first and second Comings of the Messiah.

Many academics hold that Chapters 40 onwards have a different author from the writer of Chapters 1 – 39. Chapters 40 – 55 are taken as perhaps being the greatest prophetic writing in the Bible, the work of one author; it is strange that his name is not known if it was not Isaiah. Isaiah had round him a band of disciples learning and treasuring his prophecies; their successors during the Exile wrote down his prophecies; these were edited into the complete book, but not consistently. Thus chapters 56 – 66 contain many different prophecies, perhaps unrelated. The phrase "The Holy One of Israel" comes 12 times in the first 39 chapters, and 13 times from chapter 40 to the end. It lends credence to the book's unity. The phrase comes only 5 times elsewhere in the OT. Arguments for and against various authors are not conclusive. About 200BC, the apocryphal Ecclesiasticus chapter 48 regarded the book Isaiah as from the one author. The Dead Sea Isaiah scroll was a copy of one document made in the 1st or 2nd century BC. The New Testament writers quote Isaiah by name as speaking 40:3 and 42:1-4 (in Matthew 3:3 and 12:17-21) and 53:1 (in John 12:38 and Romans 10:20,21). Peter in 1 Peter writes 5 quotes from Isaiah without naming him. Chapters 1-39 were of Isaiah's local and contemporary scene, and they were clear and focussed poetry. The later sublime poetry was less specific, more verbose, about matters far a-field and in the future. It is important to recognise that the inspiring Holy Spirit was at work through the prophet Isaiah, revealing to him both matters of his day, at his hand, and matters well beyond his life and times.

Some Psalms reflect the situation into which the prophets ministered.

<u>Psalm 106</u> begins with praise and thanks to the Lord; he is good, full of enduring love for Israel, executing mighty acts. The psalmist applauds just leaders, and wants to share in the good things that the Lord plans for his people: favour, help, prosperity, joy and worship.

[6] But he admits continuing failure to live in right relation with God. From the past he lists forgetting the Exodus miracles and the rebellion by the Red Sea; the rescue from Pharaoh's army was soon forgotten. They craved food, and they envied Moses and Aaron; at Horeb, while being instructed by the Lord, they worshipped a metal calf-idol.

[24] At Kadesh Barnea, they rebelled and did not trust God to take them to victory in the Promised Land. A generation later, they joined in local idol worship.

[32] Their nagging had goaded Moses into error at Meribah.

[34] When they eventually entered the Promised Land, they did not obey the Lord and did not completely destroy the resident Canaanites, so they became snared by idolatry, and enemies conquered them.

[47] The psalmist pleads that the Lord will rescue them all from the nations, so that they can bring praise to the Lord.

The Prophets' message, universally, was for the kings, priests, and people to return to the Lord with real faith, and to live accordingly. They described their current situation, often in graphic terms, warned of the judgement that would come, and called for complete repentance.

An appreciation of two major Prophets:
Jeremiah lived in Judah where Jerusalem and the Temple had been inviolate for 10 generations since king David's day. His call to be a prophet came as a young person, and he shrank from the task, not merely as young and inexperienced, but because he felt unable to speak with the authorities in the restless days of world empires struggling uncertainly. But the call was irresistible. He prophesied in the reigns of the last five kings of Judah, beginning with Josiah the reformer. When Josiah was killed by the Egyptians at Meggido, Jeremiah composed lamentations for him [2 Chronicles 35:25]. From then, Jeremiah spoke with courage against the apostasy of the people deserting their Lord and the covenant, for worthless idols, for the practices of worship in high places, including shrine prostitution and burning children in the fire. He condemned the hollow formality of Temple worship, and the decay of moral standards, and greed in false dealings. He prophesied that the Lord's judgement would fall on all this, specifically by Nebuchadnezzar of the Babylonians. Nebuchadnezzar took Jerusalem over from the Egyptians in 597 BC, deporting all trained and skilled people. But Jeremiah remained with the puppet king Zedekiah. He pleaded for people to reform and obey the covenant, to return to the Lord. His sensitive soul was in anguish as he perceived it was all too late and Jerusalem would be destroyed. Both the tragedy of the destruction of Jerusalem and Temple, and the faithlessness of the people and leaders towards their covenant Lord, wounded him very deeply, and he uttered cries of grief and anguish while he prophesied the dark and bitter day of gloom. As the king's adviser in the latter days of Zedekiah's reign, he pleaded for

surrender to the besieging Babylonians, to comply with the Lord's word, and perhaps to save life and property. He even completed a land purchase as a sign of trust in a future restoration. But he was accused of treason and had to be rescued from his enemies' clutches. He wrote a letter of reassurance to the captive exiles in Babylon and prophesied a return in 70 years. As well, he looked far ahead to the last days and a new covenant under a righteous king. After the sack of Jerusalem in 587 BC, he chose to stay there. But in the end, when the new governor was assassinated, fearing reprisal from Babylon, the soldiers fled to Egypt, taking an unwilling Jeremiah with them. A lasting tribute to him is that people in Jesus' day likened Jesus to Jeremiah. [Matthew 16:14]

Ezekiel In the book Ezekiel, the prophet comes over as an extremely able person. He was well informed, knowing about politics, shipping, and ethnic origins. He possessed developed musical gifts. He was a priest by birth and training, and he grew up in Jerusalem in the reforming reign of Josiah. He was tender and loving to his wife, and in her early death experienced sudden personal tragedy. He was sensitive and passionate, with deep perception of the saving history of the Israelites. He stood aloof and above his contemporaries, with a fiery zeal for his Lord and for Israel. Perhaps he started his priestly service in the Temple, but he was soon deported to Babylon in 597 BC. He was called to be a prophet about 594 BC, and served the exiles for about 17 years. He held in tension the training as priest and the calling of prophet. He prophesied the destruction of Jerusalem, condemning Zedekiah for breaking his oath of allegiance. When Jerusalem fell he suffered deeply, but that fall broke down the exile's resistance to his ministry. Thence, he was able to preach to his people a message of future return and prosperity.

With his priestly training he would have understood that, being exiled in an unholy land, he was out of range of God's presence. But he received a breath-taking vision which gave him new hope and ministry. God addressed him as "Ben-Adam" – son of man. Thus the creature, born of dust (<u>adamah</u>), transient and weak, an inadequate vessel for the Lord's eternity and grace, had to be lifted up by the Spirit. He was shown that the supernatural glory of God was not restricted to Zion's sanctuary, for he was seeing God in the unclean land of the exile. The Lord showed him that he is God of the whole earth, distinct from Temple and Israel. Yet the distressed Father had not finished with his son. Ezekiel preached to them to believe the promises, to turn the heart, to conform the lifestyle. "Why will you die, O house of Israel?" Ezekiel's visions of the dry bones raised to form a living army, and of the new Temple with the issue of healing waters, reflected God's longing for erring people to "turn and live."

Ezekiel saw God's "appalling and unassailable" majesty and his absolute transcendence, his high sovereignty, his holiness and his glory, which shattered his creatures who fell flat on their faces before him. Ezekiel carried this sense of awe and mystery through his ministry, for once he had encountered the Lord he was permanently changed by this glory of God.

Why did all this devastation and deportation happen? Why the destruction of Jerusalem with its Temple? The Lord had brought these people through fire and water and had given them the Promised Land. The kings David and Solomon had established good government, faith, and security in Jerusalem. But weak and erring kings had discounted faith, and their attitudes, trickling down, were reflected in the administrative and priestly classes. So the ordinary people, farmers, traders, soldiers and the families were led astray. Mass behaviour and personal lives became worldly, ignoring the Law of the Lord in favour of less demanding religious superstitions – various Baals, down even to sacrificing children in the fires. The few prophets of the Lord were barely noticed. When a reforming king arose, like Josiah, his patient purifying work was quickly thrown out after his death. How this reflects on the responsibilities of leaders !

From the Prophets, we can discern:
1. <u>The state of social life</u> in both Israel and Judah, which had become sick societies, publicly religious but riddled with

idolatry, and rejecting right behaviour; it was dressed up in religion, and unacceptable to God.
      Hosea 8:1-6; 12:7-8; 13:1-2   Amos 2:6-8; 3:10-4:6
Isaiah 1:10-20   Habakkuk 1:1-4

2. <u>Prophetic pleas for right living</u>: a change of heart and not just pious rending of garments; 'Turn back! Live uprightly!
      Joel 2:12-13; Hosea 12:6   Micah 6:6-8;   Jerermiah 7:1-20

3. <u>Specific warnings</u> about coming invasions and destruction; the northern Ten Tribes were about to be overpowered by Shalmaneser.
      Habakkuk 1:5-11; Zepheniah 1:4-9, 14-18 Amos 3:11-15

4. <u>Promises</u> of future hopes – then, for them at their times;
      Hosea 14:1-9; Zepheniah 3:14-20; Jereremiah 29:1-12; Ezekiel 11:16-20.
      With hindsight, we can see much fulfilment for them; these gracious promises were still being given during the Exile.
Jereremiah 31:31-34; Ezekiel 32:11-15; 37:1-14

5. <u>Visions of distant futures</u>
both of <u>the First Coming of the Lord Jesus Christ</u> the suffering servant;
      Micah 5:2; Isaiah 9:2,6-7; 52:13 – 53:12; then the Coming of the Holy Spirit: Joel 2:28-32
and of <u>the Second Coming of the Lord Jesus Christ</u>, Lord of lords and King of kings;
      Isaiah 11:1-9; 35:1-10; Daniel 7:9-14.

Selected hot spots in the ministry of:
ELIJAH – his confronting Ahab, and the contest with the prophets of Baal: 1 Kings 17-18
ELISHA – healing Naaman the Aramean: 2 Kings 5:1-16

Some experiences of faithful believers who spoke out:
      MICAIAH – 1 Kings 22:1-28: prison
      JEREMIAH – Jeremiah 38:1-13: prison

SHADRACH, MESHAK, and ABEDNEGO – Daniel 3: the furnace

DANIEL – Daniel 6: the lions

What is our reaction?

In our day, do the strictures of the OT prophets concern us? Now that we have redemption in the cross of Christ, and have received the Holy Spirit, how do these impact us as individuals, as a church, as a nation, and as a whole world in trouble?

Can I see myself standing fast, as did Daniel and his friends, in the face of persecution, torture, and death, for the sake of Jesus? Suggestion: read 'The Heavenly Man' Brother Yun (Monarch)

On, now, to the stories of the surviving Israelites who undertook to return to Jerusalem.

Chapter 15   A Kind of Restoration!

This required some extremely hard work and persistent faith.

Some 200 years before it happened, at the time of Hezekiah, Isaiah had prophesied not only that the Israelites would go into captivity, but also that they would return [Isaiah 35]. The prophet specified that a ruler named Cyrus would send them back [44:24 – 45:7].

Babylonian Rule

The first batch of Jews in Exile in Babylon contained most of the significant people deported from Jerusalem. But Jeremiah was stuck there in Jerusalem. He sent them his letter of encouragement [Jeremiah 29:4-14]. He told them to settle in for the long haul, marry within their own community and raise families. After 70 years they would return. It is a letter of great encouragement; it is often taken as a beacon of hope for Christians, too.

Ezekiel was there with the captives, and they discovered that the Lord was with them in Babylon, contrary to their understanding and expectation. Soon the Temple and Jerusalem were in ruins, but Ezekiel received visions of a new Temple and a new life for the Jews. [Ezekiel 37:1-14 the Valley of dry bones, and 47:1-12 the River of life from the new Temple.] The distressing fact of the Exile was balanced by such encouragements.

Persian Rule
THE RETURN

Ezra 1:1-4. The book Ezra links with the last verses of Chronicles. Now we are at 538BC. [It is helpful to take the chronology based on archaeology; it is in very reasonable accord with the Bible. Academics have said that the dates for Ezra and Nehemiah are uncertain. However, "The Biblical order of events which makes Ezra reach Jerusalem in 458BC and Nehemiah arrive there in 445BC is perfectly consistent under close scrutiny." (New Bible Dictionary 1962)]

Reconstruction Time-line:

	BC
Temple and city destroyed	587
Cyrus' edict started the Return	538
Temple begun but work halted	537
Temple works restarted	520
(70 years after its destruction)	
Temple completed	516
City Wall work started but halted	486
(Ezra sent to Jerusalem	458)
Nehemiah completed the Wall	445

Cyrus, after 11 years of campaigning elsewhere, overthrew the new and dissolute deputy king Belshazzar of Babylon. At once he implemented his policy of reversing the deportation of captive peoples, to send them back to rebuild their temples. Perhaps his motives for this repatriation were to nip any revolt in the bud, and to reduce the need for heavy policing and for governing grumbling communities. Cyrus did not compel, but he encouraged the Jews to go home, making this project self financing by applying local and ethnic revenues. <u>He put it in writing</u>, which became vital a generation later. This policy was carried on by his successors Xerxes and Darius III.

Sheshbazzar, leader of Judah, was given all the treasures confiscated from Jerusalem by Nebuchadnezzar. A number of other people of importance led the 40,000 or so released Jews [Ezra 2:64]. Perhaps they set out in spring, so they had the summer for their 6 month journey of 800 miles (1300km). They arrived at Jerusalem, and by September/October they had settled in nearby villages. Soon Jeshua and his priests, and Zerubbabel with his civilian associates, restored the Altar of Sacrifice, made offerings, and they all kept the feast of Tabernacles. [Ezra 1:1 – 3:6]

After the winter they laid the foundations of the Temple. However, [Ezra 4:1-5], the locals created such opposition that they discouraged the builders, and work stopped for 16 or 17 years [v.24]. In time, [Ezra 5:1-2], the prophets Haggai and Zechariah stirred the leaders, Zerubbabel and the priest Jeshua, and building began again. [Haggai 1:1-11] It went on while local officials wrote questioningly to the new king Darius I who found Cyrus' original edict in the archives of Babylon; he replied that the work was to proceed with all support and finance from local revenues [Ezra 6:1-3]. The building of the Temple took nearly 5 more years, and it was completed in February, 516BC, 70 years after its destruction by Nebuchadnezzar. There was Dedication and a Passover celebration, and the feast of Tabernacles was due in October. [Ezra 6:13 – 22]

About 30 years later, they began to repair the city wall; but the locals objected again [Ezra 4:6].

<u>Potential for confusion:</u> *the scribes composing the book Ezra have lumped together the passages in which officialdom raises objections and refers to the king; Ezra 4:1 is about rebuilding the <u>Temple</u>, started 538BC (and not finished till 516BC – Ezra 6:15); Ezra 4:6 & 12 are about rebuilding the <u>city wall</u> started 486BC (and stopped 465BC – Ezra 4:23. It was only restarted under Nehemiah 445BC, and then completed in 52 days!)*

In 486BC, local objections to rebuilding the city wall were made to Ahasuerus (Xerxes I). [Ezra 4:6] In 465BC, local officials wrote to the next king Artaxerxes I, who replied that work on the wall was to stop completely [v.7-23].

458BC <u>Ezra</u>, priest and scribe, came to Jerusalem from Babylon, by order of Artaxerxes in his 7th year, and he enforced the Law of Moses, especially concerning the issue of mixed marriages. He led repentance and reforms. (Rain made matters more distressing!) [Ezra 7 – 10]

445BC One man, with significant access to the Persian king, (whose queen could have been Esther,) was his Wine Server, <u>Nehemiah</u>. In December of the king's 20th year,

Nehemiah at Susa heard from Hanani, recently come from Judah, about the hard times of the remnants of the exile. He petitioned the king, who made him governor of Jerusalem. [Nehemiah 1:1-2:6] The book <u>Nehemiah</u> tells of his meticulous attention to detail. He faced down strong hostility from local leaders, resisting corruption and opposition. He came and began rebuilding the city wall in mid July. His patrician leadership was hands-on! [4:16-23]. Despite strong local opposition he finished the task in 52 days, by early September [6:15,16]. The book is a personal diary, and recounts the work of this powerful and devout civilian governor, beginning in the 20th year of Artaxerxes I, through to his 32nd year. [Nehemiah 6:15-16.] He withstood Sanballat to the north, Tobias in the East, and Geshem the Arab from the south. Tobias had penetrated the society of Jerusalem by business and marriage, and had occupied the Temple premises. Nehemiah threw him out. The dedication of the wall was a joyful ceremony with two choirs processing on top of it. [12:27 – 43] Nehemiah's engineering and political work was aided by the priest Ezra, and together they campaigned for reform of faith and life in the community. Later, Ezra again publicly read the Book of the Law of Moses, in one September, and the Israelites celebrated Tabernacles afterwards. They made confession and agreed to reform in October. [Nehemiah 8 – 10]

433BC   Nehemiah went back to Artaxerxes.

Nehemiah returned to Jerusalem before 424BC and, with Ezra, purged mixed marriages between Jewish men and foreign wives. These women were idol-worshippers. Ezra and Nehemiah were emphatic on the pedigree of those who claimed to belong to the community. This problem had brought national disaster before, so they grasped the nettle and expelled non-Israelite families. [Nehemiah 13] The rejected peoples lived near Samaria, and their descendents became the NT Samaritans. Jerusalem was now a viable city for the Jews. One thing of considerable importance was this: the Exile experience seems finally to have removed idolatry from those who returned. The Return from exile to Jerusalem was far from universal, and many Jews remained settled where they were.

Isaiah 35 Isaiah recorded his prophecy of a return from captivity. It is the ecstatic return to Zion of the Lord's ransomed with singing, joy, and gladness. The whole natural world will join in the rejoicing, with the wilderness blooming, and the hills and the plains reflecting the glory of God. However, the limited return under Cyrus was not the real fulfilment of this word. There was indeed great rejoicing when the new Temple foundations were laid [Ezra 3:10-13]. However, complete fulfilment of Isaiah's prophecy awaits the Lord Jesus Christ's Second Coming.

Psalm 126 recalls the excitement of those Israelites who returned to Zion in 538BC. They were like incredulous dreamers, full of laughter and song! The local people were forced to admit that the LORD, the Covenant-maker with Israel, was in this. The prayer of the returned captives was for refreshing streams, for grace to toil and raise bumper harvests.

Psalm 147 celebrates the LORD building up Jerusalem and bringing home the exiles. His great work of creation, of providing the rain for cultivation, food for domestic animals, and for wild birds is good. The horse is strong and useful, and men can run; but the LORD asks for our fear, and our confidence in him. We should speak his praise, for he preserves and blesses; he gives peace and satisfies our need of daily bread. He is in the cycle of weather. Sublimely, he has revealed himself to Israel, and told us how we should live. Nobody else knows! Therefore... Praise the LORD!

Apart from some years under the Maccabees, the Land of Israel was never permanently ruled by the Jews again. Henceforward, they lived in enemy occupied territory.

There were Jewish stories at the time, with some preserved in the O.T. apocrypha. They are not part of the Canon of scripture, but they give some account of the chaotic history of the 400 years before Jesus was born. It was an era of incipient decline, as history was repeated. Ezra and Nehemiah had fought spiritual battles to re-establish amongst the people the high moral principles of the Laws of Moses, in attitudes and actions, and in separation from the non-Jews all around. But it didn't last.

Malachi

After Nehemiah's reforms, Persian domination went on for another 100 years. In that time, Temple worship continued, but spiritual decay set in. During the 5th Century BC, the last OT prophet Malachi pleaded with the leaders in Jerusalem. They seem to have reduced faith to religiosity. Malachi prophesied with warnings and challenges. The evils he complains about are just those which Nehemiah had sought to eradicate. Old habits die hard! Malachi prophesied the Lord's judgement – "Who can stand when he appears?" [Malachi 3:2] "You will again see the distinction between … those who serve God and those who do not" [3:18]. He spoke of Elijah, sent before that judgement Day [4:5-6]. Jesus equated the Elijah of this prophecy with John Baptist [Matthew 17:10-13].

A Study of Malachi: 7 Questions and 7 Answers – Questions 'Q' by the priests, Answers 'A' given by the Lord through Malachi.

[This is a limited study; it does not set out to be an in depth commentary on the book. It gives an interpretation of the Questions & Answers, and it summarises spiritual leadership.]

Malachi prophesied in the time between the last work of Nehemiah, 424BC and the sudden arrival of Alexander 333BC. So he ministered at some time during the last 90 years of Persian rule.

The pattern of the Qs & As is:
a) Malachi gives some **Word** from the Lord, which
b) provokes the hearers to Question;   Q:
c) the Lord gives his Answer and may enlarge on it.   A:
d) Sometimes they snap back at Malachi.

Out of these exchanges comes the interpretation given in the Comments.

1.   [1:2-5]   **Word**: "I have loved you"
   Q: How have you loved us?
   A: I have loved Jacob, not (his brother) Esau.

<u>Comment</u>: The Q implies "I don't believe you." (They are thoughtless and indifferent! God is loving, and reminds them that he has lovingly chosen them for himself, out of his grace, and not because they deserve it.)

2.   [1:6 – 7a]   **Word**:   "Where is the respect due to me?"
   Q: How have we despised your name?
   A: You put defiled food on my altar.

<u>Comment</u>: The Q implies "Contempt? Never! What about all those sacrifices which we do for you?" But they are disrespectful and contemptuous. God is to be held in awe; nothing but wholeheartedness will do.

3.   [1:7b – 13a]   A second question arises from the Lord's use of the **word** "defiled".7b
   Q: How have we defiled you?
   A: You offer second class sacrifices and say it is contemptible, a bore! You sniff!!

   1:13b – 14. Then comes a warning to the priests, and an appeal (to all) to keep faith.

<u>Comment</u>:   This Q equals "What! me? I do everything! You must be joking! (Silly old God – [sniff!])" The fact is, they are formal and defiling. God is HOLY. Yet he does not give up on them, and he spells out what he expects of them [see 2:1 – 16 in separate study, below].

4.   [2:17 – 3:6]   **Word**:   "Your have wearied the LORD with your words."
   Q: How have we wearied him?
   A: By saying 'Evil-doers are good in the eyes of the Lord – where is the God of justice?'

<u>Comment</u>:   Their Q rudely rejects God's assessment. His A penetrates to the reality of their cynicism: "Why do we get

punished and they get away with it?" God reads us all like a book, in total truth.

5. [3:7 – 8a] **Word**: "Return to me, and I will return to you."
   Q: How are we to return?
   A: Will a man rob God? Yet you rob me.
Comment: God is calling, and they are heedless. Their Q snaps back: "Return? (God, we're allright!") The Lord's A implies "But you are keeping things back from me."

6. [3:8b – 12] The second Q arises from the **word** "rob."
   Q: How do we rob you?
   A: In tithes and offerings
Comment: They (and we?) are calculating and stingy; God is so generous! He challenges the lifestyle of the whole community.

7. [3:13 – 4:6] **Word**: "You have said harsh things against me."
   Q. What have we said against you?
   A. You have said 'It is futile to serve God … even those who challenge God escape.'
   (But) the day (of judgement) is coming.
Comment: This Q implies "Never!!" ie the response of disagreeing self-righteousness. God's A: "Your focus is entirely missing the mark. I am the Judge, and I am coming."

Malachi 2:1 – 9 God's summary of requirements for spiritual leadership.
   Malachi brought God's word to Israel's spiritual leaders, the Levitical priests. (And now we are all priests with access to the Lord.)
A) *Personal Profile*
   They must <u>listen</u>, and hear God's voice [v.1]
         <u>set the heart </u>to honour the Name of the LORD Almighty, and obey in total conscience. [v.2]

live in the covenant of life and peace, with God, and practice agreeing with God [5]
    live in reverence of God's Name [v.5]
    stand in awe of God's Name. [v.5]

B) Public Profile

They must speak truthful instruction to the people, nothing false, and so be wholesome teachers [v.6]
    walk with God in peace and uprightness before people as examples [v.6]
    turn many from sin, with persuasive preaching [v.6]
    preserve knowledge, keep knowing God [v.7]
    be a source of instruction for people, being a resource [v.7]
    be a messenger of God to people, a prophet [v.7]
    follow God's ways without partiality, looking to God for exercising discerning judgement, regardless of peoples' status. [v.9]

Greek Rule

Persian rule of the whole region was eventually broken by Alexander the Great's conquest in 333 BC. Alexander, a former pupil of Aristotle, was the 21 year-old king of Macedon. He came from Greece like a shooting star, a brilliant soldier, master of war, and with a burning vision for world unity. In 8 ½ years his army marched 11,000 miles, conquering from Asia Minor, Egypt, Persia, then north into the Hindu Kush, and south to the mouth of the Indus. He imposed his Aristotelian philosophy across the East, from Greece to India, from the Black Sea to the Nile. This brought in Greek as the universal language, and introduced Hellenistic culture to the Jews. After Alexander's death, 323BC, his kingdom was carved up between his four generals, and Jerusalem came under Ptolomy of Egypt.

About 250BC, Ptolomy II, of Egypt, sent for Jewish scholars to translate the Hebrew Law of Moses into Greek, since the majority of Jews living in Egypt no longer understood

Hebrew. So about 70 scholars were settled in Alexandria, and they produced the Septuagint or LXX. The complete OT translation was finished sometime before 117BC, and it was the common Greek version of the OT in Jesus' day, and for the first Christians.

In 198 BC, Antiochus III of Syria took over the Land of the Jews from Egypt. His son Antiochus IV persecuted Jews who refused to worship the Greek gods. He adopted the blasphemous title 'Theos Epiphanes' [God revealed by me] and proclaimed himself Zeus in the Jerusalem Temple. This desecration precipitated rebellion, and the priest Mattathias raised revolt. His son Judas Maccabeus led the fighting. They reconsecrated the Temple in 165BC, and war went on till 143BC when they became independent from Egypt and Syria, then with Simon Maccabeus high priest and political ruler.

But politics and Hellenist philosophy grew to be of greater concern than faith. The liberal ruling classes became the Sadducees. The Pharisees were a group that were especially committed to the detail of the Law of Moses, with its high moral principles; so they separated themselves from the Sadducees.

Roman Rule

While the ruling family was busy with its quarrels, in 63 BC the Roman general Pompey stepped in and appointed Antipater, a non-Jew, as Procurator to rule this new province Judaea. About this time the Essenes withdrew to live in monastic communities on the shores of the Dead Sea and in the deserts. They reacted against the narrow exclusiveness of the Pharisees, and the worldliness of the Sadducees. John Baptist grew up in the deserts, possibly amongst one of these groups, once his aged parents had died [Luke 1:80].

Antipater's son, Herod the Great, ruled by Roman appointment from 37BC, till death in 3BC. He began to rebuild the Temple, to impress the Jews. He was unscrupulous and distrustful, ruthlessly murdering all possible claimants to his throne, including his own wife. About 4BC he was alarmed to hear of a baby born in Bethlehem to be king of the Jews and the Saviour of all mankind, so he instantly ordered the massacre of all babies there. [Matthew 2:1-18]

Moving on to the 1st century AD, the Roman general Titus, under Vespasian, finally crushed the Jews in the four years of war 66-70AD. A few groups were able to hide their libraries in caves; some of these were discovered in 1947AD, and are the Dead Sea Scrolls,

Psalm 146 A man of faith stands firm before the Covenant Lord, through all the changing circumstances he meets in life.
Adoring God, in Psalm 146:

Praise the LORD! The psalmist addresses himself, 'my soul,' <u>me</u>! He commits himself to a disciplined attitude: 'yes! I will praise; I will sing praise to my God all my life. God is eternal. By contrast – princes are mortal and cannot save, so don't repose trust in them.

There is blessing for him who has help from the Lord, who holds confidence in him. God is Maker of all, and he is the faithful one for ever. He takes concern for the oppressed, gives food to the hungry, and sets prisoners free. He brings sight for the blind, he lifts up the crushed, and loves the righteous. He takes care of the vulnerable as he watches over the alien and sustains the fatherless and widow; he frustrates the wicked who would victimise them.

This is your God, O Zion, who reigns for ever! Praise the LORD!

Rulers of the Israelites from 600BC to 4BC:

A = Named in the canonical scriptures θ = Named in OT apocrypha

BABYLONIAN	BC	
A Nebuchazdnezzar	597	
Nabonidas	556	
A Belshazzar	539	
PERSIAN		
A Cyrus	539	
Cambyses	530	
A Darius I	522	
A Xerxes (Ahasuerus)	486	116 years

Artaxerxes I	465	
Xerxes II	423_	
Darius II	423	
Artaxexes II	404	
Artaxerxes III	358	
Arses	338	90 years
θ Darius III	336	
GREEK		
θ Alexander the Great	333_	
EGYPTIAN		
Ptolomy I, … V	323	
SYRIAN		125 years
Antiochus III	198_	
Seleucus IV	187	
θ Antichus IV (Epiphanes)	175	17 years
MACCABEES	_	
θ Mattathias raised revolt	168	
θ Judas	166	
θ Jonathan	160	
θ Simon	143	
John Hyrcanus	134	105 years
	104	
ROMANS		
(Pompey)		
Antipater	63 _	
A Herod the Great	from 37 to 3 BC	

Chapter 16

God's Son

> The Good News of God's Messiah, Jesus who burst upon humanity, after 400 years of prophetic silence since Malachi.
> **"Glory to God in the highest, and on earth, peace to men on whom his favour rests!"** [Luke 2:14]

Mary's Psalm   Luke 1:46-55   This is the song of an OT believer who has received by faith the gift of motherhood of the Son of God. Mary said Yes to the Holy Spirit coming on her. She has just heard confirmation of this through the excited welcome of her aunt Elizabeth. This older person has been childless, but now is six months pregnant, visibly so, and with a kicking baby! Mary's maternal aspirations overflow into song.

[46] Her praises come from deep within her soul and spirit, with joy in God who is rescuing her, even now in her youth, from the dreaded infertility which burdened Aunt Elizabeth for so long.

[48] God has noted her lowly country status, and she knows that she is now going to be held by everyone down the ages as blessed by God Almighty, the Holy One.

[50] She praises God for his mercy and active concern for others who fear and trust in him, throwing down the proud and powerful. This has echoes of Hannah's praise in 1 Samuel 2.

[53] The needy hungry are not only fed, but receive good things – not so the self-made rich! The Lord has helped Israel, and Mary senses that he is doing so again, being faithful to his covenant with Abraham.

WHO IS JESUS?   The Gospel writers paint the picture of Jesus to answer this Question.

Jesus - The Early Years
(The story is told with imagination.)

Matthew begins his gospel with a genealogy. The faithful of the day were steeped in the OT, hanging in on prophecies of God's long awaited actions, promised, and summed up in their expectation of the Messiah. The faithful were to be found amongst rural communities, rather than in the city ecclesiastics, scholars, or rulers. There were a few truly faithful in Jerusalem waiting for the Messiah, such as Simeon and Anna. In the country, Joseph and Mary in Galilee, and Elizabeth and Zechariah in the Judean hills were godly people, formed in reading the OT Scriptures, and open to God's working through their family lives.

Now, after centuries of silence, God moved. This was at the tail end of Herod the Great's reign. God sent the angel Gabriel. God broke into the man-made rules and delighted the longings, as he had done before when, through Abraham, he made Sarah pregnant at age 90 [Genesis 21:1-7]; and when God had said that a virgin would be pregnant and bear Immanuel, "God with us," as prophesied in king Ahaz' day. [Isaiah 7:14, the name Immanuel is reinforced in 8:8, 10, a son for David's throne: 9:6,7] Zechariah, a Temple priest, and Elizabeth were an elderly couple who were surprised to become parents after years of infertility. Elizabeth gave birth, to the sheer delight of Zechariah and the village community. Their little boy was John. Elizabeth was a relative of Mary, to be mother of Jesus; perhaps Mary's mother was sister to Elizabeth, so that Jesus and John were cousins. Young John needed a secure home when his elderly parents died, and perhaps he was cared for in one of the desert sects.

Satan attacked: Joseph nearly divorced his now pregnant fiancée, Mary; but God spoke in a dream, and happily he took courage and they married. Caesar Augustus' census took Joseph and Mary from Nazareth to Bethlehem, 6 miles (10km) south of Jerusalem, a 6-day trek from home avoiding Samaria, and an uncomfortable donkey-ride for Mary. Worse was to come, as Bethlehem was jam-packed – "You can use the cowshed, if you must," said the desperate innkeeper. At least there was straw for bedding. Mary gave birth and they used some cloths she had brought with her in which to wrap her newborn, and the manger came in as an improvised cot. Soon, they were to be amazed by excited shepherds visiting them that very night. These men spoke of a great angelic revelation to them, announcing the birth of a Saviour, the Messiah, the Sovereign. There would be the sign to them of the strips of cloth and the baby in the manger; and then came a great angelic song of praise. Now, there was the baby, and with the signs! They left to spread the word to everyone they met.

When the census was over, Joseph found a proper house to rent, and they settled for the first weeks of Jesus' life. They circumcised him on the 8th day. Then after 5 weeks they went to the Jerusalem Temple to present him to the Lord, and for purification after childbirth. As poor people they offered two birds. [Leviticus 12:1 - 8, Exodus 13:2]. They were intercepted by the aged Simeon, who rejoiced to hold the baby, and he praised the Lord for him. Then, really aged Anna joined them with thanksgiving; she told all at hand about the child.

Joseph and Mary were perhaps intending to go home to Nazareth soon, but another event intervened. Back in Bethlehem, on a clear night, Stargazers from the east came to visit them, and to give gifts: gold, incense and myrrh. Traditionally these were offerings for a King, for God, and for a Sufferer. They had come through Jerusalem to obtain directions, where they had met murderous King Herod. They went home again, avoiding Herod, who was furious. Satan attacked again. Herod sent soldiers to kill all baby boys under age two in Bethlehem; but God warned Joseph, and he and Mary left immediately by night for safety in Egypt. They stayed there some months, until, with Herod's death, it was safe for them to return. Joseph led up the coast road to avoid Jerusalem, and in time they were back in Nazareth. They settled, and Joseph took up his carpentry again.

Jesus grew; as a small child he learned much OT faith and truth from Mary. In time, brothers and sisters joined him. Regularly in spring-time the family went to Passover in Jerusalem. When he was 12, Joseph and Mary were there again with everybody else, and it was Jesus' barmitzvah, the occasion of admitting a boy to the full covenant membership of Israel. Now he could go into the Temple for himself. He was fascinated, and he stayed on there as Joseph and Mary set out for home with their company. When they realised that he was missing, they turned back to Jerusalem and searched for him everywhere, except the Temple. After desperate days, eventually they did go to the Temple, and there they found him surrounded by the best brains in Jerusalem, all amazed at this 12-year-old's depth of understanding. Both Jesus and his parents were upset by this misadventure, which Mary remembered clearly [Luke 2:41-52]. They went home again, where Jesus grew in physical strength and in spiritual wisdom. Joseph could now take him into the synagogue; he trained him in carpentry, which included housebuilding as well as making tables and stools. Perhaps sometimes Joseph and Jesus went off for a few days to go the 20 miles (32km) to Lake Galilee, and Jesus met some of the fishermen.

At some point, Joseph died leaving Mary with Jesus, his four brothers, and at least three sisters, maybe more. [Matthew 13:54-56] So Jesus worked as carpenter to feed at least 9 mouths; he trained his brothers, too; it was the duty of sons to support their widowed mothers. Meanwhile John, son of the late Zechariah and Elizabeth, was nurtured in a desert community, one of several which had rejected the worldly leaders and the empty religion of theologians and legalists. When John was about 30, he began to preach in public, and it released a wave of Messianic expectation amongst ordinary people. They turned out in thousands to hear John and be baptised in repentance in the river Jordan.

Jesus – Three years Ministry

Jesus was now a mature man, and aware of his divinely human constitution; he had experienced family and village life, which always included annual visits to Jerusalem for Passover. About age 30, he left home in his brothers' hands and went to the river Jordan, to hear his cousin John preaching:

"The kingdom of God is at hand! Repent and believe this good news, and live life accordingly: share food and clothes with those in need, have honest integrity, be just and fair!"

John had been checked out [John 1:19-28] by the Jerusalem religious leaders, ever control freaks – No, he was not the Messiah, not Elijah, and not the Prophet. He saw himself as the King's herald, the voice in the desert calling for people to prepare for the sovereign Lord now coming in power. [Isaiah 40:3-11] Unlike the ever-vigilant Pharisees, Jesus joined the queue for baptism. But John recognised that Jesus needed no repentance. However, Jesus insisted; when he came up from the waters, John saw the Holy Spirit of God as a dove descend upon him, and heard the Voice affirming his divine and pure nature:

"You are my Son, whom I love; with you I am well pleased."

John spoke prophetically to his own disciples about Jesus, as God's lamb for sacrifice, and some of them, Andrew included, became Jesus' disciples. But Jesus, full of the Holy Spirit and led by the Spirit, at once left the crowds to spend time alone in the deserts. This was his opportunity to pray and reflect on his mission; and also the time of attack from Satan again.

After 6 weeks out of the public eye, Jesus returned in the power of the Spirit, first to Capernaum, perhaps when Andrew brought his brother Peter to Jesus, and Philip joined the group. John Baptist was arrested, and eventually murdered. Jesus picked up preaching where John had been cut off. He went home to Nazareth where he preached in the Synagogue from Isaiah 61:1,2. This was his 'manifesto' for ministry: 'The Spirit of God upon him, anointing him (as Messiah) to preach good news and liberation, healing, and rescue in a time of the Lord's grace.' But the hearers would not move on from seeing him as Joseph's boy, and finally they rose in wrath at some of his words, in order to lynch him. However, he was able to foil this. Soon he and his brothers moved the family from Nazareth to Capernaum, where some of his disciples worked as fishermen on Lake Galilee. He taught the attentive crowds with parables, and with pithy sayings which Matthew collected for the Sermon on the Mount; it is in Matthew 5,6,7.

So Jesus was now baptised with the Spirit; he was full of the Spirit, led by the Spirit [Luke 4:1], and in the power of the Spirit returned to Galilee [Luke 4:14], to start the public ministry of the next 3 years. Much of this action is encapsulated in Mark's Gospel chapter 1. As summary of these years, the gospels record Jesus as:

<u>Preaching</u> John's message and taking it further [Mark 1:14-15], <u>Calling</u> disciples [Mark 1:16-20], <u>Teaching</u> [Mark 1:21-22], <u>Exorcising</u> [Mark 1:23-28], and <u>Healing</u> [Mark 1:29-34].

Later in Mark,

Jesus <u>protested</u> against the religiosity of the establishment [Mark 7:1-8 traditional hand-washing, 9-13 traditional votive offerings, 14-19 traditional foods].

Jesus <u>forewarned</u> he disciples of his own death and resurrection [Mark 8:31, 9:31, 10:32-34]

Jesus <u>prophesied</u> the siege of Jerusalem with the destruction of the Temple [Mark 13:1-23]. This happened at the end of the Jewish War 66-70 AD when the Romans crucified over 2000 Jews and then ran out of wood! Jesus also prophesied that he himself would fulfil the prophecy of Daniel 7:13-14 [Mark 13:24-37]

Jesus <u>sent</u> his disciples out, to continue his ministry [Mark 6:7-13, Matthew 28:18-20], empowered by his Holy Spirit [Act 1:8] after his resurrection.

Jesus maintained all this ministry for 3 years, and by it trained his apostles for the future.

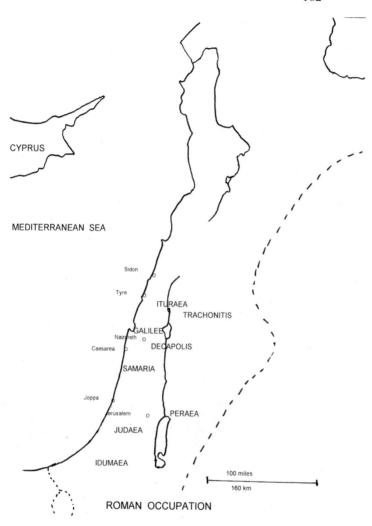

A look at the map: Start at Galilee where Jesus began his ministry; move north to Tyre, where Jesus, perhaps on holiday, healed a small foreign girl [Matthew 15:21-28]; move to Decapolis, the Ten Towns, south of the Lake Galilee, a Greek area which was no bother to the Romans, and where many Christians fled in AD70; see the River Jordan where John baptised [Matthew 3:13], and Samaria which was avoided by true Jews

[John 4:4]; note Jerusalem amongst the hills, and Judaea in the south.

Messianic Expectations   "Messiah" (Hebrew) or "Christ" (Greek). God set up creation and made humans. Right from the start he has sought to walk with us, as in the Garden of Genesis 3:8. When we foolishly turned away from him, nevertheless he still prepared to come lovingly, to redeem our situation. The OT is the setting for Jesus the Christ, ie Jesus the Messiah. He is the important person in the big picture. All the OT is the preparation for the coming of Jesus. After the storm of the crucifixion, on the first Easter Day, when Jesus walked with the two dis-masted disciples going home from Jerusalem to Emmaus, he began with Moses and all the Prophets and he explained to them what was said in all the Scriptures concerning himself. [Luke 24:27] "Moses" = Law & History, from Genesis to Samuel to Esther; "Prophets" = Isaiah to Malachi; with all the Scriptures or "Writings" = the Wisdom books and Psalms.

The Jews of Jesus' day, under the Gentile occupation in their Promised Land, were sure that the Messiah was coming in victorious power as, for example, in Zechariah 9:13 – 17:

"I will bend Judah as I bend my bow ... The Lord will appear over them, his arrow will flash like lightning. The Sovereign Lord will sound the trumpet; he will march ..."
But they did not discern v.9 – 10:

"See, your King comes to you, righteous and having salvation, gentle and riding on a donkey ... He will proclaim peace to the nations ..."

So they rejected the concept of the suffering servant of Isaiah chapters 49 – 53 as being about the Messiah. Jesus complained: "You search the scriptures ... that testify about me, yet you refuse to come to me to have life." [John 5:30-40] Without the benefit of hindsight, the prophecies of the 1st and 2nd comings merge, much as we might be unable to separate hazy distant mountain ranges. So one reason for Jewish confusion was an undiscerning theology; but also politics, pride and sin came into it. We need to study the OT to see as best we may the 1st and 2nd Comings, and grasp the enormous operation that the Lord is doing, and how we are involved.

Handel's Messiah portrays the Messianic Hope well, and also it is well presented in the traditional Christmas Eve Service of Nine Lessons and Carols:

"Genesis 3   God announces in the Garden of Eden that the seed of the woman shall bruise the serpent's head. [v.15]

"Genesis 12   God promises to faithful Abraham that in his seed shall the nations of the earth be blessed. [v.3]

"Isaiah 9   Christ's birth and kingdom are foretold by Isaiah. [v.6-7]

"Micah 5   The prophet Micah foretells the glory of little Bethlehem." [v.2]

These last two are OT people answering the question WHO IS JESUS?   Here are ten more in the NT who answer that question:

Those two Emmaus road disciples echoed the expectations of the many who had followed Jesus: "We had hoped that he was the one who was going to redeem Israel." (ie the Messiah) [Luke 24:21]

The prophet John Baptist said "Look, the Lamb of God, who takes away the sin of the world! ... this is the Son of God." [John 1:29, 34]

Disciple Andrew said "We have found the Messiah" [v.41]

Disciple Philip said "We have found the one Moses wrote about ... and the prophets – Jesus of Nazareth, son of Joseph" [v.45]

Disciple Nathanael soon said "You are the Son of God, the King of Israel!" [v.49]

Disciple Thomas said to Jesus "My Lord and my God" [John 20:28]

The Father said of Jesus: At his baptism, "This is my Son, whom I love; with him I am well pleased."   And at his transfiguration, "This is my Son, whom I have chosen; listen to him."

So consider what Jesus said of himself: "I am gentle and humble in heart." [Matthew 11:25-30]; yet boldly, when asked at his trial "Are you the Christ (Messiah)?" "I am" [Mark 14:61]

And consider what Paul wrote of Jesus: [Philippians 2:5 – 11]

Then here is the twelfth testimony to Jesus' identity:
      [Matthew 16:13-20]
On one Away-day in the mountains, Jesus probed the disciples' understanding of him: Peter professed what all Twelve were saying privately amongst themselves. " You are the MESSIAH!" Jesus confirmed this to be a correct statement, and at once said that God the Father has revealed the truth, with blessing [v.16 – 17]. Jesus appointed Peter to be leader of the little called-out group (ecclesia, the church), which ultimately has involved heaven and earth, with power over forces which are violent and cosmic [v.18-19]. But he carefully hedged it: "for the present, keep this news private"[v.20].

   The reason for keeping mouths shut was their inaccurate and limited ideas about God's Messiah which they had, and all other Israelites had, and indeed many beyond Israel had. They expected an enforcing ruler, a rousing political soldier-king who would restore David's sovereignty over the Promised Land, at least from the River Euphrates to the River of Egypt, perhaps to be extended to the whole human race. (The River of Egypt was the major one of several rivers, becoming dry wadi in the summer, which flowed into the Mediterranean, and marking the northern boundary of Egypt. See map of chapter 10) The Messiah would purge his people from evildoers amongst them, and establish his people as a community dedicated to God that would live by his law. But Jesus knew how limited their understanding was behind their words: he knew what was in man [John 2:24,25]. There and then, he warned them [Matthew 16:21 – 27]. Peter was rebuked and the disciples were cowed. As if to reassure them, Jesus took Peter, James and John up the mountain and was transfigured before them; he revealed them his Messianic glory. At the same time, the others down in the valley discovered their powerlessness to heal [Matthew 17].

   As the time for his ministry drew to a close, Jesus warned his disciples three times that he would suffer, be killed, and rise again on the third day. [Mark 8:31, 9:30-32, 10:32-34] Not long after, he was heading for Jerusalem, for the final encounter with the religious establishment, and for the cross.

Jesus – the Last Weeks

Some weeks before the last Passover, the family of Martha, Mary and Lazarus at Bethany had a catastrophe. Jesus had often stayed with them on his visits to Jerusalem, and he had a warm affection for them. The sisters sent an urgent message to Jesus, that Lazarus was ill. The story is told in John 11. Jesus came after a delay, to find that Lazarus was already dead and had been laid in a tomb, four days previously. Jesus called him with a loud shout: "Lazarus! Come out!" He had to be untied from the burial shrouds. News of this event reached the ears of the High Priest, who now plotted against both Jesus and Lazarus. Jesus withdrew to minister in Peraea, to the east of the Jordan. But as Passover drew on, Jesus returned to Bethany, where the family celebrated him, and Mary, sister to Lazarus and Martha, anointed him with fragrant oil. However, Judas Iscariot began to criticise, and perhaps was thinking how to precipitate a victorious Messianic conflict between Jesus and the Priests and the Romans.

Next, Jesus staged a Royal entry to Jerusalem, riding a young donkey and deliberately fulfilling Zechariah's prophesy of the King coming in peace [Zechariah 9:9]. Anybody who pondered would have understood the Messianic implications. But they thought in terms of the Messiah coming as the great deliverer from the occupying powers, so the point was missed at the time. Jesus went to the Temple, acclaimed by the country crowd with their children: "Hosanna to the Son of David!" But the Pharisees were just cross, and the city crowd merely asked "Who is this?" Jesus was upset by all the commercial trading within the Temple precincts, but he went back to Bethany for the night. Early next morning, he arrived with a whip and furiously drove out cattle and traders and money-changers. "My house shall be called a house of prayer, but you have made it a den of thieves!" He took up position to teach the dense and listening crowds in the cleared space. They so hung on his words that neither the Temple Elders could intervene, nor their police could arrest him. There were many memorable verbal exchanges between Jesus and the authorities, and the big crowd was delighted by his exposure of error and hypocrisy. Passover was upon them, and the city was now a heaving throng, so he sought the peace of the small group. He and his Twelve disciples celebrated the Feast probably in the large Upper Room of John Mark's family.

At the meal, with its special food and liturgical conversation, Jesus changed the words from remembering the hurried Israelite meal in Egypt and the death of the firstborn, to remembering the death of Jesus himself so soon to happen. John Mark overheard his departure from the traditional words, and wrote them into his story [Mark 14:22-24]. John the disciple remembered the intimate teaching Jesus gave them on that occasion; he wrote them into his gospel [John chapters 14-17]. (More information about the Last Supper can be found below.) Afterwards, Jesus and the party left the house and the city for the Garden on the Mount of Olives, the Olive Press or Gethsemane. They lodged here in the out-buildings, while the women were lodged in the house in the city, or back in Bethany. Now Jesus prayed desperately, maybe for an hour, but the others were overwhelmed by sleep.

Suddenly Judas Iscariot arrived with a large posse from the priests. He identified Jesus with a kiss, and they arrested him. The rest of Jesus' party panicked and fled, probably out to Bethany, though Peter and John followed the posse back to the city, at a distance. Jesus was arraigned before Annas, and then before Caiaphas the High Priest, with many of the Sanhedrin, the ruling council. It was illegal to hold court at night. They lacked consistent witnesses, and could not concoct a capital charge, until Caiaphas put Jesus under oath and asked him "Are you the Messiah, the Son of the Blessed One?" "I am," said Jesus, "and all of you will see the Son of Man coming in the clouds of heaven!" This was his outright claim to pre-eminence over any Jewish Priest. Caiaphas exploded with anger, and the whole Sanhedrin sent Jesus to the Roman governor, Pontius Pilate, to be executed. Pilate was reluctant, but the Jewish accusers raised a city rabble who howled for blood, and Pilate gave way, knowing full well that Jesus was a good man, innocent of the accusations of the Jewish leadership. Jesus was mocked, scourged and crucified. He suffered and died on the cross after three hours of darkness and desolation, in a manner that convinced the Roman Centurion of his innocence and something of his godly character. He finally gave up his life some time before sunset when the Jewish Sabbath was due to start. Joseph of Arimathea, helped by Nicodemus, gave him a decent but quick burial in a nearby fresh tomb; then the tomb was sealed by the Jewish authorities to prevent any body-snatching. Several women amongst his closest disciples witnessed it all. These ladies had to observe the Sabbath (from sunset Friday, to sunset Saturday), and then they prepared spices for the next day, to give Jesus a proper burial.

Psalm 22, perhaps composed by David in lonely desperation, screamed of life and times falling in on him.
[1] 'My God, My God, why have you forsaken me? Why are you so far from saving me, so far from the words of my groaning?' It was Jesus' cry of desolation on the Cross. It was not answered. [Matthew 27:46]
[3] David recalled that God is Israel's Holy One, enthroned, praised, trusted, and has been their faithful rescuer.
[6] But since he was not rescued, and sunken in depression, his self-esteem was that he was a worm, not even human. He was denigrated by real men, scorned, despised, mocked, insulted, and dismissed.
[8] The hurtful scorn goes on: 'He trusts in the Lord; let the Lord rescue him; let him deliver him since he delights in him.' The priests quoted this in derision about Jesus on the Cross. [Matthew 27:43]
[9] David told God how from birth 'You made me trust in you.' He prayed for God's presence with him now, to rescue him from such wild beasts.
[14-18] David's description of his own suffering and condition has remarkable prophetic resemblance to the extremes endured by Jesus on the Cross.
[19] David prayed explicitly for rescue.
[22] He was quick to sense that God is not party to the mockery, but has heard his cry for help. At once he proclaimed the name, I

AM, of the LORD to Israel, so that they should worship, praise and honour him. The worm was transformed into the leader of the great crowd in the Temple, bringing sacrifices of thanksgiving; the abundance will feed the poor, too!

[27] The news of God's response to the terrible cry of desolation will spread across the globe and foreigners will turn to him down the generations.

[31] "He has done it" might be the triumphant cry of Jesus ringing out from the Cross – "Finished!" [John 19:30] It was followed confidently by 'Father, into your hands I commit my spirit," [Psalm 31:5] and then he died.

The Character of Jesus

The Table may help understanding, but it is not a theological statement! It may make us think of Jesus as Son of God and Son of Man, both divine and human. This also implies much that is encouraging about redeemed human beings.

God – **Father**	Impeccable:	Invincible:	Omniscient:
Spirit, Truth	unable to sin	unable to	knows everything
[John 4:29]		be defeated	

God – Son

The Perfect	Able to sin	Vulnerable	Some ignorance
Man	[Hebrews 4:15]	[Luke 22:53]	[Mark 13:32]

Nevertheless, by complete dependence upon God the Father, Jesus could live perfectly [John 8:29].

Humankind
1. Fallen   sinful   beaten   erring

2. Redeemed and Spirit – filled, with <u>potential</u> for new
                clean Life   power for Life   knowing Life
                [1 John 1:7]   [Act 1:8]   [2Corinthians 5:16]

The Human Jesus

The personal character of the living human Jesus shines through the gospels, even though no writer expands on this:

His *bodily needs*: he accepted the domestic provisions of people, such as obtaining a drink from a stranger at a well [John 4:7], and receiving the care of the women with the group of disciples. He enjoyed food, and once he was called "a drunkard and a glutton" [Matthew 11:19]. He got tired, [John 4:6] and slept on the boat [Mark 4:38].

He had *real emotions*: he had happiness with the disciples after their mission [Luke 10:21]. He was very upset and angry at Lazarus' grave [John 11:32-36]. He was furious with synagogue leaders who objected to his healing one Sabbath [Mark 3:5]. He was sadly moved over Jerusalem [Matthew 23:37]. He was outraged with the commerce in the Temple [John 2:13-17].

He was genuinely *compassionate*: he rescued the wedding at Cana [John 2:1-11]. He felt for the crowds who followed him, and fed them [Mark 6:30-34]. He showed mercy to an unjustly exposed prostitute [John 8:1-11]. He acted by raising a dead son for the widow of Nain [Luke 7:11-15]. He loved his disciples right through it all [John 13:1-17]. He cared for his mother at his cross [John 19:25-27]. He encouraged the penitent thief: [Luke 23:39-43]

He told stories with *humour*: the splinter and the plank in the eye [Luke 6:41-43].

He had clarity of *mental grasp*: the Sermon on the Mount [Matthew 5,6,7]. Parables – the Sower, [Luke 8:4-15], the Lost Son, [Luke 15:11-32], the Good Samaritan, [Luke 10:29-37]. Skilfully, he turned hostile questions: the challenge to his authority [Mark 11:27-33]. "Must we pay taxes?" [Mark 12:13-17]; he had understanding of Psalm 110: [Mark 12:35-37]

He had an unchallengeable *integrity*: his prayer and his life – 'I always do what pleases [my Father]' [John 8:29]. 'Which of you can convict me of sin?' [John 8:46].

He *prayed*: at his baptism: [Luke 3:21], as a habit often [Luke 5:16], before appointing his apostles [Luke 6:12], at the Transfiguration [Luke 9:28,29], with glee at the return of the 70 he had sent on mission [Luke10:21].

He had a focussed *commitment*: the night of prayer when selecting the apostles [Luke 6:12]. He was 'sent only to the lost sheep of Israel' [Matthew 15:24]. "The Son of Man must suffer" [Luke 9:22]. The scary last journey to Jerusalem [Mark 10:32-34], and the agonised prayer in Gethsemane [Mark 14:32-36].

His *courage*: through the trials, the flogging and the cross.

Jesus – the Resurrection

The third day, Sunday, Mary Magdalene, Mary mother of James, Salome, Joanna, and maybe others, were up before dawn and went to the tomb, with their spices, only to find the stone rolled aside, the body of Jesus gone, and radiant angels saying **"He has risen! Why are you looking for the living among the dead?!"** They ran back to the men, who could not believe them. [John 20:1-9] Peter and John went to the tomb and found it as the women had told them. Meanwhile the risen Jesus showed himself first to Mary Magdalene [John 20:10-18], then to the other women, and finally to the men. Later in the day, two were walking home sadly to Emmaus, a near village, and Jesus joined them. [Luke 24:13-35] When suddenly they recognised him, they ran back to tell the others in Jerusalem; then he appeared to the group in the Upper Room. (Was it his appearing and vanishing, or was it their eyes being able and unable to see him?) Over the next few days, their incredulity turned into amazed belief. (The next chapter contains more about the Resurrection.) After 6 weeks of appearances, Jesus made an unmistakeable withdrawal, ascending into the clouds of heaven; they went back to Jerusalem. There, in the Upper Room, about 120 gathered and prayed for 10 days, and waited for the next move.

Now follows a survey of the Apostolic Testimony about the Resurrection of Jesus from death on the first Easter Day.

Chapter 17 Truth, the Resurrection, and the Apostles' Testimony

> The relevance of this for the present day for followers of Jesus is the creeping Secularisation of life and government in the UK. The Secularists are in power and seek to ban the proclamation of the name and gospel of the Lord, Jesus Christ. They lump all 'religions' together as dangerous and potentially terrorist.

"What is Truth?" Pontius Pilate when trying Jesus – John 18:38. We live in a world where many speak knowingly of there not being absolute truth. Truth, they allege, is relative; what is true for you is not necessarily true for another person. They say it depends on who you are, your setting, your upbringing, your philosophy. (Logical Conclusion: there is, absolutely, no truth in what they say !!) However, let today's Christians beware! We may not be in a position to gainsay this assertion, but we can remember the first Christians like Peter, arraigned before the Jerusalem rulers who within months previously had sent Jesus to execution, saying "Salvation is found in no-one else, for there is no other name under heaven given to men by which we must be saved." We may read of countless other more recent heroes of faith, as Martin Luther before the Emperor at Worms, saying "Here I stand," affirming his faith in Christ, and defiant of church abuses.

Especially we should note well, that while we believe in Christ, we should avoid being deceived, or even consenting for a moment, that our faith is founded on relative truth. No! We need to stand on the solid rock of historical fact which our faith rests upon. The evidence for the life and death and resurrection of Jesus is absolutely and historically true for all time and eternity! IT HAPPENED !!

The apostles are saying "We were there!"

Peter: "Men of Israel, listen to this: Jesus of Nazareth was a man accredited by God to you by miracles, wonders and signs, which God did among you through him, as you yourselves know. This man was handed over to you by God's set purpose and foreknowledge, and you with the help of wicked men, put him to death by nailing him to the cross. But God raised him from the dead..." [Act 2:22-24]

Then Peter, filled with the Holy Spirit, said to them "Rulers and elders of the people! If we are being called to account today for an act of kindness shown to a cripple and are asked how he was healed, then know this, you and everyone else in Israel: It is by the name of Jesus Christ of Nazareth, who you crucified but whom God raised from the dead..." [Act 4:8-10]

"We did not follow cleverly invented stories when we told you about the power and coming of our Lord Jesus Christ, but were eye-witnesses of his majesty." [2 Peter 1:16]

John: wrote in his gospel, John 20:24-29: "Thomas (called Didymus), one of the Twelve, was not with the disciples when Jesus came. So the other disciples told him, "We have seen the Lord!" But he said to them, "Unless I see the nail marks in his hands and put my finger where the nails were, and put my hand into his side, I will not believe it." A week later his disciple were in the house again, and Thomas was with them. Though the doors were locked, Jesus came and stood among them and said, "Peace be with you!" Then he said to Thomas, "Put your finger here; see my hands. Reach out your hand and put it into my side. Stop doubting and believe." Thomas said to him, "My Lord and my God!" Then Jesus told him, "Because you have seen me, you have believed; blessed are those who have not seen and yet have believed.""

Paul: "... The gospel [God] promised beforehand through his prophets in the Holy Scriptures regarding his Son, who as to his human nature was a descendent of David, and who though the Spirit was declared with power to be the Son of God by his resurrection from the dead, Jesus Christ our Lord." [Romans 1:2-4]

"What I received I passed on to you as of first importance: that Christ died for our sins according to the Scriptures, that he was buried, that he was raised on the third day according to the Scriptures, and that he appeared to Peter, and then to the Twelve. After that, he appeared to more than five hundred of the brothers at the same time, most of whom are still living, though some have fallen asleep. Then he appeared to James, then to all the apostles, and last of all he appeared to me also, as to one abnormally born." [1 Corinthians 15:2-7]

Resurrection and Science

Dead biological material does not live again. <u>Dead people do not revive.</u> This is an ordinary and normal experiential observation, a scientific FACT. This must be accepted.

This fact has led on to a scientific HYPOTHESIS, that <u>Dead people cannot be revived.</u> Established Fact is one thing. Hypothesis is not Fact; rather it is a provisional working assumption.

The apostolic personal testimony as witnesses is that Jesus was raised bodily from death. The Romans, and the Jews, knew that he was dead. Luke (physician, and careful historian) records 40 days during which the apostles – at first stubborn sceptics (Mark 16:14) – became securely convinced of the resurrection. Their united testimony from experience made the resurrection of Jesus, Christ, Lord, Son of God, from the dead, a Fact.

So, believers in the Facts positively state that the Hypothesis is wrong, since it makes the Facts irreconcilable. Also, it is a Fact that miracles do happen. OT, NT, and Early Church history (1st, 2nd, and 3rd Centuries) record miracles, including a number of resuscitations. But Resurrection is more than resuscitation; people whom Jesus and the early Christians raised to life died again, ultimately, and their bodies decayed. Jesus was dead and buried, bodily. But he was raised to bodily life, and that without decay. He is alive now. The resurrection was not merely a spiritual event (a Platonic idea), but it was also an established historical physical event.

Daily Miracles: God creates natural human life, with the potential for knowing him. He calls erring humans to turn to him. When humans do turn to him, he regenerates them with personal spiritual life. When natural death occurs, the human spirit "sleeps" and the body disintegrates. At the 'consummation of all things', the human spirits will "awake" to face God's verdicts. The regenerated human spirits, clothed in 'spiritual bodies,' will join God's service in the resurrection scene where Jesus is already enthroned in power.

Regeneration is an ongoing miraculous process: God is intervening in his creation, and the ongoing miraculous is assured by the fact of the historical resurrection of the Lord, Jesus Christ. As with Thomas, it is not the intellectual historical evidence, not the personal testimony of preachers or friends that convinces; it is my personal encounter with the living risen Lord Jesus that turns my doubts into belief. This beginning becomes a living daily experience. It is then that the evidence and the testimony of others make sense and add to conviction.

These are notes from Norman Anderson's pamphlet **The Evidence for the Resurrection.** They provide sound intellectual evidence for the Resurrection:
(Sir Norman Anderson, OBE, was QC, Professor of Oriental Laws in London University, &c)
He began by writing 'If the Resurrection is not true, the whole of Christianity must be fraud, the product of liars or deluded simpletons. (1 Corinthians 15:14-15 refers). So we must test the historical evidence, and we must test our present day experience amongst ourselves and our friends.'

A.   Documents The primary ones were written by Matthew, Mark, Luke, John, Paul, and Peter.

The secondary ones were the product of the primitive church. All these writings are very early, and this is agreed by scholars. Thus:

1. Paul: there is no doubt that Paul wrote 1 Corinthians between 52 – 57 AD, so his first *speaking* to them on his travels was

about 50 AD. He had received the message authoritatively at his conversion and on his first visit to Peter and James about 35 AD; this is within 5 years of the event.

2. Mark: it is believed that his gospel followed Peter's spoken teaching, and is an early account.

3. Luke: the author of the gospel and the Acts is renowned for his detailed historical accuracy.

The other writers gave eyewitness accounts of the events of the 10 years before and after the death of Jesus, which are to be accepted as such.

Challenges:

B. <u>Was it a deliberate invention?</u> Certainly not!

a) there were too many witnesses for this to be possible. (i) At one time, 500 saw the risen Christ, most of whom were still alive in 56 AD. (ii) There was the united authority of all the first believers.

b) this is not a lie; the integrity of the high moral teaching, lived out, as opponents admitted, contradicts it being an invention.

c) the disciples' lives changed from being cowards to heroes who faced death; nobody ever admitted any invention.

C. <u>Was it a legend?</u> This is not possible.

a) the records are too early to allow the time for the growth of legends.

b) unlike legends, the records are true to life, for example <u>not</u> going into the scene of the moment of resurrection, nor into the details of Christ's face to people – to Mary, or James.

Few scholars use these theories today. They accept the sincerity of the records, and seek to explain.

D. **Explanations which have been proposed.**

1. *The disciples stole the body* (an idea now abandoned). They could not, psychologically, as they were terrified and in hiding; nor could they sustain such a lie ethically.

2. a) *The Jewish or Roman authorities removed the body.* (For what purpose?) If so, they could have produced evidence of the removal, and indicated the true second grave, in order from the start to put an end to the preaching (Acts 3:14,15 and 5:28). But they did not; and they could not.

b) *Joseph of Arimathea removed the body.* But he would have told either the apostles, or the Jewish authorities, according to which side he took.
3.   *The women mistook the tomb.* But then the authorities could have pointed to the real tomb and shown the body.
4.   *Swoon and resuscitation.* "Jesus never died on the cross. He revived in the tomb, broke out of it and persuaded his terrified disciples that he had conquered death." (Even sceptics rule this out!)
  a) the experienced Roman executioners knew a dead body when they saw one.
  b) it seems unbelievable that Jesus could do this when half-dead.
  c) it would be utterly out of keeping with his character of truth and integrity.

E.   Further comment about the Tomb:
1.   The early preaching (Acts and some epistles) majored on the resurrection, without reference to the tomb or the women's stories.
2.   The tomb was never a place of pilgrimage.
3.   Not only was the tomb empty, so also were the grave clothes.
Initially, there was no need to speak of the empty tomb as evidence, since all accepted the resurrection. Only later when the gospels were written for the instruction of converts were the tomb stories recorded.
F.   Explaining the Appearances – *were they not hallucinations and psychic phenomena?* No!
  a) only some types of personality are liable to this, and not 500 all at the same moment, and not to all in the smaller group, containing a variety of personalities, a tax-collector, fishermen, &c.
  b) Hallucinations are individualistic, whereas this was the same for all.
  c) They usually happen only to people who are longing for them. But the disciples were <u>not</u> expecting them. It seems they stubbornly refused to believe at first.

d) They usually happen at suitable times and places; but Jesus appeared at many kinds of times and places.

e) Obsessions occur over a long period. But these appearances lasted for only 40 days, then ceased; the disciples never claimed any repeats.

Further: 1. No spiritualist medium was ever involved.

2. The risen Jesus was no ghost or immaterial spirit. He could be seen, heard, touched and handled; he could walk, cook fish, and eat; his wounds could be seen and felt.

G.   *Other evidences*

1. The church can be traced back to its origin in the Holy Land in about 30 AD, that is to the resurrection of its founder from death.
2. The Day of Rest was changed from the Jewish Sabbath, the Seventh Day, to the First Day of the week, by the original church who were nearly all Jews; they had been rescued by Jesus from fanatical Sabbath-keeping, and celebrated the startling event of the resurrection on the first day of the week.
3. The success of the Early church's preaching against furious opposition derived from incontrovertible evidence that Jesus had risen.
4. The delay of 7 weeks, from Resurrection to Preaching at Pentecost and from then on, would not be part of a fabrication. The record is true to the happenings.
5. Jesus predicted his death and resurrection, and his disciples did not understand his words.
6. Peter and the apostles changed totally; from Peter's fear before a servant girl to being unstoppable witnesses before the entire Sanhedrin.
7. Jesus was God in flesh; he died, and it is no mystery that he rose!
8. The change of people's lives down the ages who have met the risen Christ is an eloquent witness to the reality of the living Jesus then and now.

However, the ultimate proof for us lies in *our* response to the living Saviour's promise: "Here I am. I stand at the door and knock. If anyone hears my voice and opens the door, I will come in and eat with him, and he with me." [Revelation 3:20]

Encounter with God

When God graciously reveals and we encounter the living Lord, we know that Jesus is alive. But are we above today's false concepts about Jesus? How can we be sure? Really only by the Father's revealing – so may we keep reading, and being open to receive blessing, with trusting obedience. Only so will we live in the experience of the presence of the Spirit of Jesus in us; only then will we begin to move in his purposes, amongst people, in pain and in power, all for him, taking up the cross. The Christian life costs everything we have got, and the consequences are revolutionary, since all other kings are deposed! [Psalm 2]

"Resurrection or nothing" – Scripture Union comment from Encounter with God by Rikk Watts, for 19 06 2003.
1 Corinthians 15:12 – 19 (NIV)
But if it is preached that Christ has been raised from the dead, how can some of you say that there is no resurrection of the dead? If there is no resurrection of the dead, then not even Christ has been raised. And if Christ has not been raised, our preaching is useless and so is your faith. More than that, we are then found to be false witnesses about God, for we have testified about God that he raised Christ from the dead. But he did not raise him if in fact the dead are not raised. For if the dead are not raised, then Christ has not been raised either. And if Christ has not been raised, your faith is futile; you are still in your sins. Then those also who have fallen asleep in Christ are lost. If only for this life we have hope in Christ, we are to be pitied more than all men. [NIV]

Like some modern 'Christians', some Corinthians were denying the (bodily) resurrection of the dead. Although their reasons might differ – the Corinthians, apparently believing that reality was spiritual and only the soul immortal, held the body of little account, whereas for moderns, resurrections simply cannot happen – the consequences are identical. If the dead are not raised neither was Christ. Whatever it was that happened it was not a resurrection. And if so everything is over.

First, the content of Paul's preaching, whereby the Corinthians experienced the Spirit's life-changing power, would be utterly compromised. If that went, then what in the world were they trusting in? Paul's own credibility would also evaporate. The resurrection was so central to his message, how could anyone trust any of his testimony if it was denied? Worse still, he would be guilty of lying about God. How so? In proclaiming the resurrection Paul declared that God had decisively vindicated Jesus in every respect. It was God's resounding 'yes' to Christ's death on our behalf and the beginning of the new creation. But if Jesus was not raised then God did not so act. …It has become fashionable to deny the bodily resurrection of Christ. Nothing could be so mistaken or disastrous. Paul fully understands what these people do not. If there is no bodily resurrection then there is no forgiveness of sins, no gift of the Spirit, nothing. This is one place where weak-mindedness, pandering to secular scepticism, or failure of nerve is fatal and, frankly, non-Christian. He was raised, and bodily. And that is that.

"Salvation is found in no-one else, for there is no other name under heaven given to people by which we must be saved." For ever and ever, world without end, AMEN.

Jesus lived but briefly, was crucified, buried, and then was raised in total victory over death, to ascend to God's glory; from there he will return. After Jesus' ascension, in God's grace, the Holy Spirit came in power, working out in the Apostles and disciples in spoken ministry and in the New Testament writings.

Chapter 18   The New Covenant

> This chapter examines the NT era with Pentecost and the energetic work of the Apostles and of the believers. Gentiles became included, and the Good News spread by preaching and letter writing. Also the Gospels and Acts were written.

Psalm 118
The first and last verses command thanks to the covenant-making God, Israel's I AM, for his goodness and ever-enduring love.
"Give thanks to the Lord, for he is good; his love endures for ever."
[2] The instruction is to all Israelites, specifically to the priests, and yet it includes all who fear God.
[5] The writer testifies that the Lord has released him from distress; the Lord is with him and helping, so he rides above his enemies and does not fear them.
[8] His refuge is the Lord, not unreliable men, nor respected leaders. In fact, when besieged by foreigners, swarming like bees, they were rapidly removed because in the name of the Lord he cut them off. They were pushing hard, but he did not fall, since the Lord helped him, with strength and song and rescue.
[15] The shouts of victory resound, that these mighty things are the work of the Lord's right hand.
[17] He says, "My reason for living is to proclaim the Lord's work, giving me life in my hardships; he has become my salvation, my total righteousness, therefore 'Open the Temple gates!' to let me in and thank the Lord."
[22] Marvels continue. The reject stone becomes the building's keystone; the day of life, given by the Lord, is for joy and gladness.
[25] Rescue, success, blessing – the Lord is God, the one whose face shines on us, so we come to joyful worship.

"You are my God – Thank you, you are exalted!"

10 days of waiting

It is a time in the early 30's AD, at the join of the Old and New forms of the Covenant of grace between God and humankind. The <u>Old Covenant</u> was started by God in the 2nd millennium BC, with Abraham. Jesus completed the act of Redemption on the Cross and he uttered those victorious words: "It is finished!" – and then he gave up his spirit. [John 19:30] At the Resurrection he proclaimed the <u>New Covenant</u> – "Greetings!" he said to the women. [Matthew 28:9] Then there was the 7 weeks span when Jesus was seen and not seen by the disciples – "Stay in the city..." he said towards the end of it. [Luke 24:49] Then came his Ascension [Act 1:4-9]. In those 10 days after the risen Jesus had ascended, the last vestige of the Old Covenant was enacted when the disciples cast lots to choose Matthias to replace Judas. [Act 1:26]

This is the moment for pause. Jesus said "Do not leave Jerusalem, but wait for the gift my Father promised... you will receive power when the Holy Spirit comes on you, and you will be my witnesses..." [Act 1:4,8] So it is a time of bated breath, because God has created the universe, brought life on the earth, and made human beings in his own image. He has not walked away when he was rejected, but provided for reconciliation by sacrifice. Through the Law and Prophets and Writings, he has prepared for Jesus to redeem. Jesus has come and finished the rescue plan, and has now gone back to heaven. So all is poised for promised power!

The Old Covenant had been made by God with Abraham, some 1900 years before Pentecost; 500 years later, it was developed and codified for the nation by Moses. The New Covenant was set up by God through the cross, ratified by Jesus in the resurrection, and brought into effect by the Holy Spirit at Pentecost.

Pentecost

The New Covenant, promised by the risen Jesus [Luke 24:49, Acts 1:8], burst on the scene with the Holy Spirit coming at Pentecost. Pentecost was the final step across from the Old to the New Testament [Joel 2:29-32]. The Holy Spirit had fallen on Jesus at his baptism; now he fell on Jesus' disciples, on all of them, not only on Peter and the apostolic leadership; and not as in the OT only on a restricted person and limited occasion for, say, prophecy, or worship (glory in the Tabernacle or Temple) or vision (Isaiah, Ezekiel, Daniel). There were 120 people waiting on the Lord, all together in one place. The Holy Spirit came and filled each of them, young and old, women and men. There was uproarious noise of praise of the Lord in tongues. This was on the Day of Pentecost about 9am, and the city was bustling with people, all awake and able to hear the commotion. Many gathered outside the Upper Room. Peter came out, stood on the steps, and began to speak. The hubbub subsided.

[Act 2:14 – 47] Peter preached to a pilgrim crowd, about Jesus crucified and then raised from death. God had sent the Holy Spirit, who had now come for them all. Peter preached on the Joel prophecy. 3000 believed his message, were baptised and were filled with the Spirit, to form a new community. They soon settled in as a new fellowship, receiving the ministry of the apostles, caring for one another, and living in holiness.

A new kind of community

Great Grace was upon them all – so that they were set free, anointed by the Spirit, to do what they would never do by themselves, by their upbringing and prevailing culture, and by instinct. They began to live supernatural lives, breaking across what were natural inhibitions, by the Spirit. The impact of the Holy Spirit on the community of faith after Pentecost made the believers different. The 3000 became devoted to the apostles' teaching, and to vital fellowship, with breaking bread and remembering Jesus at the Last Supper, and prayer. There was awe, with signs and wonders. There were practical actions in their life together, sharing things, pooling resources, giving to the needy, which was quite contrary to instinct and culture; they held daily united worship, separately in homes and together in a large group in the Temple Yard. There was a natural flow of witness - joy, reality, and praising the Lord, which impacted others in town who received this with approval. The fruit was kingdom growth.

Instead of effort, duty and religious drive with various levels of intensity, they were impelled by love that flowed supernaturally, to love the Lord totally, and their neighbours with honour, respect, and care. Luke, writing the Acts, told of the first weeks of this new growing group of believers in Jerusalem, how they continued Jesus' ministry, preaching, healing, praying, organising community care, setting standards of integrity, and then being persecuted by the Jewish authorities.

The Holy Spirit – "the Spirit of him who raised up Jesus" (Romans 8:11) – filled them, dwelt in them, possessed them as they yielded to him [Act 2:38 – 43]; he empowered them to heal [3:6-8], refreshed their spirits [3:19], emboldened them before their accusers [4:13, 5:29-32], made them radiant in testimony [6:15], encouraged them in martyrdom [7:54-60], guided them in a tricky situation [9:10 – 16], authorised them to declare healing and raising the dead [9:34], and he led them across cultural barriers [10:44-46]. All this was repeated later through Paul in his ministry and letters. There are more examples in Acts.

Stephen

[Act 6:8 – 7:1] Stephen, a Greek Jewish Christian, was appointed to administration in the growing church. As well, he spoke and ministered powerfully in the Spirit with signs and wonders. This attracted Jewish hostility, and he was arrested on false charges. His defence before the Sanhedrin is given at length in Acts 7; however, they stoned him. Wholesale persecution erupted, and the disciples were scattered from Jerusalem, telling the Good News to all they met. Philip, a colleague of Stephen, ran a mission in a Samaritan town with blessing and healings [Act 8:5-8]. At the time, Simon Magus sought to blend the new doctrine (as he saw it) with his own Gnostic power-base. But when Peter and John came to minister alongside Philip, they discerned his heart and spoke accordingly [Act 8:21-23].

> The Greek word GNOSIS means "knowledge". The Gnostics claimed that they had an inner knowledge of spiritual affairs, which superseded Christian knowledge of God through Jesus, Son of God, crucified and risen from death. They denied the historical facts of Jesus' life, death and resurrection. There were many brands of gnosticism, derived from syncretism with various cults. Simon Magus' Gnostic influence was widespread. Caesar Claudius I had a statue of him put up in Samaria.

Saul

Soon Saul of Tarsus, a young fanatic Pharisee, who had been educated under Gamaliel at Jerusalem, being ardent for Judaism, set out to demolish the disciples and to quench this new sect. He journeyed to Damascus with authority, but God revealed the risen Jesus to him [Act 9]. He turned from persecuting, became filled with the Holy Spirit, and started to preach the Good News.

Peter

Peter's ministry took him to the sea coast where he healed Aeneas, and raised Dorcas from death. Then the Spirit overcame Peter's deep-seated prejudices and he broke all the Jewish rules by preaching the Good News to Cornelius, a God-fearing Roman centurion, and his friends. The Holy Spirit fell on them [Act 10,11].

Paul

From Acts 13, Luke's focus moves from Peter and James in Jerusalem to Paul and Barnabas based in Antioch in Syria. A strong Gentile church was growing there. Luke wrote about Paul (his Greek name; Saul his Hebrew name). The Holy Spirit guided Paul and gave him opportunities for preaching. The preaching of Act 13:14-41 was probably spoken many times in synagogues across the Roman provinces of Asia Minor. Back in Antioch in Syria, Paul reported to his 'sending' church, on how God had opened the door of faith to the Gentiles. But some from Jerusalem insisted that Gentiles had to become Jews to be saved

[Act 15:1-35]. There was sharp disagreement, and Paul went up to the Jewish Christian leaders in Jerusalem to sort this out. He was backed by Peter. In the end, James summed up the meeting by absolving the Gentiles from Jewish rites and Moses' rules and regulations. (This James was Joseph and Mary's son, next after Jesus. He wrote the epistle of James. He had become the resident leader of the church in Jerusalem.) This pronouncement caused gladness and encouragement in Antioch, but the Jewish faction continued to create problems for Paul, who needed to defend the gospel from their religiosity again and again.

Paul's group of friends at times included Luke; he wrote "We" in Acts when he was involved. They travelled out with the Good News along the south half of Asia Minor and across to Macedonia and Greece, preaching and planting churches, and encouraging believers. The Roman colony of Philippi, and Athens, Corinth, Ephesus, were key places in the mission; there were growing house-churches in many other towns and villages. He took gifts back from the new Christians to the poor in Jerusalem. Paul travelled back to Jerusalem several times, but finally he became the target of unconverted Jewish fanatics who made a riot, so that the Romans intervened [Act 21:27-36]. From then on he was a prisoner, falsely accused and yet able to give his testimony at courts of enquiry. No judicial progress happened for over 2 years, until he 'Appealed to Caesar' [Act 25:9-12]. So he travelled under relaxed arrest to Rome, by stages. Act 27:13-44 is a graphic description of a storm and shipwreck that landed Paul and the total ship's complement of 276 on the island of Malta, with no loss of life. After the winter, he arrived in Rome and lived in a private house with a soldier as guard, and for two years he preached boldly and taught about the Lord Jesus Christ [Act 28]. Luke was his faithful friend and companion. Paul's prolific ministry was supported by the many letters that he wrote. We have 13 of these. While under arrest, and before then, he wrote letters to his friends and believers; also he wrote letters to churches, dealing with theological matters, right living, marriage and families, morality &c. He defended himself twice before Caesar (probably Nero), surely giving his testimony yet again. Tradition says that he was beheaded.

The story in Acts is limited to the record of Peter in Judaea, and Paul in the north Mediterranean and into Roman Asia. It is a fulfilling of Act 1:8. That we have this much is thanks to Luke, who gave us the only Bible account of the spread of the gospel in the NT. There are hints and traditions of others who went to other places: there was the Treasury Minister who went back to Queen Candace of <u>Ethiopia</u>; the apostle Thomas, it is believed went East to <u>India</u>; and later on Peter went to <u>Bithynia</u> – the north of Roman Asia, along the south coast of the Black Sea, while, interestingly, Paul was directed away from this region [Act 16:6-10] to go over to Macedonia and Greece.

The apostolic message was given with utter integrity, excitement and conviction of both the <u>fact of the resurrection</u> of Jesus, so that his teaching (as written in the gospels) had been validated by God his Father, and of the <u>experience of the Holy Spirit</u>, who was giving gifts and power in the name of Jesus, for ministries as apostles, prophets, evangelists, pastors and teachers [Ephesians 4:11] to fulfil God's purposes.

The Epistles were letters written to churches in definite situations, such as facing false teaching, or persecution, or problems of living in their pagan society. The writers set out the theology of grace, first found in OT Israel. Grace was now bursting out for all nations, for all time, and for ever. This grace (God's undeserved love in action) brings forgiveness of our sins whereby we have life, not condemnation, in the light of the death of God's Son. Indeed, it is life with new calling and empowering for the purposes of God, that same life and power that God demonstrated in the resurrection of Jesus from the dead and imparted to us by the Holy Spirit entering us.

(It should be remembered that these letters were read out at the church meetings; those present were able to recall the steps in the presentation as they listened. Not all could read and write, but they could all remember accurately, talk over, understand, and apply what they heard. We do not have this beneficial Oral tradition.)

We have 13 of Paul's many letters.

Romans Paul planned to visit the church at Rome, though this never happened as he was arrested before he could do so. In the event he travelled to Rome as a prisoner to appear before Caesar. In this profound letter to *people most of whom he did not know*, he was at pains to bring together the Jewish and the Gentile Christians on equal terms, so he expounded in depth the grace of God that justifies all to be in the same right relationship before God and also with each other. They were to understand and respect each other as equals, and to live uprightly in peace and blessing, as equal beneficiaries of life and the Holy Spirit and suffering and glory. 15:5-13 summarises his aim for these Christians. (More detail is below.)

In Galatians, Paul wrote to *a church he did know*, who were being pressed into religiosity by visitors from Jerusalem. He expounded justification before God by faith and not by religious observance, nor pedigree; he demanded that they live according to the Holy Spirit. [5:22,23]

In the two letters to Corinthian believers, he was carefully and forthrightly answering questions asked by the leaders of this vibrant, seething, Christian community. He had worked among them for 18 months. He dealt with important issues, including a challenge to his own apostolic authority.

In Ephesians he expressed the lavish nature of God's love and purpose in our redemption, his removing barriers between people, his commissioning, his calling to holiness, and his strength for us in the cosmic work in which he involves us all. [3:14-21]

In Philippians he encouraged with example and happy joy in the Lord, even under arrest. [4:4]

In Colossians he exalted Christ as the true image of God, the Firstborn over all creation. This was counter- cultural to the Gnostic claims infesting Colosse. He set before them the intention of lives lived before Christ in a hostile environment. [3:12-17]

He wrote two letters to the Thessalonians, encouraging and exhorting them to live to please God, whether Christ should return in their lifetimes or not. He wanted them to stand firm and live constructively.

In the three Pastoral letters, two to Timothy and one to Titus, and in the letter to Philemon, he wrote personally, and we can detect his deep concern for them and their work for the Lord in their situations as leaders.

Romans is a key document for establishing Christians in faith in Christ. Paul wrote to people in the capital city whom he did not know, other than a handful (30) whom he named in chapter 16. So he took extra care over choice of words, and in selecting illustrations which would be understood and accepted, rather than taking them from his personal situation.

Romans is formidable, and often the keen Christian has been taught from separate parts of Romans – pieces like Justification [3:21-25a], Victorious living [6:11-14], Sonship [8:14-17], Prayer [8:26-28], Consecration [12:1-2], the Weaker Brother [14:15-17, 15:1-3]. One theme we never hear expressed is the equality of believing Jew & Gentile, because as such it is not a living issue for us. However, unity between groups in a church, or region, is much needed for receiving blessing; therefore it is important to read all the epistle, to have a guide such as Gordon Fee's, below, and so discover how foundational and comprehensive it is. Some of it is hard work! It is a tremendous blend of clear teaching with instruction on practical daily Christian living. It challenges us to grow assured faith and appropriate lifestyle. We can study it, two or three verses at a time, with commentaries; or we can read it right through (as Paul knew they would hear it in Rome). It is good to use both methods!

AN OVERVIEW OF ROMANS (derived from teaching by Gordon Fee. He is NT professor in Regent College, Vancouver. These notes come from his lectures in London, September 1996)

The Epistle would have been read aloud to the church at one sitting. Unlike us, they learned by oral means. They would have been used to picking up themes mentioned earlier, being better at synthesis than us who think more analytically.

Paul sought to unite Jews and Gentiles in the church, starting explicitly at 1:17 and concluding at 15:13.

1:1-7   Paul signs in as an apostle for the <u>gospel</u>, namely: God's Son, descendant of David, through the Spirit was declared with power to be God's Son by his resurrection – JESUS (Saviour, Son of Man), CHRIST (Messiah, Son of God), our LORD (our Sovereign). Emphatic words of v.4
   Paul's apostleship is to call people from the Gentiles.
1:8-15   Paul is longing to have personal contact with the Roman believers, both Greeks and non-Greeks, ie non-Jews and Jews.

1:16-17 **Manifesto statement**: The gospel is the power of God for salvation of all believers, both Jew and Gentile.
   "<u>The righteous will live by faith</u>".

Claim A
1:18-32   God's wrath is revealed against all men's <u>wickedness</u>; they have no excuse.   They wilfully became idolaters, exchanging God for images, so God let them degrade their bodies sexually. They worshipped and served the creatures rather than the Creator. They rejected knowledge of God, so God allowed them to have depraved minds.
2:   Whoever you are, (Jew or Gentile,) you do it, so you have no excuse to pass judgement on others, Jew or Gentile. Do you steal, commit adultery, desecrate other peoples' temples, cause dishonour to God? "Yes, but we Jews have the Law…"
N.B. Physical circumcision is nothing; circumcision is to be of the heart, by the Spirit, not by written records.
3:1-8   So, what advantage is there in being a Jew? Much! (especially) as repository of God's words [which include words of God's judgement!]
3:9   **Conclusion:** Jew and Gentile alike are under sin.
3:10- 20   <u>Guilty.</u> (The Law makes us conscious of sin.)
Claim B
3:21   BUT right relation with God, other than through the Law, has been made known.

3:21-31   Righteousness from God comes through faith in Jesus Christ to all who believe. There is no difference (between Jew and Gentile in this) – all have sinned, all are justified freely by his grace. This upholds the Law.

4:     The example of Abraham; righteousness was credited to him by faith. Abraham believed before circumcision was given (the sign of God's covenant with the Jews). Therefore he is the father of all who have faith, not just of the Jews. God credits righteousness for us who believe in him who raised Jesus to life for our justification.

Claim C

5:     STATUS   We now stand justified, in peace with God, we rejoice in the hope of glory, even if we suffer, in God's love poured into our hearts by the Holy Spirit, saved from wrath, [flashback to 1:18], reconciled by the Son's death, saved by his life.

Adam = sin & death; hence the many died, under condemnation, the result of one disobedience.

Jesus = grace & life; to the many with eternal life, upon justification, from one act of obedience.

     Grace is more abundant than sin.

Claim D

6:     ACTION   [flashback to 3:5-8] Grace's outcome: No! to sin. Our union to Christ is proclaimed at Baptism – dead and buried with Christ, raised to new life with Christ. So live the new life! Count self dead to sin but be alive to God. You were slaves to sin, now be enslaved to God.

7:1-6   The example of the Law of Marriage: obligation ends at death of one partner, and then the other may remarry; the law of sin and death ends for us through the body of Christ, so we may belong to the risen Christ, to bear fruit for God, to serve in a new way in the Spirit, not bound to the old way of Law.

7:7-13   [flashback to 3:20] the Law is good and holy; it points up the nature of sin.

7:14-25   The struggle to live according to the good and holy Law; the old Law is powerless.

8:1-4   [flashback to 5:1-11] our Status means NO CONDEMNATION, so we are FREE.

8:5-17 <u>The new way of life controlled by the Holy Spirit.</u> The Spirit of God, the Spirit of Christ lives in you, with power to live according to the Spirit in mind and deed and peace (especially between Jew & Gentile). We have received the Spirit of adoption, sonship, we relate to the Father, Abba, the Spirit testifies inwardly that we are the children of God, co-heirs with Christ.

8:18-39 The impact of our redemption on the rest of the living creation: it groans, and we groan (in suffering) too, looking to the future hope and glory. The Spirit empowers prayer, God works for good; glory is coming. We are more than conquerors now, through all hardship; there is NO SEPARATION from the love of God in Christ.

Claim E

9:1-5 <u>Tragedy</u> <u>The Jews are missing out</u>, the very people to whom God revealed himself.

9:6-29 Descendants of Abraham are not necessarily God's children. Gentiles are also called by God. This matter is entirely in his gift.

9:30-10:3 Israel has <u>mistakenly pursued</u> righteousness by works of the Law, and not by faith.

10:4-21 Righteousness – by Law works, and by faith – contrasted. The word in the heart, the good news which Israel has obstinately rejected.

11:1-10 Q.1 Did God reject his people? No!

11:11-32 Q.2 Did they stumble so as to fall beyond recovery? No! It has been the opportunity for the Gentiles to be reconciled; But Gentiles must not brag over Jews. Israel will also be delivered. <u>God is having mercy on Jew and Gentile equally.</u>

11:33-36 Our amazing God! THEREFORE
.....

Claim F

12: <u>Consecration:</u> In the light of this equal-handed mercy, Paul calls for total dedication by all, not distinguishing Jew and Gentile again till 15:5. Many members, many gifts, but one body. He spells out how to live in community in harmony, indeed as far as vengeance and enemies go.

13: Submit to government, pay taxes, pay off debts. Love your neighbour. Behave! for Christ's Day is imminent.
14:1-15:4 The strong in faith are to care for the weak, in particular over "unclean food."

> **Overall conclusion:** 15:5-13 Paul prays for <u>Jews and Gentiles together</u> to have joy and peace and
> hope in the power of the Holy Spirit.

Personal 15:14-32 Paul has ministered Christ Jesus to the Gentiles of the Eastern Mediterranean; now he plans to visit Rome on the way to Spain. [v.29 !]
16:1-24 Greetings to individuals, men, women, Jews, Gentiles, slaves and free.
Praise 16:25-27 Glory to God!

Psalm 118:29 Give thanks to the Lord, for he is good; his love endures for ever.

<u>Questions to consider</u>
What on the day of Pentecost shows us God's gracious loving-kindness?
What were the notable activities of the new community? [Act 2:42-47a]
What impact did all this have on outsiders? [Act 2:47b]
How much of that community lifestyle is appropriate for us?
Who now represents Jesus to the outside world?

Have we met Jesus in this? How might we respond?

Times were hard for Christians, and, in the next chapter, Paul and John wrote against diversions by persecutions and philosophies.

Chapter 19   The New Testament Writings

<ins>The Letters sent in Hard Times</ins>

Others besides Paul sent letters – Peter and John, apostles; and James and Jude, brothers of Jesus. They wrote to Christians about right attitudes and lifestyles in the situations of the 1st century AD; they wrote encouragement to sustain Christians under persecution; they wrote about the loving fellowship, which was a new phenomenon in the Roman world, a witness to all society. [John 13:34; 1 John 4:14-21]

<ins>Hebrews</ins> is written in good literary Greek, not the ordinary market place language of the day. It addresses a Hebrew Christian church under serious pressure to return to OT Judaism, because this would save them from persecution. At that time, Judaism was a permitted religion in the Roman Empire, but Christians faced barbaric treatment. The writer might have been Apollos, (a strong Christian of Jewish stock, well versed in Tabernacle worship, and an able teacher), or Priscilla (who had added to Apollos' knowledge), or Barnabas (originally colleague and friend of Paul). The writer gave 4 serious warnings about total loss if they apostatised, and expounded in detail how so much better the NT faith is than that of the OT.

<ins>James</ins> was Mary and Joseph's eldest son after Jesus. He wrote as leader of the Jerusalem church, so from a strongly Jewish context, about a living faith seen in consistent and enduring goodness with concern for others.

<ins>Peter</ins> wrote two letters. These were to Christians scattered by persecution, and he encouraged them to stand fast, to praise God for the death and resurrection of the Lord Jesus [especially 1 Peter 1:3-5], and to live holy lives committed to God – we have "everything we need" [2 Peter 1:3] !

<ins>John's</ins> first letter passionately declares that

Jesus is LIFE: he is both a real human being, and true eternal God.

Jesus is LIGHT: he had none of the darkness of sin, his was the atoning sacrifice.

Jesus is LOVE: he laid down his life for us, and we are to love like that. [More on this follows.]

John's two short letters were written to people and the churches behind them.

Jude was brother of James, Joseph and Mary's fourth son after Jesus. He wrote urging Christians to build one another up in the face of those who would try to divide, dilute, and destroy the faith of the apostles.

Paul's letter to the Galatians

The churches in Galatia were those in the centre of Asia Minor, to the west of Pontus and Cappadocia, and to the east of Bithinia and Roman 'Asia'. While Paul's letter to the Christians in Rome was written for people he did not know, apart from a few, he wrote this forthright letter to people whom he did know, whom he had won for Jesus, and were still unformed in faith. They were Gentiles who had been filled with joy and with the Holy Spirit when they had received the Good News. He was seriously troubled by their response to the persistent Judaisers. Judaisers insisted that for Gentiles to be saved, they had to become circumcised and keep the full ritual law of the Jews. Paul's view of these Judaisers is pretty low, as damaging purveyors of religiosity. He aims to bring the Galatians back on board to faith for continuing in Christ, restoring the joy of the Holy Spirit in their lives, and establishing a Spirit led lifestyle. As well he seeks to provide them with suitable ammunition to counter the arguments of the Judaisers. There are only two brief prayers in the letter, one in the greeting at the start, and the other at the very end. Reading 6:12-15 makes a good introduction.

1:1-5 Paul greets the Galatians, who are composed of several Christian groups. He writes who he is, an apostle sent by Jesus Messiah. (Perhaps this is a significant word, a challenge to the Judaisers.) Paul prays Peace upon them, since they are having to survive in the restless strife of their evil age. He gives the Lord his praise.

1:6-24 Alarm! Grace has been deserted! The Gospel perverted! Paul expresses his double anathema.

The Good News that he told them was not man-taught (as if a student pleasing the teacher; furthermore, the perversion was God-displeasing). Paul had received it supernaturally by authentic revelation from Jesus, who accredited him to preach to the Gentiles. He gives his pedigree: his preaching the Good News was not second hand from other apostles. He took time out in Arabia, (perhaps for a visit to Mt. Horeb), then back to Damascus where he had previously encountered Jesus. After 3 years there, he spent a fortnight with Peter to get to know him, and he met James. He went north to Syria and Cilicia, not to the Judean churches, who none the less had heard about him and were praising God for his remarkable change.

2:1-10 14 years later, he went to Jerusalem to defend his preaching; the visit was by revelation from the Lord, and Barnabas and Titus came with him. He set before the leaders his preaching, to keep its freedom from legal religiosity and rules. The leaders saw that Paul had been entrusted with the Good News for the Gentiles, as Peter had been for the Jews. James, Peter, and John gave him the right hand of fellowship. They even accepted the Gentile Titus without pressing circumcision on him.

Later, when Peter came to Antioch in Syria, his fear of offending the 'circumcision' party affected his lifestyle, and the infection started to spread. This drew down Paul's open rebuke: "We Jews by birth know we are justified not by rules but by faith. [19-20] God's law condemns us to death; the sentence was exacted on Jesus on the cross. Therefore I died (with crucified Jesus), and now I live (with risen Jesus), meaning 'not I but Christ lives in me.' My life in my human body I live by faith in God's Son – he loved me and gave himself for me. Love means laying down life, taking action, giving. This means being dead to rule-keeping, crucified with Christ. If right standing with God comes by keeping rules, Christ died in vain!"

(The density of Paul's thoughts increases.)

3:1-14 You foolish Galatians! Clearly I portrayed Jesus Messiah as crucified [which is contrary to the Judaisers' perceptions about the Messiah].

You received the Holy Spirit by faith, not by rule-keeping – are you trying Spiritual living by human effort?

Are you suffering (persecution) for nothing? Were the Spirit and miracles given by God for rule-keeping, or by faith?

Consider Abraham: [Genesis 15:6] he believed, and this made him right with God. Therefore all who believe are 'children of Abraham;' Gentiles too are made right with God by faith [Genesis 12:3]. Law-keeping – never perfect – brings a curse [Deuteronomy 27:26], but right relating with God comes by faith [Habakkuk 2:4]. So law keeping is not the same as faith.

The inexorable Law sentences the sinner to death. Jesus bore this sentence. Christ redeemed us from this curse by the cross, being hanged on a tree and therefore cursed [Deuteronomy 21:23]. Thus we have the blessing given to Abraham, and so by faith we may receive the promise of the Holy Spirit.

3:15-29 Human covenants cannot be abrogated, so Abraham's still stands. This was made with him "and to his seed" [Genesis 12:7], singular, so looking forward to Christ. The Law was given 430 years later than Abraham's covenant, and does not set the gracious promise aside.

So, why was the Law given? "Because of transgressions." The ritual law provided a system for forgiveness, until Christ came. [A suggestion to interpret Paul here:] "The Law came via angels and a mediator; (generally a mediator represents both parties, but) God is one, so there is no bargaining, because he has dictated, albeit graciously." The Law concurs with the promises, and does not oppose them. But Law observance fails to bring life. The OT says that all people are in prison to sin. The promised rescue from prison is through trust in Jesus Messiah, given to believers. The Law held us prisoners until God revealed his rescue, which is by trust in Jesus. It was a child-pedagogue [3:24] to lead us into faith for eternal forgiveness.

Therefore we are all sons of God through trust in Messiah Jesus. We have been baptised and gone public with water, and more significantly baptised with the Spirit, so owned by God who gives him to us, and clothed in Christ. Perhaps this hints at the Garden where God replaced the fig-leaves – excuses

– by skins of sacrificed animals. Now there are no divisions: between Jew & Gentile (religious divisions), slave & free (social divisions), men & women (gender divisions). [Some of this was obvious at Pentecost in the Upper Room.] To be Messiah's is to be Abraham's, and that is to be lawful inheritors of the promise to Abraham.

4:1-7 Heirs! The status of a child is no better that that of a slave. He is under trustees and guardians until a set time. Under the rule of Law, we were slaves according to the world's system. But the time has now come; God sent his Son, as a human under the Law, to redeem, so that we are given full rights as sons. We sons receive the Spirit of Jesus into our hearts, and the Spirit in us cries out "Abba!" No more ceremonialism, but Christ! No longer are we slaves, but sons and heirs.

4:8-5:1 You were slaves, according to the world's system; but now you and God know each other, so why revert to slave status? That's religiosity! You welcomed me proclaiming the Good News with joy – where's that gone? The Judaisers are keen to alienate us. I care for you as parent. I'm so puzzled about you. I tell you a deep allegory: (It may be far-fetched to us; but it appealed to the Pharisee mind!)

Abraham had one son by natural birth from a slave girl, and one son by supernatural promise from the free woman, Sarah. Hagar represents the covenant from Mt Sinai in Arabia; its children are slaves, corresponding to present-time Jerusalem, enslaved with her children. But Sarah is the free mother, the new heavenly Jerusalem, free, our mother. You are free, and like Isaac, children of promise! Ishmael persecuted Isaac – it happens today! But Ishmael was turned away, and had no right of inheritance. We are the free children! Being set free, stand firm! Don't accept slave status and duty.

5:2-12   Freedom in Christ! To become circumcised obligates full subservience to the Law. It binds people to do in order to live. Trying to be right with God for the past and in the present life by Law-keeping (by 'doing') is rejecting Messiah, which is rudely refusing Jesus, falling from grace. We have secure right-ness with God by faith, and the Spirit in us is the pledge. In Messiah Jesus, physical circumcision is irrelevant.

What matters is faith, issuing in love. You were living well and true, but someone has barged in with lies, like yeast penetrating dough. That person will face judgement. Preaching the cross causes offence, hence I face persecution. I am NOT preaching circumcision; those who do should go the whole hog and become eunuchs! [Self immolation was a pagan religious rite.]

5:13-25   Freedom means loving service, not free rein for our unredeemed nature. The false gospel brings quarrelling. "Walk by the Spirit, and you will not gratify the desires of the unredeemed nature ("flesh")... They are in conflict, so you do not do what you want" [5:16,17]. The "flesh" is there, latent in the believer. "In my flesh dwells no good thing" [Romans 7:18]. By the Spirit in us, we say No to the inclination of the unredeemed nature; this No is the strong word of the person set free in Christ. The unredeemed nature thus denied, the Spirit of the living God powerfully leads, for he is the Eternal Spirit.

Live by the Holy Spirit, follow his leading. Paul addressed them as a community of believers, more than as single individuals. Having got them right with God through faith in Christ, he was at pains to get them right with each other – No quarrelling! He warned them directly not to bite and devour each other in the unity of the Holy Spirit. If they did, then all the other horrid 'fleshly' actions would follow: [5:13-21 has 15 named actions, and there are 7 more elsewhere in Galatians.] This was the competitive self-centred life they used to live. However the community fruit of the Spirit [22,23; 9 are named] promotes the love and care of its members. The Lord expects that individuals with this growing supernatural fruit will meld with others in the community of faith. Paul's teaching about the fruit of the Spirit is for the Christians as a group, so that the Spirit synthesises them into his fellowship.

People with immoral behaviour as a regular lifestyle will not inherit God's kingdom. The Holy Spirit grows fruit in us: love (v 6,13,14), joy, peace, patience, goodness, kindness, faithfulness, gentleness and self-control. We members of Christ Jesus reckon the unredeemed nature to stay dead, crucified with Christ (at the level of passion, desire, and indulgence). Our life is by the Spirit – so keep walking in him.

5:26-6:18   No conceit, no envy! Pastoral care should sustain the fellowship, though test yourselves! Leaders need material support. You cannot cheat God: unredeemed living reaps destruction, while life in the Spirit reaps eternal life. Keep at it! Do good to everyone, especially to fellow believers.

Paul takes the pen to write in big letters a summary of his letter's conclusions [6:11-15]. His body bears the marks of beatings for Jesus. Finally he prays a grace on them. (This, and 1:3-5, are the only prayers in the letter, so unlike his other letters.)

Questions to consider
    Why does Paul give his pedigree?
    What was wrong with Peter's behaviour at Antioch?
    Why was Moses given the Law at Mt Sinai?
    With reference to 'all one in Christ,' how should Christians try to influence society? How do we cope with legislation which tells us to be 'all one <u>without</u> Christ,' to be politically correct?
    The obvious acts of the unredeemed nature can be divided up: the first five are misfunctions of the human body and its spirit. Then follow eight within the dysfunctional community (of Christians !). The last two are the inevitable product of broken relations, as alternatives to loving communities, by those who try to dissolve differences in alcohol. Paul mentions seven more to join the eight: conceit, provoking, envy, self-deception, comparing with others, boasting and devouring people. All this behaviour was normal in the non-Christian world of Roman rule, with its paganisms. Would it be true to say that, alas, it is also common today between churches, or within them, to some degree?
    What can we do for tetchy quarrelsome folk, those with a tendency to pick a bone? [5:13]
    Is the fruit of the Spirit soft fruit?

Paul's Letter to the Ephesians – a contrast to his letter to the Galatians.

Paul's letter was perhaps a shared letter to several churches in the district. He is exuberant with the love and goodness of God, and this he wants his readers to grasp and by which to be blessed in a living understanding and in a new lifestyle. We can feel the sensual and hostile world in which these Christians were immersed at the time. They were all converted Gentiles, pagans who were steeped in magic arts. Also they were aware of hard-line Jews who kept a separation from them, with their own exclusive claims. So Paul's ink flows for four and a half chapters to them with excitement that God has now abolished the distinction between Gentiles and Jews through the life-blood of Christ shed at the cross, and has fused them to make one brand of believers out of the two previously distinct strands of humanity. This 'called out' group, in God's plans, has a role both in lifestyle testimony to the world, and also to the cosmic world of spirit forces, some benign, but some adversarial, evil and demonic. In the final chapters, Paul writes with clarity about behaviour and attitudes, and with directions for households. His advice also draws illustration from the Roman soldier's equipment.

Chapter 1   After the Greeting, verses 3 – 14 are all one sentence in Paul's Greek. Vital phrases: *v.7 'God's grace... lavished on us.' v.13 'Marked in him with a seal, the promised Holy Spirit.'* It is a non-stop rush of amazement with God's grace. He has blessed us, chosen and adopted us into his loving family; he has graciously given us redemption and forgiveness, riches and wisdom, so that we perceive what he has revealed. All this is according to his purpose in Christ, to be for the praise of his glory. His gift of his Holy Spirit in us is the down-payment now for the guaranteed future complete redemption.

1:15-23   Vital phrase: *v.19 'His incomparably great power for us who believe.'* Paul draws breath for strong prayer, that through his revealing we may know him better, with enlightenment, forward looking with resurrection power. Now

Christ is enthroned as head over everything for all time, head for called-out believers in God's purposes.

Chapter 2:1-10   Vital phrase: *v.4 'His great love for us.'* Paul begins with a recall of the past dark existence of death in our human spirits; but God in his great love has brought rescue, new life through his grace and our faith to receive it. No good deeds by us, however intense, earn this; rescue is entirely his gift, even our ability to believe to receive life is his gift. Then on, God has good things for us to do.

2:11-22   Vital phrase: *v.18 'Through [Christ] we both have access to the Father by one Spirit.'* You Gentiles were excluded from the Old Covenant. You were without God, you were No Hopers. But Christ bought you in. His life-blood shed at the cross has broken all barriers, all the distinct and separating backgrounds of all human beings. Two old hostile systems have become one new body. It is peace for both, for through Christ we all have access to the Father by one enabling Spirit. So we form one household, one building, one Temple.

Chapter 3.   Vital phrases: *v.5 '[The mystery] now revealed by the Spirit.'   v.19 '[Power...] to know [Christ's] love.'* Paul's role and God's intention: Paul explains the reason why he is telling them this: he was given this as a past and hidden mystery which is now revealed by God for them, namely, that the Gentiles are heirs together with Israel. Through Christ, "his intent was that now, through the church, the manifold wisdom of God should be made known to the rulers and authorities in the heavenly realms" [3:10]. Therefore Paul prays strength into the company of believers by the Spirit, so that Christ dwells in their hearts. May they have power to know the unknowable, this love of Christ; may they be filled full of God, so there is glory in the church and in Christ, for ever!

Chapter 4:1-16 Vital phrase: *v.7 'To each one of us grace has been given.'* Paul stresses the need for worthy living, with positive unity of believers. Be humble, be gentle, and keep the unity, for we all have one Spirit, one hope, one Lord. God has given various gifts within the one household of faith: apostles, prophets, evangelists, pastors, teachers. They all contribute to building up and to resourcing believers for working for God.

4:17- 5:20 Vital phrase: *5:15 'Be very careful how you live'* For the rest of the letter, Paul writes with directness. No to evil living, Yes to a new Godly life: In the light of this, live intelligently, not as unconverted Gentiles. Put off the old self, put on the new. Speak truth, cope with anger, work and share; there is to be no foul talk, no malice. Be kind, compassionate, forgiving. Imitate Jesus' lifestyle; no hint of sexual immorality, no obscenity, coarseness, greed. Live as children of light, and take care how you live. Don't be drunk, but be being filled with the Holy Spirit. Sing, speak to Christians in spiritual songs; make music in your hearts to the Lord.

5:21-6:9 Vital phrase: *v.21 'Submit to one another out of reverence for Christ'.* Have mutual respect for one another. He uses wives and husbands in marriages as picturing the relationship of Christ with his church. He continues with children and parents, slaves and masters.

6:10-24 Vital phrase: *'Be strong in the Lord.'* Now he instructs them to put on God's armour, deliberately, to serve in the Lord's forces – There's a war on! Speak and pray in the Spirit. Be encouraged, and have peace and love and grace.

Some analysis can reveal Paul's loving heart and clear mind in always seeking to encounter the Lord. Grace and Rescue come 15 times, with the Holy Spirit 10 times; the world, the flesh and the devil come some dozen times. Paul wrote "Christ" frequently, no doubt his habitual affirmation of Jesus as Messiah against any opposite Jewish view. The epistle focuses on God's amazing Grace in rescue by the Sovereign Messiah Jesus, and equally in his empowering believers to be overcomers by the Holy Spirit. We are to stand united with fellow Christians, and as private individuals, in a toxic milieu of contrary forces, to pray and make known the Good News of the Kingdom of God.

That little phrase given as "the heavenlies" in AV and as "the heavenly realms" in the NIV comes in 5 times:
1:3 "[God] has blessed us in the heavenly realms with every blessing in Christ.

1:20 - 1:19 "...that you may know his incomparably great power for us who believe. That power is like the working of his mighty strength which he exerted in Christ when he raised him from the dead, and seated him at his right hand in the heavenly realms, [resurrection plus ascension] far above all ... power..."

2:6 - 2:4 "But because of his great love for us, God, who is rich in mercy, made us alive with Christ even when we were dead in transgressions ... And God raised us up [us! resurrection!] with Christ and seated us [yes, us!] with him in the heavenly realms in Christ Jesus... "

3:10 "His intent was that now, through the church, the manifold wisdom of God should be made known to the rulers and authorities in the heavenly realms."

6:12 "Our struggle is not against flesh and blood, but against the rulers, against the authorities, against the powers of this dark world, and against the spiritual forces of evil in the heavenly realms."

This is astonishing!

We are there in the heavenly realms, and in receipt of every blessing.

Christ is seated there, at God's right hand with total power, way over all other powers.

In Christ, we are seated there with Christ.

God's purpose is to demonstrate through the community of believers his comprehensive and right force of mind over all spiritual powers, good and malign. We are actively involved.

Our struggle is not really against other people, but against evil spiritual forces behind them and in the spirit world.

So we are right there, involved in life-long battle, but we sit with Christ in his seat of power – we have work to do! It is spiritual warfare in Christ! Compare with Joshua 5:13-15.

Note Paul's breathless exuberance!   Here are ten examples:

- 7-8   grace, lavished upon us... all wisdom and understanding
- 14   the Holy Spirit guaranteeing our inheritance
- 19   incomparably great power, mighty strength
- 3:8   the unsearchable riches of Christ

20   able to do <u>immeasurably more</u>
4:13   <u>all</u> reach… [maturity], to the <u>whole measure</u> of <u>fullness</u> in Christ.
5:15   to be <u>very careful</u>
6:7   serve <u>wholeheartedly</u>
 19, 20   <u>fearlessly</u>… <u>fearlessly</u> declare…
 24   Grace to <u>all</u> who love [Jesus] with an <u>undying</u> love

In fact, there are over 50 expressions of stressed or extreme meaning in this letter.

Questions to consider:
   Paul's prayers [1:15 on, and 3:16 on] erupt; how is it that they flow so copiously? Can we emulate this enabling?
   What gift/s have we been given? What is the purpose of each gift? Are we cultivating a gift with an aim in view?
   Are we prepared to make changes to lifestyle according to 4:17-5:20 ?
   Society has changed.   How can the passage 5:21-6:9 be worked out by Christians in the world of today?

The First letter of John

   John wrote with warmth out of his own experience of the three years of close life with Jesus, beginning with his call to leave his father Zebedee's fishing business on Lake Galilee, through the experience of the Transfiguration of Jesus and hearing the Voice – "This is my Son: listen to him!" Then onto his exposure to Jesus' cross, resurrection, ascension, and the anointing of the Holy Spirit at Pentecost. Then out of his life ministry as a totally committed apostle.

Working through his letter:
1:1-4   John testifies to the physically real Jesus, and to him as the Word of Life, making tangible his heavenly Father God, in fellowship with us all. He declared that God is Eternal LIFE.

1:5   John declared that God is LIGHT, and contrasted our bias and self deception to darkness of disobedience and sin. Three times he assessed common erroneous claims of the day: first a claim to company with God, while behaviour remains in darkness; this is a lie, not living to the Truth. (Yet if our life is in the light, we company with other believers and Jesus' death completely purifies from sin.)   Then a claim that we are sinless. But this is deception! It is not the Truth. (However if we confess to sin, God forgives, and purifies from all unrighteousness.)   And then a claim that we do not sin. This makes God a liar, for we are not hearing him speak.

John wrote to turn people from sin. Yet Christians do disobey, and then Jesus defends us since he is the atoning sacrifice for us, and indeed for all.

2:3   John wrote to affirm believers of God's LOVE as they obey his word We come to know him the Truth in us, his Love made complete in us. We should behave as Jesus did. God's Truth is as of old, and now the new word is added to the old Truth and Light: Hating is out, and we should Love our brothers. John wrote a short poem about children, old fathers, and strong young men, that sins are forgiven, knowing the eternal Father God, overcoming the evil one, and God's word alive within.

John wrote that human life is lived in the context of the world, our society organised with no reference to God, with sinful cravings, lusting eyes, and boasting. Roman society was particularly self-assertive, despising other people. John wrote that all this passes away, and Christians in contrast are to love and do the will of God. He noted that false believers leave the community of faith, and so Christians are living in 'the last hour.' These false believers deny that Jesus is the Messiah, so they are denying God the Father as well. The Holy Spirit's anointing is in us, so they cannot teach us. John urged believers to remain in the real anointing, just as he remains within. True believers are to continue in Him, ready to meet him confidently.

2:29   John teaches that right living unites the family of faith, and we experience the Father's lavish Love, of which the world is ignorant.   Our forward-looking hope makes us purify ourselves.

Now, sin breaks the law, which is the expression of the character of God. Sin is lawlessness. We are to live in him, and not be led astray by the devil, sinful from the start. God's Son came to destroy the devil's work, so God's sons have his seed, his Son, continuing in us. Right living and loving distinguishes a child of God. Love is evidence of Life, unlike Cain, the first murderer; the world hates and murders and has no eternal life.

3:16   John gave a definition of LOVE. Intrinsically, there is nothing emotional nor sentimental about this kind of Love. It is costly serving Love.
   "This is how we know what love is: Jesus Christ laid down his life for us. And we ought to lay down our lives for our brothers."

Love is not just words, but is to be delivered with our material possessions, with pity and action and truth. God knows all about this. Obedience here, prayerfully, brings deep assurance in the Holy Spirit.

4:1   John was well aware of false prophets, purveyors of pseudo-religion. He cautioned against being gullible and told his friends to test their spirits: 'does the spirit acknowledge that Jesus Christ came in the flesh?' If No, this spirit is anti-christ, from the world and acceptable in the world.
4:7   Love! Love for Christian friends; it is from God, for God is love. God sent his Son as the atonement so that we could live, not die for our sins. We should love one another. We know that we live in him because he has given us his Holy Spirit. Awareness of him in us gives us confidence as we look forward and see the coming of the day of Judgement. Do not fear. There is no fear in Love. Love God, Love brother.
5:1   This is family love – Father and Son, and born children. Therefore reinforce it by obeying God's commandments – they are not burdensome! Family obedience overcomes the hostile world; victory is one of faith, that is, belief that Jesus is the Son of God. John gave three evidences of this. Jesus came by water (perhaps the waters of normal human birth, or possibly the water

of his public baptism), by blood (his life-blood shed in atonement at the cross), and Jesus came in the Holy Spirit, the Spirit of Truth, God's testimony. He is to be believed! God has given us eternal life, and this life is in his Son.

5:13   John wrote to establish assurance in his friends, so that they knew where they stood before God, and their prayers for each other would be answered. Born of God, kept safe by God's Son, we Christians have security, understanding, and knowledge of him who is True; we know Jesus, the True God; we have eternal life. Don't let false gods attract! Keep away from idols!

John wrote in the context of the boastful Roman society that despised any attitude of loving kindness. Also, his letter contained refutation of Gnostic lies. Thus he wrote that Jesus was a real human being, that the human Jesus was the Son of God, and that Jesus' death was the atoning sacrifice for all. He refuted the idea that we do not sin, and also, that we are sinless. Gnostics, the pseudo-prophets, held that only the human spirit mattered, so how we behave is irrelevant: but John taught quite the opposite! His 20 things that 'we know' quietly cut into the Gnostic claims of superiority over Christians knowing God by the Spirit in Jesus.

<u>Some Questions to discuss:</u>
Can you distinguish between striving to obey God's commands to become christian, and striving to obey God's commands as a Christian to reinforce the family of God?
How are we to test the spirits of preachers?
Do we fear to be dead? Why?/Why not?
John wants to give us Holy Spirit-hope; what do we do about this?

The Gospels

These were written later than the Epistles. As the Apostles moved away from Jerusalem, the Writers (the

Evangelists) realised the value of collecting together the stories of Jesus that the Apostles had regularly told.

There are four gospels, and the writers, the Evangelists, tell the story according to their different characters. The first three were probably written before the Jewish War, ie before 65 AD.

<u>Mark</u> was probably the first to be written; using market-place Greek, he wrote in a forthright style that would communicate well with the Roman mind; he seems to have derived his material from the stories told by the apostle Peter.

<u>Matthew</u> incorporated most of Mark. At that time, much communication was by the Oral tradition, and mental recall was very reliable; Mark and Matthew would have listened carefully to Peter telling the stories of Jesus again and again. Matthew had also heard Jesus teaching in Aramaic, and he translated his 'sayings' into Greek. This forms Jesus' Sermon on the Mount. (It is interesting that an Aramaic language scholar has found that when Jesus sayings are translated back from Greek into Aramaic, they are particularly memorable, a bit like rhyming couplets.) Matthew's gospel is linked strongly to the O.T. and it was probably written for Jewish enquirers.

<u>Luke</u> has an educated Greek style. He used much of Matthew and Mark, and had his own material, carefully researched. He seems to have met Mary, the mother of Jesus, who was his source for the first chapters of his gospel. As well as writing his gospel, he wrote <u>the Acts</u>, describing much of Peter's work in Judaea, and Paul's work for the Gentiles, taking the Good News to Rome. He was a physician, and a loyal companion to Paul, on his journeys and in prison.

<u>John</u> wrote later, perhaps about 90 AD, as an old apostle recalling precious and meaningful events and teaching of Jesus. His gospel uses simple words and is profound, reflecting the depth of Jesus' ministry and his own deep human friendship with Jesus.

Of the four Gospels' text, 6% covers Jesus' and John's births and first 30 years of their lives; 60% present Jesus' 3 years of ministry; and 34% runs for the seven weeks from his entry to Jerusalem on the donkey, through crucifixion and resurrection, until his ascension.

Chapter 20   Witnesses to the ends of the Earth

> The story of the New Covenant grows. This chapter moves on from the mission of Paul and the apostles into the difficulties of the next centuries.

The New Life
The people who had known the human Jesus, namely his family and the disciples, all Israelites, had journeyed through amazing and positive and shattering situations. They had emerged knowing God himself and themselves in a totally new relationship. This had been borne out of their past history, the secure old Covenant of faith and tradition. Now they had been bundled unceremoniously into their present stories, to find that the Holy Spirit of their Lord and Master Jesus was not only empowering their lives, but was present within each person. This was true whether they met as an early group fellowship, or were alone, singly, perhaps working or travelling or visiting. No longer did they depend on a ministry of human priests who would intercede for them before God. In their hearts and lives, they were all able to enter and remain in God's holy presence, the inner presence of Jesus himself, resurrected, alive for evermore. There was great celebration when Christians were able to meet together and worship and hear what good things were happening across their world. They strengthened themselves by prophetic ministry [eg Acts 15:32], and with spiritual gifts [1 Corinthians 12, Ephesians 4] for everyone, leaders and led. As well as finding the new liberty [2 Corinthians 3:16-18] they grew into a new community of believers.

The Passover, the Last Supper, and the Lord's Supper.
On the occasion of the 10th plague of Egypt, all Egypt's firstborn sons died, animals as well, while Israel's were spared. In fact there was death in every household in Egypt; but in Israel it was a lamb that died, not a son. Egypt howled when the Lord passed through them, and the Israelite firstborns were safe when the Lord passed over them. In the annual celebration for the

Israelites, they were to remember for ever the terrible means by which they had been rescued from slavery and death in Egypt. This was both a memorial of the original event, displaying God's grace to their forebears, and also it was an opportunity to teach the rising generation. Passover commemorated the past, celebrated the present, and anticipated the future.

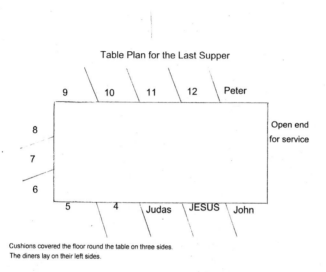

Cushions covered the floor round the table on three sides.
The diners lay on their left sides.

[The diagram is derived from Edersheim]

In Jesus' day, the festival was kept, centred on the Temple. The Israelites killed the Passover lambs in the Temple courtyard, and then celebrated Passover in their homes, roasting the lamb and eating; it was both a family affair, and a community occasion. Then at the Last Supper Jesus changed things! The NT doesn't write down what were all the well-known actions and words and songs sung in homes on Passover night. It records only the changes and additions that Jesus gave the group in the Upper Room that evening.

At the Last Supper, the ceremonial form was to recline on the left, on pillows round 3 sides of a low table; the fourth side, the end, was open for supplying the food. Peter and John had made the arrangements. Jesus had John on his right and

Judas on his left, with Peter opposite John. Jesus as head of the group, took the first of four wine-cups and spoke over it "Blessed are you, Lord our God, who has created the fruit of the vine."

Next, the head would rise and wash his own hands, but Jesus changed this into the <u>footwashing</u> for them all. Then dishes were brought to the table; Jesus dipped some bitter herbs in vinegar, spoke a blessing, and handed the bowl round. Next he broke one of three unleavened cakes, put half to one side, and passed the others round.

Then the youngest (presumably John) asked the meaning of all these observances. The standard answers fully explained the festival, the occasion, and the ritual.

Now, suddenly, there was great tension at the Last Supper; Jesus announced that he would be betrayed to the authorities by one of them - there was consternation! Peter made signals and whispered to John: "Ask him who is it?" Jesus whispered to John: "I'm giving the sop to him!" He gave the sop to Judas, but then he gave sops to all of them, so nobody knew who! This sop consisted of the flesh of the lamb with bitter herbs and unleavened bread; it was passed round on dishes. At this point, after eating, Judas left hurriedly, into the night.

The meal continued. The other half of the unleavened cake was taken, broken, and Jesus added his own words of institution: "This, my body given for you; do this in remembrance of me." Note the switch from remembrance of the original Passover, to remembrance of Jesus our Passover.

Then came the 4th cup, and he said " Drink from it, all of you. This cup, the New Covenant in my blood. Do this in remembrance of me." They sang a hymn as they left, to go to the Garden of Gethsemane for the night. They lodged out there; Jerusalem was crammed full of pilgrims.

In 1 Corinthians 5:7, Paul wrote "Christ our Passover has been sacrificed." Jesus had changed the Passover meal at the Last Supper, and Christians ever since have made the Lord's Supper to be a lasting celebration of God's rescue for all people from enslavement and death. We remember our rescue from God's righteous judgement on our rebellion and failures, by Jesus on the Cross, the life-blood of Jesus painted on us; we have his life and he has our death. At the Cross, the first born Son of God was not spared, not passed over; Jesus was forsaken by his Father; for 3 hours of darkness and terror he bore the sentence of justice; he was pierced for our transgressions, he was crushed for our iniquities, and the Lord has laid on him the sin of us all. He himself bore our sins in his body on the cross. There has ever only been one sacrifice, and all others have been imperfect shadows of the Lamb of God on the Cross of Calvary. Then came the Resurrection.

Today, the Lord's Supper is organised into a pattern; we say words together – such as 'Christ has died, Christ is risen, Christ will come again.' We hear of the body broken, that we are to take and eat bread in remembrance, to feed on him in our hearts; we recall the precious lifeblood shed, we drink the red wine, the blood of the grape, in remembrance, and are thankful. We are to remember for ever the terrible means by which we have been rescued from the penalty of our sin. It is a symbolic meal, a fellowship gathering in oneness, a united family celebration, a comm-union: yet each of us takes part individually. This transformed meal points to the future meal, to the wedding banquet of the Lamb and his bride, in the vision of Revelation 19:6-9. For now, the Lord's Supper looks back to the Lamb of God, slain at the Cross, the First Coming; and it also looks forward to Jesus' return, to the Second Coming, to the consummation of everything.

Howard Marshall has expressed it thus:
Messiah has died to bear human sin and consequences, and to overcome supernatural forces of evil.
Messiah is risen with power over the whole of creation, material and spiritual.
Messiah will come again to complete history and establish the universal and invincible realm of God.

Paul wrote about the church – the whole body of Christian believers following Jesus and being filled with his Holy Spirit. In Ephesians, the letter written to other centres too, he painted a great panorama from Creation to the End of Everything, and he put the church at the centre, for God's purpose of purveying the Good News of God's rescue plan world-wide. The church as the community of love and peace displays God's wisdom, even to the watching spiritual rulers and powers, good and bad. Maybe they see things they have not seen before, such as the transformed relationships between peoples (Jews and Gentiles) and individuals (Paul and John Mark), bringing forgiveness and unity. Their fellowship of love ran counter-cultural to the coarseness and lack of care in Roman society. Paul taught them to submit to one another, as an act of reverence to Jesus: husbands and wives, children and parents, slaves and masters. Such respect, such valuing each other, was completely foreign to the streets of Roman Ephesus. This testimony to the Lord invited outsiders to receive the Good News.

TIME CHART BC 2000 TO AD 100

Century	Jews	Christians	Writings	Sects	Year	Events	Romans
					BC		
19th BC	Abram & Sarai					Abraham entered the Holy Land	
14th	Moses					Moses led Israelites out of Egypt	
11th	David 2nd king				1000	David reigned over all Israel	
8th			Torah		722	Samaria overwhelmed	
6th	Zedekiah last king		Psalms		586	Nebuchadnezzar deported Judah	
5th	Ezra, Nehemiah		Isaiah			Restoration of Temple, Law, city wall	
			Jeremiah				
			Zechariah		333	Alexander the Great	
4th					250		
3rd			LXX of Torah				
2nd	Judas Maccabeus		Judas collected OT rolls		168	Revolt of Maccabees	
1st BC	(Herod the Great)				31	Actium victory for Augustus	Augustus to AD 14
					BC 4	Birth of Jesus, visit of Magi	
						Death of Herod the Great	
AD	(Tetrachs)				AD 8	Jesus as boy at the Temple	
1st		Apostles			27	Baptism, preaching and ministry	Tiberius to 37
					30	Crucifixion, Resurrection, Ascension	[Pilate]
		Peter and 120			30	Pentecost	
		Stephen, Barnabas			34	Paul converted	
		Philip		Simon Magus	35		
					48	Paul started missionary journeys	Caligula to 41
	Philo	James, Peter, Paul			49/50	Council in Jerusalem	Claudius I to 54
	Agrippa		3 Gospels, Letters		58	Paul taken to Rome	[Felix, Festus]
					66	Jewish rebellion, War for 4 years	Nero to 68
		Christians ...	completed LXX		70	Jerusalem sacked by Titus	Galba to 69
							Otho 69, then
							Vespasian to 79
							Titus to 81
	Council of Jamnia		John's Gospel written		90		Domitian to 96
		Clement of Rome	OT recovered	Cerinthus	95		
	Josephus				100		Nerva to 98
2nd	Aquila, Theodotian	Ignatius of Antioch	NT canon emerging		107		Trajan to 117
			Didache				Hadrian to 138

216

Romans, Jews, and Christians.

For us, two millennia later, significant Romans were the **Caesars** (listed in the Time chart). Also the provincial governors, such as Pliny, the governor of Bithynia, who oversaw the persecution there. His letter to Caesar asking for advice, and Caesar's reply, have survived.

In the Military, Vespasian was the general who waged the Jewish War from 66AD. He was made Emperor in 69, and it was his son Titus who sacked Jerusalem in 70AD. One escaping Pharisee had prophesied to Vespasian that he would become Caesar; the delighted general let him off being executed!

The defeat of **the Jews** in 70AD brought the destruction of Herod's Temple, and in 73AD the overthrow of their fortress of Masada on a crag high above the Dead Sea. The self-governing Jewish communities were dispersed permanently and finally. Later, the Romans allowed the surviving Hellenist Pharisees to hold a conference, 90AD, at Jamnia where they reconstituted the Sanhedrin, retrieved their literature and re-established their OT faith, but without a Temple.

The Christians in Jerusalem, being ethnic Jews, were caught in the conflict, and some were executed – such as James, their leader – while others had heeded Jesus' warnings [Matthew 24, Mark 13] and fled with other Jews to Decapolis. Elsewhere, the Christians were mostly not ethnic Jews and were safe until persecution broke out. That depended on who was Caesar at the time. Persecution continued on and off for 300 years from the middle of the 1st century AD.

Luke's careful researches were conducted before the Jewish War 66-70AD, and he wrote his Gospel and Acts before Paul's execution in the AD60's. At that point the story in Acts ends abruptly. The apostle John, possibly in Ephesus, wrote his gospel anonymously. Then, with persecution raging, he was exiled to the Greek island Patmos, where he wrote down the apocalyptic vision which we have – the book Revelation.

In the NT Acts and Epistles there are snap-shots of individuals serving the Lord – Barnabas (who originally befriended Paul), Luke himself (companion of Paul), Timothy (protégé of Paul, later left in charge of the Ephesian church), Aquila & Priscilla (colleagues of Paul), Titus (leader of Christians in Crete).

The Historic Faith

The Christians were united by faith, and by common lifestyle, and by Worship. They lived in a twilight spirit world of pagan syncretism, magic and astrology. Their claim of the human birth of Jesus, his crucifixion under Pontius Pilate, his resurrection which declared him to be the Son of God with power [Romans 1:4], and that he will come again as judge of the world, was founded on history. This claim was extraordinary within their society, because by contrast with their times, the faith was not a cosmic or psychological myth, part of an esoteric mystery cult.

Leaders of the Christian communities met or wrote letters, and agreed certain matters of worship. One early document is the Didache, in which some of the form of words for use in the Communion is mentioned.

Gnostics

> The Greek word GNOSIS means "knowledge". The Gnostics claimed that they had an inner knowledge of spiritual affairs, which superseded Christian knowledge of God through Jesus, Son of God, crucified and risen from death. They denied the historical facts of Jesus' life, death and resurrection. There were many brands of gnosticism, derived from syncretism with various cults.

Both Paul and John wrote emphatically about the nature of Jesus as Son of God (to the Colossians and in 1 John) so that Christian communities could discern the sea of gnostic lies and perversions about Jesus, and not be deceived. Gnosticism became a big problem as the apostolic generation died out. A dozen rival sects broke with the Christian church 80-150 AD. Many unblended raw materials of gnosticism had existed before Christianity: from Plato, from hellenised Zoroaster, and from Judaism. But in the 2nd Century, the sects were claiming 'knowledge' to transcend the faith of Christians. Significant leaders were Simon Magus of Samaria (Acts 8), Basilides of Egypt, Valentinus of Rome. One such heresy was Docetism (*that the divine could not inhabit a human body, as this was understood to be only material, either of no consequence or evil. Therefore Jesus was an illusion, a mere semblance: dokesis.*) This was asserted by Marcion, and he was excommunicated in 144. He founded the Marcionites

Canon

While many of the new Christians, Jew and Gentile, were not able to read and write, they could all remember accurately what they heard spoken. This oral tradition was reliable and was maintained into the 2nd Century AD. As the apostles and early disciples came to the end of their lives, Christians realised the value of authentic writings from that generation, and they collected these resources as far as they could. "Canon" means "measure". The canon of Scripture is the measure of belief and behaviour set down in the Bible. Clearly it was necessary for Christians to agree what writings were a correct record of the Faith. The OT scriptures have come down from earliest times. Their core is the Law; the Prophets and the Writings were built round this. For the NT, the entire body of apostolic writing was in existence within a few decades of AD70. It was quoted by Marcion and Tatian. The canon was certainly recognised by AD 190, and quoted by Irenaeus and Tertullian. The canon was the churches organised response to developments, to establish truth against false gospels claiming to be apostolic.

The NT is an authentic history. It comes from 8 men and the writer of Hebrews who were in close contact. Most of their writings, the letters and the gospels, were penned within 5 decades from mid 30's AD. These form a united testimony.

Much has been made of the cache of ancient writings found at Nag Hammadi in Egypt in 1945, and coming from a later and different era from the New Testament scriptures. They are all written in Coptic (Egyptian). They were buried about 400AD, hundreds of years after the NT writings. Of course they are valuable to academics because they have not been seen for 1500 years. The most important one is The Gospel of Thomas. It is not a gospel, but 114 collected sayings of Jesus, under Gnostic guise. They represent a different world from the Jesus of the NT. *The body is evil, containing the true self which cannot be touched by physical pain. Jesus did not have a body, so he did not die on the cross. They crucified a substitute man, and Jesus stood by laughing.* Gnostic texts have influenced the Qur'an, which in its telling of the crucifixion (4:157) says Jesus was not killed nor crucified, but it was made to seem so. "This Gnostic error lives on, in the beliefs of more than a billion Muslims, to this present day." (Michael Green)

Next comes a trace through history from the 4th century, on through the Dark and Medieval ages, to the Protestant Reformation, which, under God's Spirit, was fired up by people meeting God through the Bible. The English Bible and the Authorised Version.

Chapter 21   Preserving Scripture

Jeremiah 15:16   "When your words came, I ate them; they were my joy and delight, for I bear your Name, O Lord God Almighty."

> This chapter covers some 1500 years of Bible History, from the 4th Century Roman Empire. The Bible is our inheritance. This wonderful book tells us about Jesus. It is our source book, "for showing us truth, exposing our rebellion, correcting our mistakes, training us to live God's way." The Message – 2Tim3. The Bible has come to us today though the lives and work of the Protestant Reformers.

Psalm 40:17   "You are my help and my deliverer – O my God, do not delay."

Constantine in the 4th Century

The Early churches flourished under the apostles who appointed their elders and deacons. They were independent, yet were guided by the apostles and their successors, who took enormous care to preserve accurately the teaching of Jesus and his actions, including the accounts of the crucifixion and the resurrection. They were helped by the Oral Tradition, which was relied on, in parallel with written matter, to about 200AD. The Holy Spirit preserved the new wine of the kingdom. In the course of time the leaders formed councils to maintain unity and ensure that the apostles' teaching was being followed.

The Roman emperors had persecuted Christians for professing "Jesus is Lord," and refusing to sign up to "Caesar is Lord." However, Emperor Constantine had marched against a rival at Rome successfully under the banner of the cross. As well, his sister Anastasia had become a Christian. So he made Christianity the Roman state religion in 324 AD, at least in part for pragmatic politics. Persecution ceased. In effect, without his realising its significance, this became a Take-Over, as it introduced the Roman governing system and power hierarchy into the separate Christian communities hitherto united by love of the Lord, and bonded by the common adversity of persecution. Freedom, equality and independence disappeared. Henceforward, Christian leaders wore the Toga, which was the purple cloak of social status in the Roman Empire. Now the bishops began to wear purple! It became respectable to be a Christian.

<u>The rise of the Roman Church</u> Church government was enhanced when the Emperor gave the church a portion of land in Rome (not the present Vatican), and the role of the Bishop of Rome became significant in State eyes. Conveniently, on the basis of Jesus' word to Peter [Matthew 16:18-19 "I will give you the keys of the kingdom of heaven..."], the Bishop of Rome took command and became the father, or pope, of the church, in spite of what Jesus had said: Matthew 23:9; "Do not call anyone on earth 'father', for you have one Father, and he is in Heaven." 20:25 – 28 "The rulers of the Gentiles lord it over them, and their high officials exercise authority over them. Not so with you... [your leader] must be your servant... your slave – just as the Son of Man." The church now claimed that the pope had Peter's apostolic authority, and the keys of the kingdom. It subscribed to the canon of Scripture, but it denied believers the freedom to understand the Bible for themselves – only the church priests were authorised to interpret the Bible, to pronounce forgiveness, administer baptism and communion. It claimed universal and absolute authority. Worldly aspiration to power invaded the church leaders. So at the heart of organised Christian faith and life, Christianity became churchianity, and the Lordship of Jesus Christ was replaced by "Christendom," the Reign of the church. (As a strong tendency, centralisation of executive power happens in all societies.)

Constantine wanted Christians to support him, and to become part of the Roman Empire. However, he maintained the Roman social structures, upwards from slaves, to freedmen, Roman citizens, Magistrates, Proconsuls, Governors, Senators, to Emperor. This was 300 years after Paul wrote "You are all sons of God through faith in Christ Jesus, for all of you who were baptised into Christ have clothed yourselves with Christ. There is neither Jew nor Greek, slave nor free, male nor female, for you are all one in Christ Jesus." [Galatians 3:26 – 28; Colossians 3:11 similar]. Of course in Paul's day, there was already some degree of hierarchy with deacons, elders and overseers in the local churches. As top Christian, Constantine presided at church Councils, anxious to establish peace in troubled corners of the Empire. The Councils debated to resolve contrary views, to agree policies and order, and to identify heresies – Gnostic, Donatist, Arian – and throw them out.

Bible Versions:
The Vulgate. The church spread as far as the Roman Empire, eastwards to Syria and beyond, with the capital Constantinople and the language Greek; westwards with the capital Rome and the language Latin. The pope commissioned an able scholar, Jerome, to translate the Bible into Latin, the 'vulgar' or common language. Jerome had versions and texts that we do not have now, so the Vulgate is valuable to academics today. He worked at Bethlehem 386AD. This common language version was borne of good intentions.

The Masoretic Text. Later, the Jewish scholars, the Masoretes, independent of the Christian church, working 500 – 1000 AD, researched to produce the best authentic Hebrew OT, from old texts, and translations and versions – Syriac, Coptic, LXX, and the Talmud (civil and ceremonial laws) and Targums (Aramaic paraphrases). Their text became the only reliable Hebrew source for Christian translations, until the Dead Sea Scrolls were discovered in 1947.

Decay, Corruption and Political Ambition
When the Roman Empire fell to invaders like Attila the Hun (406 – 453), the church structures remained. However the church leadership was preoccupied with worldly matters. "Power tends to corrupt and absolute power corrupts absolutely." (Lord Acton, historian, 1887). So, as in Israel of old in the era of the Kings, money, sex and power took over within the papal structures; oppression in order to achieve political ambitions in

the name of religion dominated the ordinary faithful. The Dark Ages descended, and stretched from Syria in the east to Spain in the west, and from North Africa to the Baltic.

<u>Crusades</u> The popes rallied European rulers to fight and take the cross to recapture the Holy Land from the Saracens and Islam. These crusades began in 1095AD and each lasted from one to a dozen years. Richard I led the English contingent to the 3rd Crusade. The 8th ended in 1272, and most of them did not achieve their intended aims. The Latins were finally driven out of the Holy Land in 1291. Muslims still hold the 200 years of Crusades against all Christians today.

There were lights in the darkness. (From Andrew Clark, editor of EWG SU notes quoting Bonaventure, 1217-1274) The Minister General of the Franciscans said all learning should be directed to God. Do not believe 'that it suffices to read without unction, speculate without devotion, investigate without wonder, examine without exultation, work without piety, know without love, understand without humility, be zealous without divine grace, see without wisdom divinely inspired.' Clark's comment: the Scriptures are there to bring us to God, so that we can be transformed.

Another attempt at forced evangelism by the church began with the voyages of exploration finding the New World. The Conquistadores, like 'stout' Cortez (1485 – 1547) who invaded Mexico, were Spanish adventurers who brought Latin to America and imposed obedience to the church.

In Salisbury, just outside the Cathedral Close is a pub which used to be called The King and Bishop. This name reflects medieval facts: the King ruled the land by his soldiers, while the Bishop wielded power over all living souls because he decided who qualified for heaven. There needed to be a working relationship between them! In later days, the Lords Spiritual and the Lords Temporal worked out their relationship by debating in the parliament of the day.

The Bible emerges again

Education slowly spread, and universities were founded: Paris and Oxford in 1208, Cambridge in 1209, Karlova (Prague) in 1348, Padua in 16th Century. But the Medieval church exerted force to keep its hold on the growth of knowledge, and with it knowledge of the Bible.

However, the Protestant Reformation was inspired by people reading the Bible. Europe began to move from captivity under Medieval Catholicism to freedom of faith. Thus:

John Wyclif 1329-1384 was Master of Balliol College, Oxford, 1360. Then he held college livings, and in 1374 moved to become rector of Lutterwoth. He expounded that all authority is found in Grace. Civil rulers have the right to control clergy. Bishops and the pope proceeded against him, but to little effect as he had the support of the nobles and citizens of London. Also the church at that time was split by the Great Schism and the election of rival popes.

From Chambers Dictionary of World History:
The Great Schism ran 1378-1417, when the Catholic church divided between the pope in Rome and the pope in Avignon. A third pope was elected at Pisa in a failed attempt to heal the schism. Finally it was ended with the election of pope Martin V at the Council of Constance in 1417.

Wyclif attacked church structures as being better without bishops and pope. He denied that priests could forgive sins, together with forced confession, penance and indulgences. He taught that every man should read the Bible for himself. He began to write in English, not in Latin, and he issued tracts. He sent his 'poor priests' out to spread his teaching. He started translating the Latin Bible into English. Also he attacked transubstantiation, and so provoked condemnation by Oxford academics and the Archbishop. They compelled his followers to recant, but left Wyclif alone. From Lutterworth for 2 years until his death he continued to write powerfully insisting on inward religion rather than the formality of the day. His influence lasted 200 years up to the English Reformation. Thirty years after his death, 45 of his articles were condemned by the church Council of Constance in 1414, and they ordered that his bones be dug up and burnt! This was duly executed in 1428. Such action shows the fear and fury of the church of the day about the independent souls who read and understood the Bible for themselves.

Jan Hus 1369-1415 was born in Husinec, Bohemia, now Czech Republic. His name derives from the village. He was a student at Karlova Unversity, Prague, and then, from 1398, lectured on theology faithful to the Bible. He was influenced by the writings of Wyclif. In 1408, a papal bull alleged his teaching to be heretical, but he defied it and continued to teach. He was excommunicated in 1411, but he published his main work in 1413. He was summoned to the church Council at Constance, and given a safe travel pass there and back. When he refused to recant they burnt him at the stake, notwithstanding the safe pass. This aroused extreme fury amongst his followers in Bohemia, and it led to the Hussite Wars (1419-1436).

[Note that Tomas de Torquemada (b.1420), a Dominican monk, was responsible for 2000 burnings in the time of the Spanish Inquisition (1480-1498).]

Martin Luther (1483-1546) studied at Erfurt University 1501-05, became an Augustinian monk and was made priest 1508. His spiritual guide in the monastery at Wittenberg told him to study for his doctorate, start preaching, and take over the university chair of the Bible in 1512. Luther lectured on the Psalms, on Romans and Galatians. He preached salvation by faith alone, not by good works, nor through the purchase of indulgencies. He went to Rome, and was deeply upset by the practices there, especially the sale of indulgencies to raise funds for buildings.

> The sale of indulgences was based on the concept: "Goodness is a pool of righteousness sustained by the worthiness of the saints, the Virgin Mary, and the Son of God." This merit is transferable to those whose accounts of guilt before God are in arrears. This covers the dead sinners in purgatory with unexpired terms of suffering, and the sins of the living. The transfer of credit was effected by the pope, on the basis of Matthew 16:19: (Jesus to Peter – "I will give you the keys of the kingdom of heaven …") This was an indulgence, and could be bought by a holy action, such as a visit to a relic, or a payment, on the behalf of oneself or a dead friend in purgatory. "As soon as the coin in the coffer rings, the soul from purgatory springs."

Luther was appalled that money was raised from the fearful and impoverished in Germany by the sale of indulgences, really for the sake of buildings at Rome.

Luther drew up 95 theses against indulgences and he denied the pope any right to forgive sins; he nailed them to his church door in Wittenberg. They were burnt by the pope's agent who issued his own theses, and these were burnt by Luther's students. At first the pope kept silent, but in 1518 he summoned Luther to Rome. However both the university and the state prince blocked this. Luther attacked more boldly, and Erasmus and others joined the conflict. Luther wrote to the Christian Nobles of Germany attacking the papal system. A papal bull was issued against him, but he burnt it in public in Wittenberg. Germany became amazed and excited. Luther was summoned to appear before the Holy Roman Emperor in 1521 at the secular Diet of Worms. He stood his ground, and he declared that Jan Hus had been right. At the end of his defence, he said *"My conscience is captive to the word of God. I cannot and will not recant anything, for to go against conscience is neither right nor safe. Here I stand. I cannot do otherwise. God help me – Amen."* Accused of heresy, threatened with excommunication and death, he spoke these fateful words as he took his unyielding stand against the abuses of the medieval church. He was outlawed, but as he returned from Worms he was arrested by the prince of Saxony and kept for his own safety at Wartburg castle for a year. But for this interception, he would have been kidnapped and burnt at the stake. While there, he translated the Bible into German from better texts of Hebrew and Greek than those of the Latin Vulgate; also he wrote other works. Civil unrest brought him back to Wittenberg in 1522, where he rebuked lawlessness of the people, and oppression by the rulers. Luther was a difficult person to know; he breached with the English King Henry 8, with Erasmus, and with Zwingli and other Swiss theologians. He married in 1525 a former nun who had withdrawn from the convent. His loyal friend Philip Melanchthon represented him at the Augsburg Confession 1530, the apex of the German Reformation.

Two extracts from "Here I stand" (Bainton)
1. Martin Luther's testimony of being born again: "I greatly longed to understand Paul's epistle to the Romans and nothing stood in the way but that one expression, "the justice of God," because I took it to mean that justice whereby God is just and deals justly in punishing the unjust. My situation was that, although an impeccable monk, I stood before God as a sinner troubled in conscience, and I had no confidence that my merit would assuage him. Therefore I did not love a just and angry God, but rather hated and murmured against him. Yet I clung to the dear Paul and had a great yearning to know what he meant. Night and day I pondered until I saw the connection between the justice of God and the statement that "the just shall live by his faith." Then I grasped that the justice of God is that righteousness by which through grace and sheer mercy God justifies us through faith. Thereupon I felt myself to be reborn and to have gone through open doors into paradise. The whole of Scripture took on a new meaning, and whereas before the "justice of God" had filled me with hate, now it became to me inexpressibly sweet in greater love. This passage of Paul became to me a gate to heaven. If you have a true faith that Christ is your saviour, then at once you have a gracious God, for faith leads you in and opens up God's heart and will, that you should see pure grace and overflowing love. This it is to behold God in

faith that you should look upon his fatherly, friendly heart, in which there is no anger nor ungraciousness."

2. The mercy and goodness of God seen in Scripture: "When I am told that God became man, I can follow the idea, but I just do not understand what it means. For what man, if left to his natural promptings, if he were God, would humble himself to lie in the feedbox of a donkey, or to hang upon a cross? God laid upon Christ the iniquities of us all. This is that ineffable (beyond being expressed) and infinite mercy of God which the slender capacity of man's heart cannot comprehend and much less utter – that unfathomable depth and burning zeal of God's love toward us. And truly the magnitude of God's mercy engenders in us not only a hardness to believe but also incredulity itself. For I hear not only that the omnipotent God the creator and maker of all things, is concerned for me, a lost sinner, a son of wrath and of everlasting death, that he spared not his own Son but delivered him to the most ignominious death, that, hanging between two thieves, he might be made a curse and sin for me, a cursed sinner, that I might be made just, blessed, a son and heir of God. Who can sufficiently declare this exceeding great goodness of God? Therefore the holy Scripture speaks of far other than philosophical or political matters, namely of the unspeakable and utterly divine gifts, which far surpass the capacity both of men and of angels."

William Tyndale (1495-1536) at Magdalene Hall, Oxford, first as student, then as Chaplain to a family in Gloucestershire 1515-1524. He approached Tunstal, bishop of London for help to translate the Bible into English and was refused. He went to Germany, to Hamburg and on to Wittenberg to meet Martin Luther. In Cologne he began printing his English NT 1525, but he had to flee to Worms, where 3000 NTs were printed. Hundreds of copies were bought by opponents on orders of Tunstal, and burnt, and the money from the sale enabled even more to be printed! He moved to safety at Marburg 1527. In 1531, secretly in Antwerp, he published his first edition of the Pentateuch, complete with comments in the margins. He sent a special copy of his NT to Anne Boleyn, and under her favour the first printing of the English NT was run in England. But he was betrayed in Antwerp in 1535, tried for heresy, strangled and burnt in 1536 (5 months after Anne was beheaded). From Tyndale's work, other English versions were made, completing the OT. Such were Coverdale's, the Great Bible, the Geneva Bible, and others.

Bible Translations

There had been vitriolic denunciation of the Reformation leaders, and Hus and Tyndale had been burnt at the stake. The Alps protected both Lutherans and Calvinists from any possible military action by the pope in Rome. Calvin, safe in Switzerland, had modern translations of the Bible made in several languages, including English. European protest against the corrupt Roman church, its false doctrines, and its stranglehold on people, ranged from Lutheranism in Germany and Scandinavia, to Calvinism in Switzerland. It is sad that Calvin is only thought of in terms of predestination; so much of his Bible exposition is inspired. He expounded the Bible and sought to recreate a church structure in line with the NT (c.1540). He sought to replace the Roman church structure with presbyters and elders; many agreed with this, but Luther favoured an Episcopalian system. Luther retained the concept of the Real Presence of Christ in the sacrament, whereas Calvin taught that there was no change of substance when the Bread was consecrated. Luther's Bible made German the main language of Germany and this helped unite the territory.

In England, Henry 8 (1491 – 1547) was a strong king, a catholic who refused papal rule and authority in his dominion. The pope excommunicated England and its king, hoping for popular support to force the king to obedience. Henry wanted his people to have religious ministry, but on his terms. Thomas Cranmer (1489 – 1556) was a bishop who assisted him in his divorces and marriages, and Henry made him his archbishop. Cranmer was a quiet and able person. He devised the Book of Common Prayer, the Ordinal (for making ministers and bishops) and the Articles of Religion. Quietly, freed from Roman shackles, he married, and Henry never discovered it! He paved the way for the Church of England to become protestant, a (true) catholic church, reformed from Rome, without moving to Lutheranism, or into Calvinist doctrines and structures. He perished in Mary's violent reign, but Elizabeth took up Cranmer's Protestantism.

Queen Mary (1516 – 1558), brought up a Roman Catholic, really wanted the pope to restore England to communion, and tried to eradicate the protestants. She put her half-sister Elizabeth, daughter of Anne Boleyn, in the Tower, while burning many for treason. But she died childless. On one woman's infertility hung the future of England as Catholic or Protestant! Elizabeth, who had been brought up as a Protestant, was crowned 1558AD.

The English Bible

The apostolic faith of the Bible had been eclipsed for about 1200 years in England, up to the reign of Elizabeth I. This means of meeting with God was reopened for ordinary people in their normal language when the Authorised Version was printed and became available. The Bible was of first importance in those times and is today. All this will help us to see how it is that we have the immense privilege of the freedom of access to God's Book nowadays, at the cost of some hundreds of people's lives.

Elizabeth I (1533 – 1603) Nobody could make her out. At times, she appeared ambivalent about the Faith, but she persistently defied Spain and papal claims. She worked hard on parliament and made them pass laws which established Cranmer's design for a protestant Church of England. This was the Elizabethan Settlement. Richard Hooker (1554 – 1600), at one time Bishop of Exeter, assisted the process by writing "Of the Laws of Ecclesiastical Polity," an 8 volume work which set the tone and direction of Anglican theology. An able man, he was insistent on practical application of Christian living: "To our security our sedulity is required."   'Anglican theology' is that framework which governs the Church of England, replacing the legislation of the Roman Catholic Church. It avoided Lutheran doctrines of church governance and its tenets about the Mass, on the one hand. On the other hand it avoided Calvinist opposite extremes, and retained the structure of Bishop, priest, and deacon, as ordained ministers.

James VI of Scotland (1566 – 1625) became James I of England 1603, a protestant who at first seemed lenient towards Roman Catholics; but he hardened his attitude to the militants. So the Gunpowder Plot (1605) followed.

The "Authorised Version." (AV) Under James' encouragement, 47 learned men in teams produced this English translation in 1611. It is said that 60% of its text derived from earlier English versions, including 19% from the Geneva Bible and 18% from Tyndale's works. The AV "unites high scholarship with Christian devotion and piety." (Skelton) Copies were placed in every church to be read in every service. 400 years later, the modernised American New King James Version (NKJV) is still taken by many Christians as the authoritative version. But over the years, new discoveries and much improved understanding of the ancient texts have called for fresh versions and revisions, such as the New International Version (NIV), which is continuing to be updated year on year, without being tethered to the AV.

There were other protestants who found fault with the new version of the Church of England, because they were more Calvinist, such as John Knox who led reformation in Scotland. Legal Acts of conformity, which were intended to force Roman Catholic priests to abandon the Latin Mass and to use the English Prayer Book, also led to dissent by some protestants. These dissenters became Non-Conformists. Some of them promoted public antipathy to Roman Catholics. John Foxe wrote his Book of Martyrs while in Switzerland 1556-9, and copies were placed in churches and cathedrals. The copy in St Paul's, Salisbury, is open at the page describing the trial and burning of 3 martyrs near the church building, John Maundrel and two other protestants. Others were godly men who preached from the Bible. John Bunyan, tinker and preacher in Bedford, spent time in gaol, and wrote Pilgrim's Progress – part 1 in 1678, then part 2 in 1682, once more in gaol.

Reformers and martyrs suffered in their faithful stance for the Lord. This is a truth reflected in the Psalms. Thus:

Psalm 40 encapsulates David in some trouble, (and to some degree, Jesus obeying Father-God, in the face of Israel's leaders).

[1]   King David, in later years perhaps, reminds himself of times past when the Lord redeemed him from a hopeless experience, helpless in a slimy pit; he cried out to the Lord, and after a patient wait he was lifted on to solid ground and given a shove in the right direction. This encouraged those who saw all this to trust in the Lord for themselves.

[4]   He can see God's goodness poured out on faithful individuals and on the Israelites in general – too many blessings to count!

[6]   It was not the religious activities that brought good things; rather they were released through his utter submission and maintained commitment to obey and serve the Lord. The willing slave would stoop to have an earlobe pierced to the doorpost of his master. Thus openly signed, he was appointed to proclaim his Lord's uprightness, faithfulness and truth to the crowds in the Temple. For David, servanthood to the Lord was greater than kingship of Israel. (Likewise, Jesus openly taught the Temple worshippers in the teeth of those who were hostile. Martin Luther stood courageously before the Holy Roman Emperor.)

[11]   Now the Lord's servant returns to his present situation with many active enemies and with his own failings. He prays for protection in God's love and truth, for help to come quickly, for opponents and mockers to be shamed, and for fellow seekers of the Lord's rescuing to have joy and exalt him in open worship.

[17]   He ends with what he is, without resources and vulnerable, and with what the Lord is, my help and my rescue:

"My God, come, now!"

Questions for discussion:

How would you respond to a Muslim who holds the Crusades against you?

Suppose that you were brought up in a practising Hindu family, in a strict Hindu State. You know of another local family in which a 16 year old daughter had been executed by her father for her apostatising to Christianity. On your radio in bed at night, you keep hearing the Gospel of Jesus Christ attractively presented in your own language. It is absolutely you! In bed, under the pillow with earphones in, you turn to Jesus, and the Holy Spirit fills you. What is your survival package?

The Protestant Reformers stood faithful to the Bible because they encountered God through it. That is why this chapter is called "Preserving Scripture." The next chapter moves on to the present day.

Chapter 22   "Be faithful, even to death…"

> The Bible has been of first importance through history. Church life in England has waxed and waned as people of influence have responded to their encountering with God through the Bible. The Scientific enterprise sprang from some Christians exploring the natural world, while others set up Mission as the world opened before them. The Bible impacts today.

Church Life

The English church declined in spirituality, but the Lord raised up individuals to bring revivals. One such person was John Wesley.

John Wesley (1703 – 1791) was brought up in a Christian home; he was ordained and lectured in Greek at Oxford. He joined a group round his brother Charles, known as the Holy Club or Oxford Methodists, founded in 1729. George Whitfield joined them in 1730. In 1738 John attended Moravian meetings in Aldersgate Street, where he heard read Luther's Preface to Romans; his heart was "strangely warmed" and he was assured of salvation. (Charles was similarly blessed that year.) John determined to bring this to others, but his enthusiasm alarmed parish clergy and bishops, and they prevented him preaching in churches. He began preaching the Biblical Gospel in the open air in Bristol in 1739, where he founded the first Chapel. He reached the impoverished masses, preached 40,000 sermons, hated horses yet travelled 250,000 miles (400,000km) on horseback, wrote educational books and ran the Methodist Magazine, determinedly keeping Methodism within the Church of England. (Charles wrote more than 5,500 hymns which were an effective way of conveying the Gospel.)

Science

Meanwhile, Scientific Enterprise had been growing. Many Christians saw this as their respectful exploration of the works of the Creator. Galileo, b.1564: The Italian inquisition excommunicated him for writing that the sun is the centre of the solar system, rather than the Earth – a conviction which was only retracted in 1992. <u>Robert Boyle, b 1627</u> wrote that his experiments were exploring the works of the Creator. <u>Isaac Newton, b.1642:</u> at the end of his life, he said "I have been but a child paddling on the shore of the ocean of knowledge." Robert Hooke, James Joule, Lord Kelvin, were pushing into different areas and discovering relationships between the quantities they measured.   Naturalists were classifying living organisms. Mendel, an abbot in Bohemia, discovered laws of inheritance from observing peas in his monastery garden (1863). Charles Darwin developed Evolution (1859). Cosmologist Fred Hoyle (c.1950) coined the term 'The Big Bang' in order to detach himself from this, in favour of his own theory of Continuous Creation, in an equilibrium state.

<u>Charles Darwin, b.1809,</u> published "On the Origin of Species by means of Natural Selection," and it precipitated a heated debate. For hundreds of years, the church had taught that creation was by miracle in 6 days, and Irish archbishop Ussher had worked out from the new Authorised Version that God had created it all precisely from the early morning of Monday 23rd September of 4004BC. (If it really was in 6 days of miracles, one wonders why God took so long. Why not all in one split second?) The controversy of Science and Religion continues needlessly and artificially today, especially in the USA, and is sometimes acrimonious. (See chapter 2)

Mission

As the world was being explored, <u>The Missionary Enterprise</u> also sought to take the Bible and the Christian Gospel to heathen lands.

Henry Martyn, (1781 – 1812), curate under Charles Simeon at Cambridge, went to Turkey, saying "Better burn out than rust out!" He died young of sickness on the field.

David Livingstone, (1813 – 1873) went to Africa, with the Universities Mission to Central Africa (UMCA).

Hudson Taylor (1832 – 1905) went to China, and began the China Inland Mission (CIM).

C.T.Studd was one of the Cambridge Seven, and from him arose the Worldwide Evangelism for Christ (WEC), mainly in Africa. This operates now in other places as well as in Africa.

> The Cambridge Seven was formed in 1884; they were young men from privileged homes who had responded to Christ through DL Moody's evangelism. They were accepted by Hudson Taylor for mission in China with the CIM. CT Studd was a brilliant cricketer, playing for England until then. Their public commitment to Biblical Gospel mission caused a great stir in universities and in London society. Their last public meeting before leaving for China was in 1885.

The Victorians took the Gospel, but also the Victorian culture and ecclesiology. Some was with imperial, political and business interest, dressed up as 'church'. Mission Agencies have now been purged of this, yet always need to watch out for religious traditions, and seek to work the works of God.

Today's Scene

<u>Gnosticism</u>   Michael Green quotes Duncan Greenlees as a modern Gnostic. He writes: *"Gnosticism is a system of direct experiential knowledge of God, the Soul of the Universe. In the early centuries of this era among a growing Christianity, it took on the form of the Christian faith, while rejecting most of its specific beliefs. Its wording is therefore largely Christian, while its spirit is that of the latest paganism of the West."*

Michael Green writes: All this matters today. Without integrity, our civilization is heading for disaster. Today's gnostics deny the historical truth of the NT, and supplant it with outright lies. In Society religious belief of any sort has greatly declined; marriage has become an option for the few. Overall apathy may turn into persecution. "Where there is no energising faith, civilizations crumble." (AJ Toynbee) The Western world has been built on the Christian faith – universities, science, hospitals, human rights. Coherent faith (contrast Gnostic ambivalence) brings Virtue; Virtue in society brings Freedom; Freedom supports Faith. This circle is being eroded as Christianity is discounted. The church is being penetrated by modern Gnostics, particularly the powerful Episcopal Church of the USA. Individually, modern Gnosticism is attacking and alluring people to believe lies. It would reduce NT Christianity to a Mystery Cult. Now, there is aversion to Christianity, and yet there is hunger for spirituality. Theism is out. People want an all-inclusive neo-paganism, no authority, all religions much the same; they accept nature worship. Fact and Fiction are confused. The aim is to replace salvation in the death and bodily resurrection of Christ in history with a return to Mother Nature and pagan pantheism.

<u>The Bible in Today's Roman Catholic church</u>   This church is now encouraging personal Bible reading. 253 bishops at the Vatican have met (Autumn 2008) to discuss the Bible, to meet the Bible Society, and support its publication of the Lectio Divina to help understanding the Bible; they want every Catholic family to have a Bible and read it and pray with it. Good can come from this.

Roman Catholic Worship: many women find mother Mary more a person to relate to than male celibate priests and hierarchy, and thus, sadly, not to Jesus. Of course, the Lord understands this, and draws them towards himself. Bible reading will help them!

<u>Charismatic Renewal</u>   Many date the first records of this 'spirituality' from the "Great Awakening" revival in the USA in the ministry of Jonathan Edwards (1703 – 1758), a forceful Calvinist preacher. The Holy Spirit came, again in the USA, with the Pentecostal movement starting in 1901. The Welsh Revival, and the Hebridean Revival were Charismatic, and the renewal reached England again, and Norway, in the 1960's. A feature of the Charismatic Renewal is its crossing traditional boundaries; at the present time, there is some renewal taking place in Roman Catholic churches in Germany and France, as well as in England; Anglo-catholics have held a renewal conference at Caister, Norfolk. But many Conservative Evangelicals, especially those in Reform churches, hold an authority to keep their members out of this renewal movement. They allege that Charismatics are in serious doctrinal error, and that Prophetic words given since the finalising of the NT canon,

(ie about the start of the 2nd Century AD) are unnecessary and are likely to be the words of the devil! Of course there is much more to personality than intelligence and proclamation alone.

David Watson (1933 – 1984) brought renewal to St Michael-le-Belfry, York. Jacquie Pullinger from St Mary's Reigate worked in China, and David and Mary Pytches took the renewal to South America, returning and founding the New Wine conferences. At Holy Trinity, Brompton (HTB), Raymond Turvey nurtured the stirrings of the Spirit (1979). He said "We have proper liturgy and robed choir for Morning Prayer; in the evening we have informal worship without robes! The vicar," speaking of himself, "wonders about this, but secretly he rather enjoys it!" He was followed by John Collins, Sandy Millar, and now Nicky Gumbel, with the Alpha Course. The Airport church Toronto (originally a Vineyard church,) received The Father's Blessing, and HTB received a fresh injection from Toronto. Diocesan Renewal Groups have grown. Church planting has brought the Charismatic renewal to many towns. The Church of England has accepted the rising up of Fresh Expressions, of which Network Churches in renewal are but one.

Underneath all these various church activities is the Bible, which is the means of encounter between the reader and God.

This has brought us from Moses in 2nd millennium BC to God's work at the start of the 3rd millennium AD. Consider the broad sweep of spiritual conflict over some 3500 years: Moses stood up to Pharaoh [Exodus 11:1-8], Micaiah to Ahab [1 Kings 22:26-28], Daniel and friends to Nebuchadnezzar [Daniel 3:14-23], Esther to Haman [Esther 7:1-7]; centrally, Jesus to Caiaphas [Matthew 26:62-64]; then Paul to Caesar [2 Timothy 4:16-18]; also Martin Luther, John Wyclif, and William Tyndale, and the 400 English protestants burnt in Queen Mary's reign. These 400 Marian martyrs included 5 bishops: Hooper at Gloucester, Ferrar at St David's, Latimer and Ridley together at Oxford in 1555, and Cranmer also at Oxford in 1556. Latimer's last words: "Be of good comfort, Master Ridley, and play the man. We shall this day light such a candle by God's grace in England, as (I trust) shall never be put out." These were heroes of faith, fit to be added to those of Hebrews 11.

Likewise, in the **Psalms**:

<u>Psalm 123</u> was sung by people who had suffered much injustice, stating their case for God's mercy, having had to endure contempt and ribaldry from the arrogant. They are faithful servants, watching for any indication in their lives from God.

<u>Psalm 116</u> was perhaps on the tongues of the Lord's servants as he delivered them for a new lease of life in serving him, or not, as 'the fire of martyrdom' began to blaze strongly. "O Lord, save me! Praise the Lord." This is both a life and a death Psalm. To the Lord, "precious in the sight of the Lord is the death of his saints."

<u>Psalm 95</u>

[1] "Come ..." This is a strong invitation for us to be together and raise the united voice of worship, singing, shouting, thanking and extolling. The Lord is the solid foundation of rescue, the Rock that poured out water in the wilderness then, and filling today's believers now with the Holy Spirit.

[3] The LORD is – I AM – HE IS – King on high, creator of land and sea, high and deep.

[6] "Come ...," it is compelling! Worship on knees, HE IS our God, our Shepherd and we are his flock.

[7b] It was at Meriba Massah that the faithless Israelites did not trust the Lord in demanding water; they upset Moses, and yet the Rock poured out water to supply their need. Already the Lord had turned them all back from the Promised Land, to spend time in the wilderness until the generation of rebels had died out. Only then would Joshua lead their successors into the Promised Land.

So today, listen for the Lord's voice; come and worship and bow down to our King, the "Rock."

Down the ages, where Christians have opened themselves to the Lord, the Lord of the Scriptures, and hearing him have become obedient doers of his word, there is important blessing for the whole world. Like the Reformers, the old Missionaries, and the current Mission Agencies, there may be a high price to pay, but our privilege is to tell others, especially the children. May we all encounter and receive the Lord of the Bible as we search the Scriptures.

Questions for discussion:

Is it really possible to keep apart our politically correct community life, and our active living the Christian Life with the offence of the cross?

How would you approach your MP to complain that your stand as a known Christian has cost you promotion, or your job?

You are an interviewing governor of a church school. Before the panel is a practising Muslim applying for a teaching post, and he has good qualifications. Others are less impressive. Can you appoint someone else?

Today, liberal and gnostic pagans assault the Bible's truth and would replace it with psychobabble and outright lies. 2000 years of wrong have passed since the Baby was born in Bethlehem…Jesus is due to come back as glorious Lord and King, any day now! The final chapter reviews the Last Day and the Consummation of All Things, from the Scriptures.

Chapter 23   The Second Coming

> So far, so good! Now we look ahead with hope, to the Christian Hope! Date: No-one knows when the Son of God will return. [Mark 13:22-23 refers: don't be deceived by false prophets; v32]

In some Psalms, the work of the Messiah is prophesied:
Psalm 21 is about David as King of all Israel, probably when he was established against all enemies from the border of Egypt to the Euphrates. But Psalm 21 also foreshadows The Lord Jesus Christ.

O LORD, I AM! *This is the First Coming.* The King (Jesus) rejoices in your strength. He has great joy in the victories you give, over death and destruction. You have given him all he wanted, with nothing refused. You welcomed him with rich blessings, pure radiant glory crowning him.

[3-7]   *Resurrection and Ascension*: Eternal life, imperishable, overthrowing death gloriously, in splendour and majesty. Abundant blessing comes, and royal panoply with everlasting life. Joy, love and security are established for sure

[8-12]   *The Second Coming*:   There is the victory with the fire and wrath of judgement. The King, (Jesus, Messiah) sits enthroned in Judgement on all enemies. (Yes, there are enemies, and there is a war on). At the King's coming again, they will be judged, consumed in wrath and fire and destruction.

[13]   All people will exalt the LORD in song and praise. Here is the ultimate worship in heaven:

"Be exalted, O I AM in your strength – we will sing and praise your might."

After the cross and the resurrection, Jesus kept appearing to his friends, establishing that truly he was resurrected from death, and not merely resuscitated. Then he left them on the hill top near Bethany and Jerusalem [Luke 24:50-51]. He was taken up into heaven, and a cloud hid him from their sight. Two angels announced, **"This same Jesus ... will come back in the same way as you have seen him go into heaven."** [Act 1:9-11]

Peter shared this message with Temple goers [Act 3:19-21]: <u>Jesus will come back!</u> The birth, human life and death of Jesus by crucifixion, with the Resurrection and Ascension, was the historical event known as "The First Coming." When he returns, it will be "The Second Coming."

This is a vast topic! There is a great quantity of the Bible about the Second Coming. When we search the scriptures with an eye to the Final Consummation of all things, we are looking through a <u>telescope</u> at the future. 'Tele' means at a distance; 'scope' means seeing, so we see into the distance; we gaze at distant mountain ranges with many details partially hidden, merging, and overlapping. Likewise we cannot know whether the various actions of the Lord's return all happen together, or whether the actions happen gradually or by stages, perhaps happening as an evolving rolling action over millions of years. And if the Consummation is like this last idea, we may not be able to perceive the true order of events. But we do know that Jesus will come back, whether there is a Big Crunch, or a staged and controlled work-out. Now, we are explorers moving forward in time. To set an overview scene once again, this diagram represents the <u>War of the Kings</u>:

> **GOD REIGNS OVER ALL**
> **CREATION**: God in complete control, working with intense interest and loving care.
> **REBELLION**: The creation is seized by the Usurper who tempts Man's loyalty to God
> **MAN FALLS**
>   BC
> **THE FLOOD**: God's judgement on rebellion;   Noah saved
> **THE RESISTANCE MOVEMENT**: God calls Abraham who responds and receives
> **GOD'S (OLD) COVENANT**   The family becomes The Nation of the ISRAELITES, but is enslaved.
> Moses and the Exodus
> David   Kings and Prophets   Failure from within
>
> **GOD DECLARES WAR**: The birth of JESUS
> **BATTLE ROYAL:**   **The decisive victory of the CROSS over the Usurper**
>
> **RESURRECTION**
> **ASCENSION**
> **GOD'S NEW COVENANT** given at PENTECOST to Christians
>   AD
> **TODAY**:   mopping up the doomed but resisting and vicious Usurper
>
> **CHRIST RETURNS:**   All resistance to the Rightful King ceases and there is new life and time
>   **GOD REIGNS OVER ALL**

Look Back

But first, we can <u>glance back</u> and see that some previous mountain ranges of prophecy have already been crossed. Here is a piece of Isaiah, perhaps written about 750BC. He has overlapping prophecies; we can see bits that have been fulfilled in the fall of the 2 kingdoms.

Isaiah 2:2-5   NB "In the last days..." v.5 is advice for the spiritually committed. But...

2:6 - 22   refers to the Israelites who will be broken because of their idols (8,17). They will flee to caves; the Lord comes to shake the earth (19,22).
3:1 – 4:1 Woes are portioned out to the wicked: corrupt judges 2, oppressing elders14, crooked craftsmen 3,14, worldly women 16.
4:2 – 6   "The branch of the Lord" is code for David's descendent. Note the repeated words "In that day…"
Isaiah 2-4, written say 750BC, has prophetic details of what happened from 730 BC onwards; but as well there are hints of the Judgment on the Last Day. Assyria overthrew Israel, and threatened Judah; but it was Babylon that overthrew Judah 587 BC; restoration came about from 538 BC, fulfilling the earlier prophecies. Isaiah goes on to have the prophecies of the suffering Messiah, and of the mighty victor. With Roman rule came the Crucifixion 30's AD, and Resurrection, Ascension, Pentecost, Mission with Persecution; then came Decline 300AD, Reformation renewals 1500AD on; so to our 3rd millennium, right up to today!! But many of Isaiah's descriptions also fit the distant scenes of the Judgement in the End times, ahead of us. Therefore keep reading the OT. It should make us watch where and how we walk, at this present time.

Look Now

Next consider "NOW". Life with the Lord today is a taster of better things to come: "[They] have tasted the goodness of the word of God and the powers of the coming age…" (extracted from Hebrews 6:5)

It is worth studying carefully Paul's 'heavenly realms' in Ephesians:
  a. 1:3   "He has blessed us in the heavenly realms…" The place of blessing is where we are now.
  b. 1:20 "He raised [Christ] from the dead and seated him… in the heavenly realms." Jesus was raised up and he ascended and now is seated. "It is finished!" [John 19:30] The plan completed!
  c. 2:6   "God raised us up with Christ and seated us with him in the heavenly realms." It is where we are now: AMAZING!

d. 3:10 "Through the church... [God's] wisdom... made known... in the heavenly realms." God plans to use us, corporately, <u>now,</u> where we are.

e. 6:12 "Our struggle... against... powers of this dark world and... spiritual evil in the heavenly realms." Individually, we war as soldiers for God, here and <u>now</u> in this dark world with spiritual evil, in these heavenly *realms* where Jesus *reigns,* not another. Our warfare is NOW, taking part in the Rightful King's mopping up operation. The enemy is a defeated enemy, despite his propaganda and persistence.

John, in 1 John 1 & 2, writes so that believers do not commit sin [1:5-2:1a]. But he also teaches that if we do sin, our wonderful Lord has provided a way back to him [2:1b-2].

Paul teaches that our citizenship is in heaven... [Philippians 3:20-21] Citizens should act as agents of their State, in the place where they are living. So Christians on Earth should act as agents of Heaven. [2 Corinthians 5:17-6:2]

Look ahead

Therefore we should <u>gaze ahead</u> confidently in assured hope. And we should get ready for the Second Coming, because to be forewarned is to be forearmed. Let us see what lies in store.

There will be *persecutions* and *terrible times* [John 16:1-4; 2 Timothy 3:1-5]. This was true for the 1st Century Christians, and is now true of 21st Century Christians in some places. It may happen to us.

There will be *signs in Nature* [Luke 21:11]. Is global warming and climate change something of a sign?

We are to *look up, stand, and have courage* [1 Thessalonians 4:18] "The ultimate encouragement for the suffering Thessalonians was that Christ would one day return and they would then fully enter into their salvation and live with him. Their foes would be vanquished and they would be vindicated." (SU) A regular feature of the NT is 'encouragement'. Barnabas was the Son of 'encouragement'. Paul wrote to the Thessalonians with strong words and pictures of 'encouragement', such as God parenting believers as his children..

There will be *Wars and rumours* of wars – Congo, Afghanistan, Iran, Korea, &c. [Mark 13:7]

The *trumpet* will sound [1 Corinthians 15:52, 1 Thessalonians 4:16] and there will be the *general resurrection* – of all shades of the dead, the *just and the unjust*, plus the merging before the Lord with those living at the time. [John 5:28-29; 14:1 –3; 1 Thessalonians 4:17] (Trumpet? The volcanic vents at Horeb!)

It is the realisation of *our hope*, for which we have purified ourselves [1 John 2:28 – 3:3].

The last *defiance is crushed* [many prophetic words: Revelation 19:11 – 21]. v.13,14 – Jesus alone has shed his own life-blood, and his troops do not. The enemies are thrown into the lake of burning sulphur, the lake of fire, the second death [Revelation 19:20; 20:10, 14-15].

Then comes *the Last Judgement* of all humankind as individuals [Daniel 7:9-14; Matthew 13:24 – 31; 25:31 – 46; Revelation 20:11 – 15].

It important to understand that these are *pictures*. Pictures of the future express a reality, but are not the reality themselves. So details of every picture are not necessarily to be fulfilled in some specific way. (Medieval paintings go OTT, with devils and toasting forks &c. and white knights in shining armour!)

The *earth is purged* [2 Peter 3:10 – 13], and *renewed* to receive the wonder of *the New Jerusalem* [Revelation 21:1 –11]. (How far this is parabolic or literal cannot be judged at this distance through the telescope!) Note that in Ezekiel's vision [Ezekiel 40 – 44] there is reconstructed a magnificent Temple at Jerusalem, but in the New Jerusalem there is no such building, for good reason [Revelation 21:22]. [Also Galatians 4:24 – 26, where Paul used Hagar, (Abraham's wife's slave) who bore Ishmael by natural process, as equivalent to the law-bound *old city* of Jerusalem, in contrast to Sarah, Abraham's wife, who bore Isaac by supernatural promise, as equivalent to the *free New Jerusalem* from heaven.]

The picture continues with the *Marriage of the Lamb*, the wedding feast and *party*, with music, and rapturous, adoring, wild *worship* [Revelation 19:6 – 9; 4:1 – 11].
There is work to do, as hinted at in Luke 19:17, where the reward for good work is more work!

Revelation 22:10 – 16 This prophecy came to John from the angel, the messenger sent by the Lord to his servants (v.6). The prophecy was to be opened, for the present time (cf Daniel 12:4,9 with prophecy sealed up.) (v.12) Jesus is coming, with rewards for faithful witness; (14) Clean clothes, given to the Bride, (19.8) entitle her to the Tree of Life in the garden of Eden. There is full access, but it is to the City not to the Garden; (16) this testimony is the Covenant.

The book Revelation is not set down in chronological order; many different passages describe the same situation again and again with new pictures and fresh insights. Some questions remain, but are unanswered. We can trust God to get it right! Wait and see! What would we like to know, in heaven?
Will we ever have time off from work?
Will we meet old friends, or will we be too busy adoring God?
What has happened to dead or aborted infants?
Will there be animals in heaven? [Isaiah 11:1 – 9; 65:17 – 25]

Some wise words about the book Revelation by Gordon Fee in "How to read the Bible for all its worth:" "John wrote Revelation because State and church were on a collision course, and initial victory will belong to the State. It is a prophecy, and beyond warning them he seeks to encourage.

Distinguish Tribulation and Wrath: <u>Tribulation</u> means suffering and death, and the church will triumph through death. <u>Wrath</u> means God's judgement on those who have afflicted God's people. God's people will not have to suffer God's awful wrath, but they will suffer at the hands of their enemies.

Discipleship must go the way of the cross; God promises not freedom from suffering and death, but triumph through it. God is in control."

1. Some OT Prophets: both what has happened, and what awaits the future

Isaiah Chapter 13:1 to 14:27 are Isaiah's prophetic outpouring on the overthrow of Babylon, some 150 years before it happened. The taunt against the king of Babylon, from 14:4, reduced him to the grave. In 14:12 he had taken the title 'Morning Star, son of the dawn (or Lucifer)', and made all the proud boasts of 13-14; but he was to be destroyed, 23. This passage has been taken to describe Satan's arrogance, though probably that was not in Isaiah's mind. The evocative titles 'Morning Star, son of the dawn' were stolen by the Usurper from the Rightful King [Revelation 22:16].

Chapters 40 to 59 contain prophecies of the Restoration which started when Cyrus invaded Babylon from the east, from Persia and Media. Isaiah paints with poetic hyperbole. Within this he describes the Servant who suffers and is crushed on behalf of the sinful [52:12 – 53:12]. Isaiah had in mind the return of the Jews to Jerusalem, as he spoke to the sinful discouraged exiles in Babylon, telling them repeatedly why they were there. However, we have apostolic authority [1 Peter 2:21-25] to see the suffering of Jesus in Isaiah's words.

From the end of Isaiah, chapters 59 to 66, while still couched in terms of the return of the Jews to Jerusalem, Isaiah's words look beyond that event. Jesus quoted Isaiah 61 in the Nazareth synagogue [Luke 4:16-22]. In 63, Isaiah pronounced future judgement; in 64 he pleaded for mercy, and in 65 outsiders were incorporated, which John 1:11-12 echoes. New heavens and new earth will be created [65:17], again echoed by John in Revelation 21:1-7.

Jeremiah: Jeremiah prophesied in Jerusalem in the last years of its kings, before it was conquered in 597 BC, and during and after its siege and sacking in 587 BC. He, too, looked ahead to the return of the exiles, and also to a new covenant, better than the old covenant, because God would write his laws on his people's hearts [Jeremiah 31:31-34, quoted in Hebrews 8]. This was established in Christ. Jeremiah went on to prophesy a permanent rebuilding of Jerusalem, stated 5 or 10 years before it was sacked. But the restoration Jerusalem was sacked by the Romans in AD 70, and so the permanent New Jerusalem must now await the future. [Revelation 21:2]

Ezekiel: Ezekiel prophesied in Babylon amongst the Jews of the 597 BC exile, and later. He, too, spoke of restoration, and of a rebuilt Jerusalem; the Spirit of God would come into the renewed hearts and wills of his people [Ezekiel 36:24-30].

Daniel: Jesus spoke explicitly of Daniel's dream [Daniel 7:9-14], the coming of the Son of Man in the clouds, both to his disciples [Mark 13:26] and to Caiaphas [Mark 14:62]. The angels at the Ascension alluded to this, and John's Revelation 1:7 reflected this.

In all the prophets, there is a hint of the consummation of all things at a future date, over and above the return of the exiles. These pleadings with the people, mostly in Babylon, do not specify that the Messiah will come again, nor give time, location, nor detail. But they prepare the scene, they raise the expectation.

2. Some important NT passages: Many of them use visionary or apocalyptical language which was never meant for identification with historical events. In summary:

Mark 13 is Jesus' reply to the questions in v.4: 'when? And what are the warning signs?' He spoke about the Fall of Jerusalem in the Jewish War 66-70 AD. He used the apocalyptical imagery of cosmic language to invest earth-shattering political and social events with God-level significance.

Romans 8:29, ultimate conforming of Christians to Jesus at his coming again

1 Corinthians 15:20-58 is seminal teaching about the physicality of the resurrection of the dead.

Philippians 2:5-10, the exaltation of Jesus

1 Thessalonians 4:13-5:11, comfort for grieving relatives of Christians who die

2 Peter 3:3-15a, reassurance for waiting Christians

1 John 2:28-3:3, an appeal for pure living in the light of our Hope

Revelation: John was told to write to the 7 churches in Roman 'Asia.' Then from Revelation 4 to 19:10 he received a series of parallel action-visions describing the heavenly dimension of his day's happenings. They disclose what is true all along in God's dimension of reality, that is, in Biblical heaven. These chapters relate to the spiritual worship and warfare that 1st Century persecuted Christians faced, that has continued for 2000 years, and that we are currently embarked on, facing very different pressures from theirs. But from Revelation 19:11, the Vision moves on into the future Return of the Lord of Lords and King of Kings, Jesus himself.

Other items
Heaven: Jesus spoke of "the Kingdom of Heaven" (in Matthew), a Jewish way of saying "the Kingdom of God" (Mark and Luke). He was not denoting a place, but rather the fact that God rules. *This expectation is revolutionary, because all other kings are deposed [Psalm 2].* He spoke of Eternal life, not meaning a spaceless, timeless existence, but referring to a new dispensation in the renewal of all things. So Heaven is not a place, nor a future state, sitting on pink damp clouds twanging harps! It is God's transformed dimension of our present reality [1 Peter 1:3-4].

Death   Our lives on earth end in death. We 'sleep' (1 Thessalonians 4:13-15) and bodies disintegrate. At the Second Coming, we are woken by the trumpet, and raised in new bodies, with work to do for God. Those who live in earthly bodies at the time of the trumpet call will be changed (1 Corinthians 15:51-52). In one sense, "the end of everything" happens for each of us when we die. We use phrases to describe it: "we go to be with the Lord – we go from this world to the next – we sleep – the Lord comes for us, - the Lord takes us - &c." But these are quasi-Christian words, and we have to take care to grow our understanding from all of the Spirit inspired Scriptures. Individually, the Christian sense that the End is near, "The Lord is coming soon," agrees with the notice on the wall at the Funeral Director – "It's later than you think." You are propelled to make your Will, and urged to pay for your own funeral in advance, because costs are ever rising – (have you chosen the hymns and readings, yet?) All this fits well with the individualist thought that for each of us the Lord comes again for us when we die. [John Lefroy, at her bedside when his wife Sally died, testified to being aware that the Lord came into the room to take her away.] Personhood is illuminated by Birth, Life, Death, Resurrection, Heaven; it all happened to Jesus.

The OT Jews saw Body-&-Soul as an entity which perished; only later was life after death perceived possible. In the NT, Martha spoke with conviction about resurrection at the Last Day. When Jesus rose from death the entire landscape was floodlighted! Paul shone light in 1 Corinthians 15:35-57 on the natural body(-soul) and the spiritual body. This is of course comforting, without being explicit!

Body-soul-spirit is a Greek concept, and it is visible in some NT places but is not developed.

<u>Resurrection of all</u> The Second Coming is for the whole of humanity, the just and the unjust. All face scrutiny, the sheep and the goats. Judgement will be complete. Jesus made this clear in his parable: Matthew 25:31-46. For Individuals, we have personal birth, personal growth with development of awareness of other persons; then we may have personal New Birth from above, personal life and service of the Lord; and then we have personal death. For Corporate humanity, there is society organised by rulers, with strife, and true and false religion; but grace with mercy has been received because God intervened by The Cross; from this the Christian enterprise has spread.

The Biblical Second Coming is the Consummation of <u>everything</u>, for the whole human race, and for angels, and for all spiritual powers including Satan. This is at a definite time, which is hidden in God, be it next minute, or tomorrow, or in millions of years. Time must continue, because life requires time for it to be lived; everlasting life requires everlasting time. We do not know if there is continuity between natural time and eternity. This is the same uncertainty as exists between the geographical Jerusalem and the New Jerusalem, and as between the natural body of Jesus and his resurrection body, now ascended into heaven.

At the resurrection, believers will be given new bodies, to live in the New City, in eternal time.

Psalm 2 This Messianic Psalm seems to announce a final battle on Earth.

[1-5] Enemy forces, the rulers and powers of this dark world, and the spiritual forces of evil, join to attack the Lord. But God in heaven taunts their puny plans! He is the Almighty, and he warns of his anger and wrath.

[6-9] The Lord put David on the throne in the city of Zion; the Father puts the Messiah, the Son of God on heaven's throne. He will reign over the entire Earth with justice and force.

[10-11] The Lord has spelled out these final outcomes, and now he advises would-be opponents to submit: "Serve the Lord with fear;" they are to 'kiss' the Sovereign in 'humble duty'. Such penitents receive the gracious promise "Blessed are all who take refuge in him."

Post script:

Much is not clear, so avoid hard ideas because they lead to needless hurt and time-wasting. See Paul's advice to Titus [3:9] and to Timothy [1 Timothy 4:7]. We have to tread carefully, to find out what the Bible teaches about the Second Coming; then be determined not to disregard it, or compromise it with syncretistic ideas in the presence of alternative concepts which we have received from other sources, and maybe have long cherished! In particular, hymns and songs reflect the theology of the writer's day; but they need to be tested against the NT.

> Let us beware of 'isms' which can become obsessive. Eg <u>Millennialism</u>, ante- pre- post- &c stemming from the single mention of 1000 years in Revelation 20:1-6; and <u>Rapture</u> from 1 Thessalonians 4:17. These arise from an over-literal understanding of the text in places where the writers are being figurative. (There was a minister who prevented his daughter going out with a young man, 'because he was not "hot on the Rapture"'!)

Perhaps there is room for debate about some details, but let it be respectful, and remember that the wisdom from heaven is peace-loving! [James 3:17-18].

Kaleidoscope:

> The Bible is vast in extent, total in time:
> *Creation & Covenant* [Genesis]
> *Redemption* [Exodus through OT to the Gospels; the preparations laid in the OT for Jesus to come, and realisation achieved in the Cross, the Resurrection, and the Ascension]
> *Mission* [Matthew 28:18, the Acts, the Epistles, and the first 18 chapters of Revelation]
> *Consummation* [Revelation 19 to 22]
>   Notwithstanding this colossal panorama, we are to get stuck into practical things, <u>now</u>.
> Let us take our cue from Paul at the climax of his chapter on the resurrection (1 Corinthians 15:57-58) "Thanks be to God! He gives us the victory through our Lord Jesus Christ. Therefore, my dear brothers, stand firm. Let nothing move you. Always give yourselves fully to the work of the Lord…"

Psalm 150   All the Temple instruments and musicians are playing **fff** !

"Hallelu Yah!" in the Holy Place and in the Lord's vast universe; praise him for his powerful actions and his exceeding greatness. The whole band lifts everyone up, with trumpets, harps, lyres, tambourines, dancing, strings, flutes, cymbals, and great gongs!
"Let every living creature praise the Lord! **Hallelu Yah.**"

Final Read: Revelation 22:16-21   'Marana tha' is Aramaic for "Come, O Lord!" Paul used it in 1Corinthians 16:22.

The Festal Shout . . .
<u>Marana tha!</u>

<u>- Come, Lord Jesus!!</u>

APPENDIX

Editing (The technical term is 'Redacting')

For some Bible believing Christians, it is the original words of Scripture that are those which are inspired by the Holy Spirit. [2 Timothy 3:16, 2 Peter 1:20] Therefore the suggestion that there has been any 'editing' in the transmission of the text to us today is unacceptable. As a fall-back amongst many English speakers, they have perceived that the Authorised Version of 1611AD has been much used by God in Britain and the USA, so they have credited it with an anointing by the Holy Spirit as the best approach to "the Scriptures as originally given." Naturally they have become reluctant to accept any later version. (In the USA, the AV is the King James' Version, KJV.)

No two modern languages use the same sentence construction, and their vocabularies do not completely match meanings. A foreigner needs to tread carefully if he is to be understood and if he is to avoid unintended offence. Even UK English is dangerously different from US English in places. The same is true where a modern language is used to translate an ancient one. The translating process involves the task of interpretation of the 'dead' text to arrive at an equivalent current version as near as possible representing the primary source. So every translation involves some editing. Consider the processes ...

1. An 'original' oral language from the Patriarchs, is translated from Aramaic by Moses into

2. Hebrew, and written on papyrus, perhaps by his aide Joshua. This text is rewritten in

3. updated Hebrew of Solomon's time. It is acquired by the Scribes of the Exile, and

4. Copied and preserved for the Restoration under Zerubbabel.

5. A copy is taken to Alexandria and translated into Greek (the LXX), the version that was used in Jesus' day. A 4th Century AD copy of this was found in mid 1800AD.

6. It is gathered, or a copy of it, and taken to Jerusalem by Judas Maccabeus; it could also have been translated into

Coptic, Syriac, Aramaic... And copied by a Desert Sect for its library; and so it escapes destruction in Jerusalem AD70.

Today we have an English translation, but there are several versions. It is impossible to access the exact 'original' word.

If tradition is to be believed, perhaps Moses drew from Egyptian archives, as well as from spoken stories amongst Israel of the antediluvians and the patriarchs. Maybe he wrote, or caused to be written, texts of the first 5 books of the Bible in early Hebrew/Aramaic, and these were held in memories as well as in manuscript. Later on, David and his musician Asaph wrote Psalms. The ancient texts were put into current Hebrew language by scribes in Solomon's reign; and this happened again in the Exile. Many written resources were brought from Jerusalem to the Exiles, including Jeremiah's letter, over a period of time. These were carefully collected, treasured, edited and copied by the scribes who added to the Law the stories and prophesies of Israel, and the Wisdom books as far as their present time. Note that the books Samuel and Kings tell their stories from a royal and civil angle, with some related words of the prophets. The books of Chronicles tell the history from a Temple and priestly angle. The written prophets brought the Lord's overview of history, sometimes local, sometimes worldwide. Records of events in the courts of Babylon and Susa were added [eg Esther]. Most of it was written in Hebrew, while some was in Aramaic (see below). More was written down after the Restoration [Ezra, Nehemiah, Zephaniah, Haggai, Zechariah, Malachi]. At the same time, ordinary people held it in memory (see below). Later, manuscripts were translated in different parts of the ancient world, into Coptic, Syriac, &c. But only fragments of these remain. Until the Dead Sea Scrolls were discovered, the earliest Hebrew MS dated from 9th **Century AD**, the work of the Jewish scholars known as the Masoretes. The Scrolls confirmed the accuracy of the Masoretic text, but there are some small differences.

The Septuagint (LXX) was the Greek version of the Hebrew text, which had been made by the end of the 2nd Century BC, and this was the OT of the first Christians. It is the version mostly quoted in the NT. There are full manuscripts of the LXX from 4th Century AD. The LXX was derived from Hebrew texts that are no longer in existence, so it is of interest to academics. They were different source texts from those of the Masoretic text. (Source RT France, Translating the Bible)

Oral tradition All down the ages, leaders of peoples and their scribes have written down matters of significance for administration and law, and for preservation of cultural norms. At the same time, their people, many of whom could not read or write in early societies, preserved stories and useful sayings in their memories. By continuous retelling and critical listening they kept the accuracy of all the information in the form of an Oral Tradition, and it was reliable. Sadly with the increase of literacy, we have lost this skill; we have become dependent on paper: "I'll have that in writing!" We no longer accept the spoken word; it has to be dated, signed and witnessed.

Manuscripts

All scriptures were hand copied, and despite rigorous procedures and checking, there were some small differences between copies. The Jewish Masoretes worked from AD 500 to 1000 to produce a reliable text of the O.T. in Hebrew. From AD 1947, discoveries of libraries on the shores of the Dead Sea hidden in caves in times of war and persecution have brought significant additions for academics working on O.T. texts. All this has produced an agreed edition of the originals, known as the 'received text'.

The first Christians wrote in Greek, the universal language throughout the Roman world. They spoke of the New Wine of the Kingdom, which burst out of the old wineskins of Judaism. They proclaimed "Jesus is Lord"! (not Caesar!) in gospel and in transformed lifestyle; they wrote letters, and taught, and encouraged. They were refreshed in the Spirit. They recorded healings and deliverances and raising the dead, all the signs and wonders and miracles of God at work in them and their communities. Oral Tradition ran parallel with apostolic writings, and continued to be authoritative to about 200AD.

Aramaic parts of the OT: Daniel 2:4 to 7:28
Ezra 4:8 to 6:18, and some verses in chapter 7
A verse in Jeremiah, 10:11.

An Aramaic inscription occurs on a 9th Century BC stele. Aramaic was the diplomatic language of Sennacherib of Assyria about 700 BC. It was used in the court of Nebuchadnezzar of Babylon. It was widespread across the Persian empire 550 to 450 BC. Aramaic uses the same alphabet as Hebrew, and they are closely related.

Jesus and the disciples taught and spoke in Aramaic, and were familiar with Hebrew and Greek, and perhaps with some Latin, too.

The **very large numbers** of Israelites in OT censuses may have arisen through the misunderstanding by a later editor of the Hebrew word for a 'thousand'. Following the suggestion by Humphreys, that the Hebrew word for 'thousand' is also the word for 'group' or 'troop', it is possible to rewrite the very large numbers of the censuses. Eg: Numbers 1:37 in the edition from which we have our many translations, the number of soldiers from the tribe of Benjamin reads 35,400. However, the original recorder, possibly Abidan (of Numbers 1:11) may well have reported 35 troops, 400 men. Troops of a few to a score of soldiers each characterised armies of pre-Assyrian times. So for Reuben: 40 troops containing 500 men; Simeon: 59 troops containing 300 men; &c. This alternative makes the total Israelite fighting force to be 5550 at Horeb, and 5730 a generation later on the plains of Moab. If on average each man had one wife and two children, the total Israelite community would be about 20,000. But on the figures given in the OT manuscripts, the whole community would number about 2,400,000. It is worth considering that the whole Middle East population of that day is now reckoned by some to be about 2 million, an indication of the merits of the alternative. Perhaps the later compilers of documents which they possessed for writing the book Numbers chose to use 'thousand' because the armies of their day were composed of much larger units.

However, the suggestion has some complications.

Non-Canonical Writings

As well as our Bible scriptures, many other ancient writings have down to us. Some are stories and wise words related to matters of faith. It became necessary to distinguish them from the formational scriptures. There was considerable agreement amongst the Jews about the OT books, as to which books were in the OT, "in the canon", inspired by the Spirit of the Lord. The well-known OT list was formalised only out of necessity in the 1st century AD.

The criterion for the canon of the Christian NT has been the test "Is this writing from the apostles who knew Jesus, or according to their teaching?" The NT canon was clear and agreed early, at least by 140AD, and then eventually formalised by church councils in 4th Century.

Other writings, described as deutero-canonical, form the apocrypha. Some churches commend them for education. A cache of these, dating from about 400 AD, was found in 1945 in Egypt near Nag Hammadi. These form the NT apocrypha. Many contradict the words of Jesus and present a confusing muddle!